Three Kings

Also by Lloyd C. Gardner

The Long Road to Baghdad:
A History of U.S. Foreign Policy from the 1970s to the Present

Economic Aspects of New Deal Diplomacy

Architects of Illusion:
Men and Ideas in American Foreign Affairs, 1941–1949

The Creation of the American Empire: U.S. Diplomatic History
(with Walter LaFeber and Thomas McCormick)

American Foreign Policy, Present to Past

Looking Backward: A Reintroduction to American History
(with William O'Neill)

Imperial America: American Foreign Policy, 1898–1976

A Covenant with Power: America and World Order from Wilson to Reagan

Safe for Democracy:
The Anglo-American Response to Revolution, 1913–1923

Approaching Vietnam: From World War II to Dienbienphu

Spheres of Influence:
The Great Powers Partition in Europe, from Munich to Yalta

Pay Any Price: Lyndon Johnson and the Wars for Vietnam

The Case That Never Dies: The Lindbergh Kidnapping

Edited by Lloyd C. Gardner

The Great Nixon Turnaround:
America's New Foreign Policy in the Post-liberal Era

America in Vietnam: A Documentary History (with Walter LaFeber,
Thomas McCormick, and William Appleman Williams)

Redefining the Past: Essays in Honor of William Appleman Williams

On the Edge: The Early Decisions in the Vietnam War (with Ted Gittinger)

International Perspectives on Vietnam (with Ted Gittinger)

Vietnam: The Search for Peace (with Ted Gittinger)

The New American Empire:
A 21st Century Teach-In on U.S. Foreign Policy (with Marilyn B. Young)

Iraq and the Lessons of Vietnam:
Or, How Not to Learn from the Past (with Marilyn B. Young)

Three Kings

The Rise of an American Empire in the Middle East After World War II

LLOYD C. GARDNER

THE NEW PRESS

NEW YORK
LONDON

Published in the United States by The New Press, New York, 2009
This paperback edition published by The New Press, 2011
Distributed by Perseus Distribution

LIBRARY OF CONGRESS CATALOGING-IN-PUBLICATION DATA
Gardner, Lloyd C., 1934–
Three kings : the rise of an American empire in the Middle East
after World War II / Lloyd C. Gardner.
p.   cm.
Includes bibliographical references and index.
ISBN 978-1-59558-474-8 (hc.: alk. paper)
ISBN 978-1-59558-644-5 (pbk.)
1. United States—Foreign relations—Middle East.   2. Middle East—
Foreign relations—United States.   3. United States—Foreign relations—
1945–1989.   4. United States—Foreign relations—1945–1989—
Philosophy.   5. World politics—1945–1989. I. Title.
DS63.2.U5G37 2009
327.7305609'045—dc22   2009014713

The New Press was established in 1990 as a not-for-profit alternative
to the large, commercial publishing houses currently dominating the
book publishing industry. The New Press operates in the public interest
rather than for private gain, and is committed to publishing,
in innovative ways, works of educational, cultural, and
community value that are often deemed insufficiently profitable.

www.thenewpress.com

Composition by dix!
This book was set in Goudy

Printed in the United States of America

2   4   6   8   10   9   7   5   3   1

History never runs backward and there isn't any chance of turning the pages backward—we must go forward—we must assume the leadership which I think God Almighty gave us and assume the responsibility which goes with that leadership.

—Harry S. Truman, May 18, 1951

CONTENTS

PREFACE AND ACKNOWLEDGMENTS

As we contemplate the difficult process of getting out of Iraq without making matters worse, it is time to reflect on the deeper history of how the United States came to be in the Middle East, especially before embarking on a new mission to rebuild Afghanistan. A place to begin is with the events leading up to President Harry S. Truman's speech on March 12, 1947—the Truman Doctrine. Remembered today as the necessary American answer to the expansionist ambitions of the Soviet Union, the Truman Doctrine was really much more than that. From the beginning it provided a rhetorical base on which to reassemble the broken pieces of the old European empires in a new constellation of states that, according to the accepted narrative, defied the wiles and threats of "International Communism" by means of military and economic aid. As such, it was a great success.

The actual history of the Truman Doctrine contains far more doubts, and many more twists and turns, present from the very outset, when the Senate Foreign Relations Committee struggled to comprehend the likely outcome of the president's initial request for $500 million to send to Greece and Turkey to bolster their internal and external fortitude. It had a prehistory dating to World War II and Roosevelt's dreams for Iran and negotiations for the first air base in Saudi Arabia. From that time onward, American policy makers continued to develop and define the nation's role at the ancient crossroads of empire—the Mediterranean. They saw themselves as successors to the Pax Britannica, not in the sense of nineteenth-century imperialists, of course, but as creators of a dynamic new era that would prove more enduring than the old empires.

The Truman Doctrine had its greatest difficulty, ideologically, in defining the enemy. Without naming the Soviet Union, the president referred to forces directed against existing governments from the outside, and their subversive allies joined together to strike from within, a lethal combination. That loose formulation tried to distinguish between agent-inspired revolutions and non-agent-inspired revolutions, an almost impossible undertaking. Eisenhower's secretary of state, John Foster Dulles, adopted the term "International Communism" to aid him in attempting to explain why, in the absence of an actual Soviet military threat, it was necessary to send arms to countries gathered under the umbrella of the Truman Doctrine. At various times, especially in the original congressional debates on the request for money, and then again at the time Dulles was trying to sell the Eisenhower Doctrine in 1957 as an advance on definitions of the threat, the rationale became brittle and almost shattered into fragments of ideological incoherence. Added to this difficulty was the ever-changing cast of American supporters who became useless or actually hindrances, from the Shah of Iran to Egypt's Nasser, Saddam Hussein, and, most recently, Hamid Karzai in Kabul.

General David McKiernan, the former commander in Afghanistan, reflected a commonly held view among American policy makers when he warned against taking the history of British and Russian failed efforts to succeed in that country as at all applicable to American prospects. Of course, as he might note, there was now no other "superpower" to provide the Taliban or Al Qaeda with "Stinger" missiles, the scourge of the Russian army and air force in the 1980s, but he went beyond that to make a general comment that all such historical comparisons were "unhealthy." It was a typically American, can-do kind of talk, tailored from traditional notions about the disinterested motives of American foreign policy, the optimism of the military commanders, and a belief that technology ruled politics. Such convictions all too often make us deaf to unwelcome messengers, and thus foster a search for alternate facts, not truth.

Flash back to the spring of 1965 and the National Teach-In. Professor Arthur Schlesinger Jr., the famous historian and chronicler of the Kennedy years, was now beginning to waver a bit about Vietnam. He nevertheless takes a stand in favor of sending in the army. He is against the bombing campaign Rolling Thunder, however, saying bombs won't do the job. And then he adds his own take on history. It's time, he says, to stop asking how we got in and concentrate on how we get out of the situation without damaging our national security. Many in the audience nod, but in the back a hand raises.

The hand belongs to William R. Taylor, a professor of history at Stony Brook. "Arthur," he begins, "I wonder if you would care to venture an opinion on when history stopped being important to our situation and a discussion of alternatives. Was it six years ago? Six months? Six weeks?"

Smiling, Arthur starts to answer: "As usual, my old colleague at Harvard asks a tough question—"

At that very moment, the District of Columbia fire marshal steps to the podium: "Folks, we have just been alerted to a bomb threat, we have to clear this room."

The dialogue ended there, without an answer. It should not end today on that same note, "we have to clear the room."

This book is the missing part of my recent look at a later period, *The Long Road to Baghdad*, also published by The New Press. Thanks always to friends for their help and inspiration, especially Warren Kimball, Walter LaFeber, Thomas McCormick, Paul Miles, and Marilyn Young. They are not responsible, of course, for any of my opinions you may find in the pages herein, nor any factual errors. These all belong to me. A very special word of thanks as well to André Schiffrin, founder of The New Press, and Marc Favreau, editorial director of The New Press. This book is dedicated to my wife, Nancy, who has heard it in bits and pieces many times over. Here is the whole picture.

Lloyd Gardner
Newtown, Pennsylvania
May 2009

1

INTRODUCTION TO A DOCTRINE

Senator Walter F. George: I do not see how the President's speech of yesterday can be characterized as a mere plea for assistance to Greece and Turkey. If it were mere economic assistance it would be one thing, and it would be easily done. But he put this nation squarely on the line against certain ideologies.

Senator Arthur Vandenberg: I want to lay everything on the table, Senator, so that the American people will understand it. I do not think they understand it this morning much better than they did before the President delivered his message, and I think one of our major jobs is to make them understand it, and I do not believe they ever will unless we dramatize this thing in every possible way.

The above exchange took place on the first day of secret hearings to consider president Harry S. Truman's pivotal speech to Congress on March 12, 1947, his most dramatic since he announced the dropping of the atomic bomb on Hiroshima, and the one that launched the Cold War. It was now the responsibility of the United States, the president had asserted, to meet the imminent global threat emanating from Moscow. The White House insisted on a prompt response to the president's request for a $500 million appropriation to rescue two countries threatened, he said, by extreme political pressure from the Kremlin, with the shadowy implication of some sort of military action behind the threats. But Senator George worried that the administration was embarking on a dangerous path that would lead the nation far beyond Truman's initial request for economic and military aid to Greece and Turkey. Senator Vandenberg agreed that the president had not made his case, so it was up to

Congress to do that for him, as well as appropriate the funds—
otherwise Truman would be left out on a limb.

Not made public until 1973—more than twenty-five years later,
near the end of the disastrous Vietnam War—these private discussions inside the Senate Foreign Relations Committee revealed the
considerable discomfort, even confusion, about the open-ended
commitment Congress was being asked to underwrite. And it
turned out pretty much the way both men predicted it would. Over
future decades the United States would spend billions of dollars in
an effort to institutionalize a Pax Americana in the Middle East to
replace the old European suzerainty over the area, while Congress
would find itself in a compromised position whenever it attempted
to question the White House's urgent appeals to expand the "Truman Doctrine." Each time Truman's successors asked for a new congressional mandate, the White House would declare the threat to
be more serious than before, and now one that could traced to a
shadowy force—"International Communism." Making the case in
that fashion avoided some problematic questions about the consequences of intervening in the internal politics of Middle Eastern
nations, though a few embarrassing (or enlightening) exchanges
did take place in congressional testimony.

The transition path had been paved by Truman himself, who did
not mention the Soviet Union in his speech, an omission that allowed his listeners to interpret his words in different ways. Either he
did not wish to make matters worse elsewhere in Russian-American
relations by offering up such a direct challenge, or he had foreseen
the need to leave himself and future presidents a broad rationale for
new initiatives. Of special interest in this regard, moreover, was the
absence of any mention of Eastern Europe or any challenge to the
Russian presence there. When his point man in the rushed hearings
on the Truman Doctrine, under secretary of state Dean Acheson,
tried to help out with the problems that concerned George and
Vandenberg, he said: "It is true that there are parts of the world to
which we have no access. It would be silly to believe that we can
do anything effective in Rumania, Bulgaria or Poland. You cannot
do that. That is within the area of physical force. We are excluded

from that. There are other places where we can be effective. One of them is Korea, and I think that is another place where the line has been clearly drawn between the Russians and ourselves."[1]

Acheson's outstanding talents as a diplomat are on display here. He manages to calm nerves about an open challenge to the Soviet Union in its at least temporarily acknowledged sphere of influence, while suggesting that the United States stood ready to defend new frontiers elsewhere—places far beyond prewar definitions of national security.

The Meaning of the Truman Doctrine

It is best to begin this narrative by setting out some propositions about what the Truman Doctrine was, and what it was not. Acheson has given us the essential clue in his testimony: it was not about forcing the Russians out of Eastern Europe. Indeed, the Red Army's presence there proved useful to policy makers seeking to find a theme for the Cold War drama. Neither, however, was it about turning back the specific threat of Russian military bases in the Black Sea Straits. That danger could have been handled without all the ideological mobilization of an overarching "doctrine." Such a simple solution was rejected, however, in favor of the summons to take up the burden where the British had once stood guard at the crossroads of empire.

Here are the propositions offered throughout the chapters below as guides to understanding the emergence of an American empire in the Middle East from World War II and the Truman Doctrine until the United States stood alone as the dominant power in the aftermath of the 1967 Six-Day War:

- The Truman Doctrine was the essential rubric under which the United States projected its power globally after World War II— casting this as a global ideological struggle and enabling the kind of massive, unquestioned military/foreign policy spending that we still take for granted at the beginning of the twenty-first century. It was the ideological foundation for the "imperial presidency."

- It was understood at the time by the key players that what was in fact at stake was not the need to fend off the Soviets but to shore up friendly governments in strategic areas.
- And, finally, the doctrine addressed a process that had already been under way for some time: U.S. maneuvers to replace the British in the region of signal importance, the Middle East.[2]

The speech Truman read to Congress on March 12, 1947, had been carefully crafted by White House and State Department "ghosts," in part to remove sentences that referred directly to both the region's proximity to the vast oil resources of the Middle East and the already growing U.S. stake in their exploitation. The first draft was not to his liking, Truman said in his memoirs, because they made "the whole thing sound like an investment prospectus." He wanted a speech that put aside material considerations and asked the nation to face up to its destiny. "This was the time to align the United States of America clearly on the side, and at the head, of the free world."[3]

Purged of any less than worthy ambitions, the key sentence then read, "I believe that it should be the policy of the United States to support free peoples who are resisting attempted subjugation by armed minorities or by outside pressures. I believe that we should assist free peoples to work out their own destinies in their own way. I believe that our help should be primarily through economic stability and orderly political process." Truman found the second draft too wimpy, he tells us in his memoirs, especially in this regard: "I took my pencil, scratched out 'should' and wrote in 'must.' In several other places I did the same thing. I wanted no hedging in this speech. This was America's answer to the surge of expansion of Communist tyranny. It had to be clear and free of hesitation or double talk."[4]

Truman's memoirs offer us a self-portrait suitable to hang in the first room of the Cold War gallery of American leaders who grasped the essential evilness of the nation's adversaries. Some continue to interpret the Cold War by studying those pictures. Still, the immediate reaction to the March 12, 1947, speech was scarcely that of a nation united in its determination to take up the challenge that Truman had put before Congress (along with a crisis watch deadline for action less than three weeks away). The *New York Times* had not yet settled into its destined role as journalistic insider with a dash of critical thinking here and there, and reported that Congress was "somewhat bewildered" by the president's mandate, especially his insistence on an almost instantaneous response. "Members, as they listened to the Chief Executive, saw their country's foreign policy undergo radical change in the space of twenty-one minutes."[5]

There were predictions of a congressional storm in the making as the nation's legislators struggled to understand and debate the tectonic shift set in motion by the speech. Had he called for "a new, world-wide Monroe Doctrine" to warn off the Kremlin everywhere? Was it even a "declaration of war" upon Russia? Or had the president simply proposed a new postwar lend-lease plan to help Greece and Turkey?[6]

It was all of these—at least by implication. It announced the beginning of a Cold War to legitimate nearly all the actions Truman and his successors in the White House would undertake to realize the American Century, from Greece and Turkey to Vietnam. After 9/11, comparisons of the two "accidental" presidents, Harry Truman and George W. Bush, suddenly appeared all over the media, even in outlets where praise for Truman had never even been whispered about, let alone proclaimed. Of course it was not praise for the "Fair Deal," but for the man who had put forward the "Truman Doctrine," where it was possible to honor the author of the charter under which conservatives and liberals alike waged the good fight for world leadership against successive "evil empires." Former Reagan speechwriter and keeper of the flame Peggy Noonan wrote in the *Wall Street Journal* on November 16, 2001: "Harry Truman was a great man. And I believe we are seeing the makings of a similar greatness in George W. Bush, the bantamy, plain-spoken, originally uninspiring man who through a good heart and a good head, through gut and character, simple well-meaningness and love of country is, in his own noncompelling way, doing the right tough things at a terrible time."

But Bush's mission went beyond the Truman Doctrine, even as Noonan saw it as the foundation for the war on terror:

> And he faces stakes as high as Truman faced, if not, as many think, higher. Truman had to stand for freedom and keep the West together while keeping Stalin from getting and then using weapons that he could, in his evil, use to blow up half the world. Mr. Bush has to stand for freedom and keep an alliance together while moving against a dozen madmen who have it within their power to deploy weapons of mass destruction that can blow up half the world. He has to see to it that this great mission doesn't end with getting or killing Osama and his men. He must lead the civilized world now to root out, get and remove every weapon of mass destruction—every chemical and bio depot and laboratory in every rogue nation—and banish this scourge from the world. It will be hard to keep the allies on board and supportive, hard to keep the American people behind him, because it's going to be a long war.[7]

In fact, as she suggests, Bush's ambitions inhered in the original Truman Doctrine and its inevitable evolution as the American ideology of its founder's day and ours. The Truman Doctrine was designed from the outset to be capable of stretching from Ankara and Athens to provide a general outlook on threats to American interests, beginning with lands bordering the ancient crossroads of civilization in the Mediterranean. The story is told and retold in Cold War histories of how Under Secretary of State Acheson politely interrupted his "boss," the venerable George C. Marshall, to inject passion into a White House briefing of congressional leaders on the consequences of British inability to carry on supporting the Greek government against a Communist-led leftist insurgency, or provide modern arms to stiffen Turkey's resolve in resisting Russian pressures for joint control of the Black Sea Straits (the gateway to the Mediterranean and beyond). When Secretary Marshall began his presentation he emphasized the need to strengthen the British position in the Middle East. That did not go down well with the congressional delegation, and led to awkward questions about pulling British chestnuts out of the fire and such.[8]

Leaning over to Marshall, Acheson asked in a low voice, "Is this a private fight or can anyone get into it?" If one were to reassess turning points in American foreign policy, Acheson's briefing—or better put, his chilling vision of the Red peril—would have a serious claim to pride of place. Everywhere one looked, he began, the position of the democracies had seriously deteriorated since the end of the war. And while the immediate crisis was in the Greco-Turkish area, the aim of the Soviets was control of the Mediterranean, north to Italy, and south as far as Iran. From there the possibilities for further "penetration of South Asia and Africa were limitless."

Point Man: Dean G. Acheson

Despite the urgency President Truman asked of Congress, the day after the speech he flew off to Key West for several days in the Florida sun. He had good reason to feel comfortable about the legislation, however, because his point man with Congress was Acheson, who, while Marshall was absent at a foreign ministers' conference in Moscow, easily managed the administration's case and parried questions about why the United Nations had been ignored. A few days after Franklin D. Roosevelt's reelection for a fourth term in November 1944, Acheson, then an assistant secretary of state, had testified before a special congressional committee that no one believed the United States could absorb its entire production under the capitalist economic system. The nation had to export goods up to a total of $10 billion a year. "We cannot go through another 10 years like the 10 years at the end of the twenties and the beginning of the thirties, without having the most far-reaching consequences upon our economic and social system."[9]

The central purpose of World War II diplomacy, beyond the obvious need to see the Axis menace scourged from the earth, had been to create something better than the nineteenth century world economic system lest a new threat arise from the ashes of war. FDR was careful to caution the nation in his January 6, 1945, State of the Union message before Congress that it could not all happen at once. "In August, 1941, Prime Minister Churchill and I agreed to the principles of the Atlantic Charter. . . . At that time certain isolationists protested vigorously against our right to proclaim the principles—and against the very principles themselves. Today, many of the same people are protesting against the possibility of violation of the same principles."

Roosevelt's warning against expecting perfection in the inevitable chaos of temporary postwar arrangements was forgotten when he died on April 12, 1945, replaced by fears that the nation was drifting. Berlin was a bombed-out shell, but already there was talk about the rising menace from the East. Truman was an unknown to most Americans. And the new president's advisers, those he inherited from FDR and his own favorites, understood the need for a unifying theme. The danger of a nation divided as it faced the tasks of securing the peace seemed even greater with the Republican victory in the 1946 congressional elections. The New Deal coalition had come apart, it was felt, with former vice president Henry A. Wallace forced out of the cabinet and now posing a challenge from the left, while southern Democrats angered by Truman's pro–civil rights stance seemed on the verge of bolting the party.

That was the situation when Acheson testified about the Truman Doctrine and offered his interpretation of American policy, combining a plea to come together to meet the external challenge with calming assurances that Truman would not go off the deep end even as American power stretched out geographically. He was not sure he had succeeded.

Writing to Marshall, Acheson wrote about his experience before the committee. The senators were not going to block the bill, he wrote, but they were still concerned about "where this is going to lead and why doesn't the Administration tell us the whole story and the whole cost now?"[10]

If he wished to be candid about it, Acheson did not know where it would lead, specifically, or how much it would cost. Also, if he were to be candid, he would have acknowledged Senator George's

concerns about an ideological war—if only to affirm such a conflict to mobilize the nation behind Truman's initiative. Republican
H. Alexander Smith had asked Acheson about a column by the
pundit Walter Lippmann, who warned that the Truman administration, with its "musts" and all-encompassing rhetoric, was spreading
American financial capability too thin. Lippmann thought, said
Smith, that we should instead bolster up some strategic areas. "That
is what troubles me." Well, Lippmann had changed his mind about
Greece and Turkey, Acheson replied; he used to think they were
strategic.

But that was not really the point, as the wording of Truman's
speech made clear. Truman's language in the speech had it that
nearly the whole world was faced by two choices—and two choices
only:

> At the present moment in world history nearly every nation must
> choose between alternative ways of life. The choice is too often
> not a free one. One way of life is based upon the will of the major-
> ity, and is distinguished by free institutions, representative gov-
> ernment, free elections, guarantees of individual liberty, freedom
> of speech and religion, and freedom from political oppression.
> The second way of life is based upon the will of a minority forcibly
> imposed upon the majority. It relies upon terror and oppression, a
> controlled press and radio, fixed elections, and the suppression of
> personal freedoms.

The Truman Doctrine initiated a policy of support for a series of
Greek governments that survived a civil war and remained within
the parameters set out for membership in the "Free World." In the
case of Turkey, especially, the doctrine laid the foundations for the
Military Advisory Groups that became an integral part of American
foreign policy in the Middle East and elsewhere. The original crisis
"locations," which supposedly called the new policy into being—
Greece and Turkey—proved not to be crises for very long, especially not in the sense of threatening the outbreak of war.[11]

The Truman Doctrine's usefulness as an ensign under which Cold

War battles could be fought on the highest planes of idealism was only beginning to be understood at the time of the Senate hearings. But there were glimpses of the future as the committee concluded that it had to approve Truman's immediate requests for funds, if only because there were dangers to be feared in leaving the president stranded on a rhetorical island.

A Doctrine for All Seasons

After watching the administration's witnesses, led by Acheson, attempt to explain the limits on the Truman Doctrine, Senator Walter George concluded, "I know that when we make a policy of this kind we are irrevocably committing ourselves to a course of action, and there is no way to get out of it next week or next year. *You go down to the end of the road.*" [12]

To understand just how prescient George was, we need to go back to World War II, where the road began, as the United States moved into the Middle East with Lend-Lease offers and requests to build air bases, and to replace British dominance economically and politically. With VE Day there was a need to reformulate the quest. The Soviet Union's advance into Eastern Europe, and its ambitions for sharing in the control of the Black Sea Straits, offered a new focus—one that would serve to justify expansion of the Truman Doctrine to Iran, leading to a CIA-engineered coup against a prime minister who sought to nationalize the oil wells; to Egypt, in an effort to control the direction of that country's revolution; and to the overthrow of a leftist government in Iraq that marked the emergence of Saddam Hussein.

Following Truman's speech, the American military seized the opportunity to expand its naval presence in the Mediterranean. Aiding Turkey to withstand Moscow's blandishments required, as a beginning point, access to existing British bases. But the United States had already begun planning for strategic strongpoints in the Middle East during World War II. Indeed, in September 1941, nearly three months before Pearl Harbor, General Curtis LeMay led a survey mission to Africa and the Near East, ending in Cairo, in search of places for American aircraft to land: "The plan was to assemble fighters at some place on the west coast of Africa and, flying them across the wastes in between, get them into the Middle East." Germany was the immediate target, but the future of American airpower could be deduced, LeMay observed, from Roosevelt's political vision. "We'd had President Roosevelt's Four Freedoms speech back in the previous January. The marines had occupied Iceland on July 7th. The Atlantic Charter was signed by Roosevelt and Churchill on the British battleship *Prince of Wales*, off the coast of Newfoundland, 14 August."[13]

As LeMay suggests here, the relationship between military and political visions is one of co-dependency. General LeMay is the first person one thinks of in talking about the history of American strategic bombing. He commanded the bomber group that dropped the first atomic bombs, and was the godfather in 1947 of the new Strategic Air Command. He understood how Roosevelt's initiatives would mature into the holy trinity of airpower—bases, delivery systems, and payloads. What began as an imagined deterrent to Germany had become by war's end a policy of burgeoning global ambitions until at last the sun would never set on the stars and stripes flying over more than seven hundred foreign bases.

As policy makers thought about how to deal with the British announcement in February 1947 that London was once again calling in the New World to redress the balance in the Old, not a lot of concern had to be given to the possibility that Stalin would risk World War III to achieve his aims. On March 13, the day following Truman's summons to world leadership, the Joint Chiefs of Staff presented their assessment of the military situation to navy secretary James Forrestal and secretary of war Robert Patterson. Truman's rhetoric and the reality were something of a mismatch: "It is believed that the Soviet Union currently possesses neither the desire nor the resources to conduct a major war. Further, the Soviet Union must now have a clear appreciation that open aggression, of the type which she undertook with something less than complete success against Finland in 1939, might inevitably result in war with the Western powers, which alone, for the present, possess atomic bombs."[14]

The only danger to Turkey that the Joint Chiefs could foresee was psychological, in the sense that if Greece succumbed to communism, the Turks might "yield" to Soviet pressure short of military measures. The real meaning of the Truman Doctrine, then, was that it would provide a means for becoming involved, establishing a presence, and projecting American power into a strategic area. Thus it is remarkable that even Secretary of State Marshall, who had only recently succeeded James F. Byrnes in that post, confessed that he did not understand the urgency of the Turkish situation in a conversation with the British ambassador Lord Inverchapel, who presented the message that His Majesty's government could no longer keep up its imperial role in checking Russian ambitions at the straits barrier. "It was his understanding," Marshall said, "that the Russians had made no move with regard to Turkey for some time and asked if the Ambassador had any ideas regarding the reasons for the Russian silence?" Inverchapel replied as Lord Salisbury might have at the height of the Pax Britannica: "The Ambassador said that in his opinion no foreigner knows why Russia takes or fails to take certain actions. Therefore, as an honest man, he must admit that he is not in a position to explain what is responsible for the present Soviet attitude towards Turkey."[15]

It would take some time, obviously, for American leaders to pick up on all the nuances of empire maintenance, especially the use of language to describe threats in a way that made everything defensive in nature. In a related exchange, at the first meeting of a special committee that Marshall appointed to consider the British notes the same afternoon, the consensus was that the United States must accept the responsibility the British were proposing to turn over. "If we did not," said the leading State Department representatives, "Greece and probably Turkey would be lost." There was but one dissent, from General James Crain, who argued that the British had arrived at their "present precarious financial state as a result of trying to do just what it was now proposing that the U.S. should attempt."

It would be better policy, he insisted, that the United States should conserve its resources "for the final trial of strength." If the question was the military defense of Greece and Turkey, that could be accomplished by advising the Soviet Union "we would use force if necessary to keep it from seizing control of those countries."[16]

Alas, General Crain had no sense about where American policy was going or how it would get there. A simple statement that the United States would defend Greece or Turkey against military attack could not provide the foundation for a projection of American power to stabilize areas of interest. It was a case, army chief of staff Dwight D. Eisenhower argued, of risking at some date being unable to traverse the Mediterranean to hold on to air bases in the Middle East to launch strategic operations in wartime. Vice-chief of naval operations, admiral Forrest Sherman, said the Mediterranean should be conceived of as a "highway" for the projection of military power "deep into the heart of the land mass of Eurasia and Africa."[17]

As legislators anticipated, even as they voted for the $500 million aid to Greece and Turkey, they had given an imprimatur to an ideological struggle that would give cover to decades of subsequent interventions, and that inevitably involved taking sides in the thorniest political struggles of Middle Eastern nations. Succeeding administrations ratcheted up the stakes as Washington justified its positions by Truman Doctrine standards, insisting that it was only protecting countries from agent-inspired revolutions dedicated to the delivery of Middle East governments to what a later secretary of state, John Foster Dulles, would call "International Communism," a purposely vague formulation used to rationalize military aid to maintain cooperative leaders in power where there was no danger of a Soviet invasion. By doing so, moreover, they would put themselves in the position of being blackmailed by ambitious leaders who called forth the "threat" to support their demands for arms. No one was better at that game than the shah of Iran, who would eventually bring about his own destruction and tip over the applecart. The process produced, as the shah's case demonstrated, a constant tug-of-war between Washington and its clients, with American policy makers determined to control the reins lest the locals kick over the traces and turn the weapons to the service of their ambitions beyond their borders instead of staying inside and maintaining good order on the safe parade grounds of the "Free World."

The principal purpose of American policy, therefore, was not to deter a Russian attack, but to ensure the loyalty of the countries receiving aid and to maintain their governments in power against internal threats. As Admiral William C. Radford, chair of the Joint Chiefs of Staff, testified at a 1957 hearing on the "Eisenhower Doctrine," "They love to have the heavy equipment that they can parade down the main street on independence days and things like that, and show the people that they have what they feel is real armed strength."[18]

Upon taking office in 1961, John F. Kennedy supplied the final words to enlarge the Truman Doctrine into full-blown counterinsurgency theory. In a speech on March 28, 1961—only weeks before the Bay of Pigs fiasco—Kennedy outlined his defense policies to Congress, saying:

> The Free World's security can be endangered not only by a nuclear attack, but also by being slowly nibbled away at the periphery, regardless of our strategic power, by forces of subversion, infiltration, intimidation, indirect or non-overt aggression, internal revolution, diplomatic blackmail, guerrilla warfare or a series of limited wars.
>
> In this area of local wars, we must inevitably count on the cooperative efforts of other peoples and nations who share our concern. Indeed, their interests are more often directly engaged in such conflicts. The self-reliant are also those whom it is easiest to help—and for these reasons we must continue and reshape the Military Assistance Program which I have discussed earlier in my special message on foreign aid.

The speech not only updated Truman's original contention about the need to resist outside support for subversive forces, but added a whole new list of rationales—intimidation, non-overt aggression, even diplomatic blackmail—thereby completing the transformation of the doctrine into counterinsurgency theory. Working from those premises, moreover, the United States would seek regime change in Iraq not once but twice, eventually bringing to power a future nemesis, Saddam Hussein.

The intellectual preparation and justification for the Truman Doctrine did not suddenly appear in a flash of insight in February 1947 when Lord Inverchapel revealed London's plight and put all of his cards on the table. "I am fully aware of the broad implications involved if the United States extends assistance to Greece and Turkey," Truman said in his speech, "and I shall discuss these implications with you at this time."

The following chapters explore the world the Truman Doctrine created. The path begins with the American forward movement into the Middle East in World War II.

2

THE UNITED STATES MOVES INTO THE MIDDLE EAST

I remember the Supreme Commander coming into Roosevelt's bed-room where [British minister Harold] Macmillan and I were having an early morning meeting with the President while he was still in bed. Eisenhower gave a very smart salute before leaving, and Macmillan whispered in my ear, "Isn't he just like a Roman centurion!"
—Robert Murphy's memoir of the Casablanca Conference, January 1943, *Diplomat Among Warriors*

On what turned out to be the last night of the Yalta Conference in February 1945, Roosevelt startled his Big Three counterparts, Stalin and Churchill, by announcing that he had to leave the next day to fly to Egypt. But, protested Stalin, there was still unfinished business! He could not stay any longer, the president replied. He had "three Kings waiting for him in the Near East, including Ibn Saud." Churchill was flabbergasted. As soon as the final session adjourned, the prime minister rushed off to find Roosevelt's confidant, Harry Hopkins. What was the meaning of this surprise? Hopkins feigned total ignorance. They were all in the same boat, he shrugged. Probably it was just "a lot of horseplay." The president wished to relax a bit by experiencing "the colorful panoply of the sovereigns of this part of the world." Besides, he teased the prime minister, they somehow had the notion he could "cure all their troubles." Churchill went away, recalled Hopkins, with the air of a man convinced of "some deep laid plot to undermine the British Empire in these areas."[1]

Having a little fun teasing "Brits" about the empire always satisfied an American itch. But who would not wonder at Hopkins's blithe suggestion that Roosevelt was rushing out of the most important Big Three conference during the war early for a pleasure trip to the Middle East? It did not take a suspicious mind to observe that World War II had provided the United States with economic and political weapons—starting with the prewar Lend-Lease Act—for Uncle Sam to commence rearranging the remnants of the old European empires into an American-styled world order. That was the sort of "horseplay" Roosevelt looked to enjoy on his last mission before his death on April 12, 1945.

In August 1941 FDR had met Churchill off the coast of Newfoundland to draw up a preliminary list of Allied war aims. The document they signed immediately became known as the Atlantic Charter, and it contained promises of self-determination for nations under German and Japanese occupation. The prime minister had sought to limit those pledges and exempt the British Empire, but U.S. policy makers during World War II hoped to extend the Atlantic Charter to the Middle East, giving those awakening countries vital space to develop their full independence—in close cooperation with American entrepreneurs and political advisers. Indeed, compared to the problems of dealing with, say, the French in Indochina or the Dutch East Indies, the opportunity for making immediate gains for American interests in the Middle East seemed a good bet. When Churchill tried to limit the scope of the charter's reach to postwar Europe, Roosevelt reaffirmed that it applied to the whole world. Around the time of the Yalta Conference he had scaled back the timetable a bit, calling the charter a great aspiration. But the Middle East was fully in play. Roosevelt's mission to the three kings signaled the beginning of something big taking place on the lifeline of Victoria's empire, the Suez Canal.

A recent State Department analysis argued the chance to provide a third path between two historical rivals for influence in the area: the fading (but still active) ambitions of the British, and Moscow's determination to block "a coalition of the capitalistic countries in the Middle East against the Soviet Union." Using its quest for security as a rationalization, it was likely Russia would seek to extend its "social and economic systems throughout the Middle East."[2]

The whole area had thus become a "fertile field for friction and activities which may threaten Middle East security and world peace." The United States had no intention or desire to station troops in the area; its only recourse to check its likely rivals was full-fledged American participation in the development of the countries politically and economically. Fortunately, "there is reason to believe that the Middle Eastern countries in realization of their deficiencies will in an increasing degree turn to the United States for such assistance." From the outset, however, there loomed a major stumbling block: the dilemma Washington faced in the "Palestine question." According to The State Department analysis, "Of all the political problems which call for solution in this area the Palestine question is probably the most important and urgent at the present time."[3]

"In general," the report summed up, "we should seek economic liberty without inequality, in all matters of trade, transit and other economic activities in accordance with the broad objectives of our commercial policy," as set forth in the wartime Lend-Lease agreements and the Atlantic Charter—both updates of the nation's traditional "Open Door" policy. The United States had made it plain both in formal agreements like Lend-Lease, and wartime rhetoric like the Atlantic Charter, that it, too, had war aims that involved global aspirations. A great believer in personal diplomacy, FDR was out the afternoon after saying farewell to his World War II partners motoring over mountain roads near the Black Sea to Sevastopol, recently liberated from the Germans. He stayed overnight on a U.S. Navy ship and then boarded a plane before daylight for the five-hour flight to Egypt. Once there he went aboard the USS *Quincy* anchored in Great Bitter Lake, a wide expanse in the Suez Canal, to await the arrival of his royal guests from Egypt, Ethiopia, and Saudi Arabia.

Roosevelt's Quest

Obviously this was a difficult trip for anyone after such a grueling conference, let alone a man with his physical disabilities. That he undertook the journey was another sign of the importance he attached to Middle Eastern problems. The first to come aboard the *Quincy* was Egypt's King Farouk. Roosevelt chatted with the king about American purchases of long-staple cotton. He hoped this new wartime trade would flourish and soon extend to other commodities. Tourist travel to Egypt, he predicted, would explode after the war. Thousands of Americans would visit Egypt and the Nile region, both by ship and air. These were not idle thoughts: trade with Egypt had in fact increased eightfold during the war. The American minister, Alexander Kirk, had advocated extending Lend-Lease aid to solidify that position after the war. After an initial hesitancy, the aid was granted, followed by efforts to secure favorable investment laws to encourage joint stock companies. Washington also sought permission for American commercial airliners to carry passengers from Cairo to the principal cities of Europe. As one policy planner put it, "Cairo is vital to air navigation, just as Suez is to shipping."[4]

Later in the day, Ethiopia's Haile Selassie joined the president for a tête-à-tête in French. Again, FDR stressed that improved communications, particularly by air, would bring the two countries closer together.[5] Roosevelt brought up the subject of new air routes crisscrossing the Middle East for good reason. U.S. postwar ambitions were closely tied to an expanding network of commercial and military air bases throughout the world. During the war the United States had become preeminent in airpower. Only too aware of what this challenge meant, British policy makers had stalled negotiations about landing rights within the empire and other places where they traditionally exercised influence—especially in the Middle East. "I haven't the least doubt," Harry Hopkins had boasted in a magazine article, "that we will come to an understanding with Great Britain about our respective air bases throughout the world. . . . We're going to trade through the air, as well as by sea, in this world to be.

And the American people are quite right in emphasizing the importance of air bases."[6]

Roosevelt repeated this message to Middle Eastern rulers he hosted, and especially to his most important guest, who arrived with a large retinue the following afternoon. King Ibn Saud arrived on board an American warship that Roosevelt had sent to Jeddah on the Red Sea for the trip to Great Bitter Lake. White House publicists emphasized that this voyage set two precedents. The navy vessel was the first modern warship to visit the Red Sea port, as well as the first American warship to pass through the Suez Canal during World War II. And there was yet a third precedent: this was the first time Ibn Saud had ever left his country's soil.[7]

The king and his forty-seven retainers, accompanied also by Colonel William Eddy, the new American minister to Saudi Arabia and a Roosevelt favorite, transferred to the *Quincy* after a journey of eight hundred miles to meet this American who led the greatest military alliance the world had ever seen. According to press secretary Steve Early, "The President, seated on the forward gun deck of his ship, received the royal visitors as the crew manned the rails, bugle calls sounded, and the shrill notes of the boatswain's pipe kept all hands standing rigidly at attention." In anticipation of the king's visit, Roosevelt had decided on an appropriate gift, a DC-3 Dakota, the two-engine, propeller-driven mainstay of U.S. commercial fleets.[8]

An American pilot, Joe Grant, who would stay on for decades as His Majesty's official pilot, delivered the plane to the kingdom. In use for years, it became "a fitting symbol of the U.S.-Saudi relationship." Ownership stimulated the king's interest in developing air travel with the aid of American commercial expertise, which is precisely what Roosevelt had hoped it would do. FDR did not miss the chance to compare American gifts free of imperial wrappings with British calculations. "We like the English," said Roosevelt, "but we also know the English and the way they insist on doing good themselves. You and I want freedom and prosperity for our people and their neighbors after the war. How and by whose hand freedom and prosperity arrive concerns us but little. The English also work and sacrifice to bring freedom and prosperity to the world, but on the condition that it be brought by them and marked Made in Britain."[9]

The king smiled at this rendition and later told Eddy he had never heard a better description of the British and their policies. Ibn Saud had sent the president a gift as well, a sword rumored to cost $100,000. "Probably this figure is an exaggeration," said the previous American minister, James Moose, "but the sword is undoubtedly expensive." Moose's 1943 appointment had elevated American diplomatic representation from chargé d'affaires ad interim to minister resident. The appointment reflected secretary of state Cordell Hull's concern to have someone near the king to protect the future interests of the American oil concession ("one of the largest oil reserves in the world") against possible rivals, and to pursue "aircraft landing rights in that country."[10]

Oil did not come up during their tête-à-tête, but, of course, it was always there, underground if you will, during any conversation about the Middle East. In addition to economic concerns, FDR had another mission. Ever since he inaugurated correspondence with Ibn Saud in January 1939, he had been trying to soften the king's attitude about the aspirations of American Zionists to establish a Jewish state in Palestine, a British mandate since the end of World War I when the Ottoman Empire was, in effect, parceled out to Britain and France. Unlike other areas that came under British and French suzerainty—such as Iraq—Palestine appeared not to have any great potential as an oil producer. Roosevelt had undertaken in his letters and now in person to explain to the king the American people's "spiritual" interest in the Palestine "situation." Political pressure in the United States had mounted as the horror of German atrocities and the "Final Solution" began to be understood, however tardily and incompletely, around the world.

British and American promises to consult with both Arab and Zionist leaders about the "Palestine question" had been a classic delaying tactic, but no one wanted to take the lead in making a real proposal. In a 1945 memorandum to Harry Hopkins, the State Department could recommend only that the British be asked to invite position papers from both sides. Without much conviction, the State Department suggested that these inquiries could encourage "moderate" elements to come forward with proposals. Somehow a plan might emerge that could be imposed by the Big Three. The weight of their approval or disapproval might, it was thought, convince everyone to settle differences. But the idea was a nonstarter then and every time afterward whenever someone floated a similar notion. To begin with, it ignored big power rivalries as well as the nascent Arab-Israeli dispute.[11]

What the king wanted from Roosevelt was exactly the opposite: a firm commitment that the United States would not support Zionist goals. Roosevelt knew going into his meeting with Ibn Saud that the State Department plan had no chance. He and his aides also knew that this issue was the single most dangerous question they faced in trying to secure an American presence in the Middle East after the war. In 1943 Roosevelt had invited Ibn Saud to send his sons to the United States for a visit. And he sent the king a special representative, Colonel Harold B. Hoskins, "in order to discuss confidentially . . . certain matters of mutual interest," code words for the Palestine question.[12] When word of Hoskins's mission and the invitation to the king's sons leaked to the press, Roosevelt was furious: "I have no sympathy with those Jews who object to my seeing the son of Ibn Saud," he wrote Hull, "any more than I have any sympathy with those Arabs who are starting anti-Semitic prejudices in this country."[13]

In the 1944 presidential campaign both political parties offered encouragement to the Zionist movement at their national conventions. Against the background of mounting political pressure in Congress for a commitment to the idea of a "national homeland" for Jewish refugees in Palestine, the State Department hoisted warning signals about Saudi Arabia's expected reactions. "The king is first a Moslem," asserted a pre-Yalta State Department memo, "and secondarily an Arab. . . . He considers himself the world's foremost Moslem and assumes the defense of Moslem rights. Hence his opposition to Zionism." Any alteration in his position would involve a loss of the respect of his co-religionists, and possibly the overthrow of his dynasty. Secretary of state Edward R. Stettinius, who succeeded Cordell Hull in 1944, added in a note to Roosevelt that the king could not be moved this side of the grave: "Ibn Saud's statement that he regards himself as a champion of the Arabs of Palestine and would himself feel it an honor to die in battle in their cause is, of course, of the greatest significance."[14]

When the king came aboard the *Quincy*, however, Roosevelt saw a man unlikely to fight anyone on the battlefield—at least not personally. Ibn Saud's crippled condition gave the president an opening to commiserate about their mutual problems getting around—and to offer to send him one of his specially designed wheelchairs. It would be said that the king prized this gift as much, or more, than the Dakota DC-3. But neither gifts nor Roosevelt's expressions of sympathy could get Ibn Saud to change his position a single degree. The Jewish people had been driven from their home-lands, began Roosevelt, and the world had a humanitarian obliga-tion to these refugees. That might be so, Saud replied, but they should be given lands within the Axis countries, not lands belong-ing to the Arab peoples. Roosevelt tried other arguments—he ar-gued up one side and down the other, he reported to his aides—but it was no use. Nothing for it then but to retreat to an old delaying tactic. In a mutually agreed memorandum of their talks, Roosevelt went back to the standard formula. He promised the king "he would do nothing to assist the Jews against the Arabs and would make no move hostile to the Arab people." Satisfied with the promise, the king thanked Roosevelt for his statement and indicated he would send an Arab mission to the United States and Great Britain "to ex-pound the case of the Arabs and Palestine." Whatever he really thought about that proposal Roosevelt kept to himself, saying only that would be a very good idea.[15]

As soon as he returned to the White House from Yalta, Rabbi Steven W. Wise, chair of the American Zionist Emergency Coun-cil, was on his doorstep. Rabbi Wise emerged from a forty-five-minute meeting ready to deliver an important announcement to the waiting reporters. The president had assured him that he had *not* changed his position about favoring unrestricted immigration into a free and democratic Jewish commonwealth in Palestine. Wise then read a statement Roosevelt had approved: "I have made my position on Zionism clear. . . . I have not changed and shall continue to seek to bring about its earliest realization."[16]

That Roosevelt had expressed such convictions to Zionist leaders came as a shock to Arab leaders. They demanded to know where American policy was heading. Roosevelt maintained a studied ambiguity. On the day of his fatal stroke in Warm Springs, Georgia, April 12, 1945, the president signed a letter to the Prince Regent of Iraq assuring him that "no decision affecting the basic situation in Palestine should be reached without full consultation with both Arabs and Jews." Close readers of the minutes of his meeting with King Saud and this letter to the Prince Regent could, however, perceive shading toward the Zionist position.[17]

On all other questions besides Palestine, Roosevelt thought he had made significant headway with Ibn Saud. The king was certainly no fool. He had not achieved control of his country without understanding how to play rivals off against one another. "I have never met the equal of the President in character, wisdom and gentility," the king said of FDR. He was not like Churchill, he added, who "speaks deviously, evades understanding, changes the subject to avoid commitment." But the British had been around longer— and were telling him to be wary about the Americans. "What am I to believe when the British tell me that my future is with them and not with America?" U.S. interest in his country was transitory, the British said. Once the wartime emergency was over, Lend-Lease aid would end and the Americans would return to the Western Hemisphere—leaving Saudi Arabia behind, within the pound sterling area economically, and defended by the Royal Navy and British Army. According to Ibn Saud, "On the strength of this argument they seek a priority for Britain in Saudi Arabia. What am I to believe?"[18]

No, that was not what the future held, Roosevelt assured the king. Vast opportunities were the future. The old world of spheres of influence was in irreversible decline; the Open Door was in ascendancy. The door of Saudi Arabia should be open to all nations, with no monopoly for anyone. That was all very well, replied Saud, but the British would continue as before to claim a sphere of influence around and over his country. Roosevelt's new representative to Saudi Arabia, Colonel Eddy, added to the king's comments that this was a well-grounded fear and could be dispelled only when the United States provided material substance to its long-range economic plans to secure the Open Door. Along with other diplomats and special aides, Eddy had been pushing the case for a stronger commitment to the Middle East for some time, especially against the supposed danger of British "imperialism."[19]

Lend-Lease as a Wedge

Before the war, American economic interests in the kingdom centered in an oil concession originally obtained in a bidding war with the British during the first year of Ibn Saud's rule. A consortium of companies headed by SoCal (Standard of California) offered Saud an annual fee of $35,000 and two loans totaling $350,000 in exchange for the right to search for oil over a huge area that covered 360,000 square miles for a period of sixty years. Desperate for funds to keep his hold on power, the king accepted the deal, which set up the symbiotic relationship forever linking American oil interests to the survival of the Saudi royal house.[20]

Not much oil flowed out of Saudi Arabia in those early years. The king's main source of revenue remained income derived from taxes imposed on pilgrims to Mecca. When World War II shut down that travel, the regime was once again in financial difficulty and the king demanded more money from the concessionaires. Oil revenues could not yet make up the difference, so where would the company get the funds? The British had anted up, supplying funds on a limited basis to keep Ibn Saud friendly to their regional interests, but London was pinched financially. With the war draining empire resources, it was doubtful they could stay in the game for the next round of bets and raises. Oilman James Moffett, a personal friend of Roosevelt and board chair of SoCal, had a proposal to offer. Why not see the king through the war with a direct subsidy? The U.S.

government could purchase up to $6 million a year in petroleum products from the king and everyone would be happy. Unless Ibn Saud received such financial assistance, warned Moffett, "there is grave danger that this independent Arab Kingdom cannot survive the present emergency." FDR liked the idea, but navy secretary Frank Knox could not imagine what to do with the oil. What was being produced in Saudi Arabia was not yet suitable for use in airplanes or even ordinary purposes.[21]

Mr. Fix It, Harry Hopkins, had another idea. What about Lend-Lease? Passed originally by Congress in the spring of 1941, Lend-Lease was the administration's answer to the problem of sending economic and material aid to Great Britain without creating a new "war debts" issue, which had plagued American relations with Europe in the interwar era. The plan was then extended to the Soviet Union in the fall of 1941, and later to other nations at war. But Saudi Arabia was not at war with the Axis powers, and, as Hopkins ruefully confessed, "just how we could call that outfit a 'democracy' I don't know."[22] A year and a half later, in February 1943, the president suddenly found "the defense of Saudi Arabia . . . vital to the defense of the United States." Lend-Lease aid started to flow into Saudi Arabia. What brought about this landmark change? Saudi Arabia was still not at war, still not a democracy, and a possible Axis threat had receded after the North African campaign. So whence came the threat?

Washington officials now suspected the British—despite their financial plight—of trying to "edge their way into" Saudi Arabia at the expense of the American oil companies. Saudi Arabia was "probably the greatest and richest oil field in all the world," declared Harold Ickes, petroleum administrator for war, and the British "never overlooked any opportunity to get in where there was oil."[23] But British ambassador Lord Halifax was so upset over presumed threats to postwar British interests throughout the Middle East that he asked for an audience with Roosevelt to clear the air. When he arrived at the White House, FDR produced a rough map he had drawn of the Middle East: "Persian oil, he told him, is yours. We share the oil of Iraq and Kuwait. As for Saudi Arabian oil, it's ours."[24]

Halifax left feeling a little better, maybe, but certainly aware that Roosevelt had been primed to be on the lookout for British attempts to block the expansion of American interests. Indeed, it had become something of an obsession with American diplomats that the British were out to close the doors everywhere they could. General Patrick J. Hurley, a trusted Roosevelt emissary and full-throated Anglophobe, told him that Ibn Saud was determined not to let the "imperialists" gain any more influence in his country; but why, the king wondered, were the Americans so lax about letting Lend-Lease aid be distributed by the British, who were shipping drilling equipment and other necessities to their oil companies in the Persian Gulf while his country's similar needs went unfulfilled? Saud's trust was a valuable asset, observed the general, and something should be done to correct the situation. Eventually, U.S. representatives did take charge of the Middle East Supply Center to ensure that governments in the region understood who their true benefactor really was. "American control of the Saudi Arabian oil resources places you," Hurley congratulated Roosevelt, "in a trading position that will enable you to obtain for all concerned an equitable allotment of the oil resources of Africa, the Middle East, and continuing through Afghanistan to the Far East."[25]

No "big government" New Dealer, Hurley even proposed that the U.S. government acquire "a degree of ownership of American companies operating in foreign territory." It could be done, he felt confident, "without destroying private ownership or private initiative." The model for such an arrangement was the Anglo-Persian Oil Company, where the British government held 51 percent of the shares but left management in private hands. Hurley's proposal coincided with an oil scare that prompted Ickes to float a plan for a government-owned pipeline across the Middle East. Ickes proposed that the American company, now called ARAMCO, simply sell out to Uncle Sam for the sake of the national interest, and accept additional compensation beyond the sale price in the form of an overriding royalty on future production. When company representatives turned him down flat, Ickes scaled back his proposal to 51 percent, exactly like Anglo-Persian's arrangement.[26]

No dice, said industry representatives. Government should stay out of the oil business, except, of course, to ensure a friendly Open Door environment for investments and an international "Oil compact" to regulate affairs among rival national bidders. American policy makers then attempted to sort things out with the British to present a united front to the local producing countries. Negotiations on various drafts of an Anglo-American oil agreement dragged on until the end of the war, when everyone gave it up as a lost cause. A few years later, however, the Iranian oil expropriation crisis reminded British and American leaders that they had a lot to lose by not pulling together.

But meanwhile, the Pentagon and the State Department focused on securing a pied-à-terre in Saudi Arabia near ARAMCO headquarters. An air base at Dhahran would facilitate shipments to the Far East for the war against Japan, and anchor future American interests in the area like an Old West fort. "An important objective of United States policy," another special emissary, James M. Landis, wrote Harry Hopkins in the summer of 1944, "should be to secure to itself, to be used either by itself or its nationals, adequate air bases and air rights throughout the entire Middle East."[27]

Because of the war, he went on, Middle East countries had now learned from Americans what air transport can really do to link key cities from Tehran to Cairo with Washington and London. What a pity it would be if the opportunity to enlarge this advantage into permanent influence passed by as others seized the initiative. The logical place to begin was at Dhahran. Let us tell local rulers, said Landis, that their future political security might depend on such air links.[28] At present, the Saudi capital, Riyadh, was largely inaccessible, but think how an air base at Dhahran guaranteed ready access to the king, so essential to maintaining the degree of intimacy that diplomacy requires: "The significance of such a step cannot be overestimated. American planes would fly regularly over Arabian soil and accustom the population to the fact of intercourse with the outer world." Since air transport offered the best way to unite the east and west coasts of the country, there could be no better way to help in maintaining law and order. It was a win-win proposition: "Our prestige would thus be greatly enhanced."[29]

Landis played a key role in the expansion of American interests throughout the Middle East. It had become clear to many that what was needed was a general plan to promote those interests against rivals who had held sway in the area before the war. But a plan was nothing without a general director to oversee American operations and keep watch on what U.S. wartime allies were doing. Landis wanted to be that man. Upon arriving in Cairo in October 1943, the new director of the Middle East Supply Center explained to reporters that his mission was to speed victory for the principles of the Atlantic Charter: "All policies must have long-range objectives, and these go beyond immediate war objectives into a period of peace."[30]

Here was a perfect example of what that quintessentially realist theologian and commentator Reinhold Niebuhr would write a few years later in a searching examination of American history and foreign policy: "Every nation is caught in the moral paradox of refusing to go to war unless it can be proved that the national interest is imperiled, and of continuing in the war only by proving that something much more than national interest is at stake." Lend-Lease was the vehicle in the Middle East that provided the bridge both materially and ideologically. Once the Germans had been driven out of North Africa, and the threat to Suez no longer existed, the rest of the Middle Eastern "front" was all about dominance in the postwar era.[31]

Landis had envisioned a combined economic and strategic approach through postwar air bases that would tie in with the desires of the rulers of those countries. Here, in nascent form, was an outline of how American policy would develop after the war, not only in the Middle East but also worldwide. The linkages Landis described would eventually extend to military advisory missions, status-of-forces agreements, and all the rest that updated classic British methods in India (where London perfected the raj) without,

it was hoped, stirring nationalist anger against an American presence or openly violating the American commitment to the Atlantic Charter's promises.

But before the bulldozers could start pushing the Arabian sand
into foundations for runways, the king had to be convinced. Three
things appeared to hold him back. First, Washington had to come
up with a solid economic aid program for the postwar era to last
until oil royalties filled his treasury. The British told him, he had reminded Roosevelt, that Lend-Lease would not last forever—and
then what? The State Department hoped Congress would solve the
problem with direct financial aid: "It is in our national interest to
extend this assistance, otherwise Saudi Arabia will undoubtedly
turn elsewhere with resulting grave long range effects on our position in that country. The War and Navy Departments agree as to its
desirability."[32]

The war ended before Congress acted, and Lend-Lease for both
the Soviet Union and Great Britain ended, too. Despite all the
noise about cutting off the British and Russians, however, aid for
Saudi Arabia continued. In a terse telegram to Eddy on September
11, 1945, Assistant Secretary of State Acheson wrote, "Lend-Lease
assistance Saudi Arabia as programmed will be continued 1945 despite general discontinuance. Please inform S[audi] A[rabian]
G[overnment] and British representative." While the new funds
would not total more than about $10 million, it signaled the United
States had indeed taken up a big stake in the Middle East. Lend-
Lease kept flowing to Saudi Arabia for more than a year while
policy makers tried to figure out how to deal with the issue of long-
term aid.[33]

The second reason for the delay in building an air base was Ibn
Saud's fears of British displeasure. While Washington continued to
debate a long-term solution, the British had persuaded Ibn Saud not
to allow an American military mission into his country. There was
no use in "scolding" Ibn Saud for his reluctance to make an early decision on the air base, said Eddy, because the king had expected the
United States to have more influence "with our greater power as
creditor and principal Ally but he fails to see proof." Without that

proof in the form of a long-term aid commitment, Ibn Saud would continue to play to the British, and they would continue to hamstring American initiatives: "I hope we never join in joint subsidy or supply again but instead attach our independent economic aid to our own strings instead of to British apron strings."[34]

Eddy believed that Ibn Saud would sit out the rivalry between the United States and Great Britain, offering something to both, but deferring big projects that might cause him political difficulty with one or the other, or his own people. He could not behave otherwise until Americans got up the gumption to provide him with a solid program so that he could defend "the Open Door against all efforts by the British to close that door."[35] Eddy need not have fretted so much. On May 28, 1945, assistant secretary of state Dean Acheson and under secretary of the navy Ralph Bard went to the White House to show Roosevelt's successor, Harry S. Truman, a specially prepared map. When they unrolled it, Truman could see the whole Middle Eastern oil area superimposed over a map of the United States. Acheson and Bard pointed out the locations of various concessions and proven amounts of oil for each. Then they briefed him about Ibn Saud's financial needs. Roosevelt had been planning to ask Congress for direct financial aid for Saudi Arabia, they told him, but there were various other ways it might be done. Truman was eager to learn how.[36]

The best way, said Acheson, was to embed it in a large-scale appropriation to give the president the ability to move money around wherever it might be needed. It would take roughly $100 million per annum, he said, to fund such a program. The president needed to have money to use at his discretion to promote American political and strategic interests in the Middle East. The Department of State, he wrote, had repeatedly run into situations where basic objectives of American policy were being hindered by the need to obtain specific congressional authorization: "In several instances it would be embarrassing and difficult to justify publicly an appropriation for the particular purpose." A case in point was the inability to comply with Saudi Arabia's desire for loans of about $10 million per annum to meet government expenditures until oil revenues began to accrue. The oil resources of Saudi Arabia, read yet another memorandum by Gordon Merriam of the Near East division, "constitute a stupendous source of strategic power, and one of the greatest material prizes in world history." But, as matters stood, the American concession was in jeopardy: "It will undoubtedly be lost to the United States unless this Government is able to demonstrate in a practical way its recognition of this concession as of national interest by acceding to the reasonable requests of King Ibn Saud that he be assisted temporarily in his economic and financial difficulties."[37]

Truman wrote Ibn Saud on September 12, 1945, reaffirming the friendship that had been cemented by the "auspicious meeting between Your Majesty and the late great President Roosevelt." He went on: "I recognize the importance of extending to you sufficient aid to enable Saudi Arabia to pass safely through the present crisis." He was happy to inform him that Congress had now acted on the pending aid measures, but in addition to those he was adding $6 million in commercial credits and a $5 million dollar loan from the Export-Import Bank.[38]

Here, also in nascent form, was the White House policy of avoiding a strict accounting of public monies. The Middle East thus became the laboratory for trying out various policies that would later be identified with the "imperial presidency." These grew out of the original Lend-Lease program designed, ironically, for the British and then the Soviets to defeat the Axis powers, but which became a wedge for both increasing postwar influence in the Middle East, and the White House within the federal government—until, by the time of Gulf War II in 2003, the president could claim almost absolute authority to do as he pleased. Acheson's proposal for a revolving fund of $100 million, furthermore, anticipated in a way Truman's request based on Greece and Turkey, but with worldwide implications. It proved much easier to sell in 1947 as an anti-Communist measure.

The third factor holding up construction of the air base was Ibn Saud's fear of his own people. The king had hesitated before granting the right to build the Dhahran air base not simply out of fear of British reactions, or an American economic commitment, but also because he faced a different threat at home from "Pan-Arab nationalism and internal fanaticism." He was held personally responsible for keeping the land around the sacred sites "free from taint of foreign occupations."[39] For this reason, Ibn Saud had refused the offer of an American military mission in early July 1945, out of fear that his old enemies might use it to denounce him as nothing more than a puppet to foreign military interests. Amir Faisal, Ibn Saud's son, elaborated on the situation during a visit to Washington. Faisal hoped Americans would understand that His Majesty could neither move too quickly in opening up his country to foreign enterprise nor always accept their suggestions. There were people both inside and outside Saudi Arabia who wished to discredit the regime: "These people endeavored to spread rumors throughout the Arab world to the effect that His Majesty was selling out his people to American imperialism and was bartering the traditions of the holiest of Moslem countries for American gold."[40]

The week Japan surrendered, ending World War II, Ibn Saud finally signed an agreement for the Dhahran air base. It was far too late to help the war effort, of course, but auspicious for postwar American interests. He ended his "holdout," reported Eddy, because foreign minister Amir Faisal had returned from Washington with satisfactory assurances of financial aid for the immediate future, and promises of long-term economic cooperation. Originally limited to three years, the American lease on the Dhahran air base was renewed several times over. During the Cold War, U.S. Air Force tankers operated out of the base to refuel the B-29s, B-36s, and B-47s that constantly circled Russia's perimeters. Dhahran was also the designated rallying point for U.S. citizens and diplomats in case of troubles in any of the neighboring countries in the area. And during Gulf War I in 1991, Dhahran was essential to the air campaign against Iraq.

The air base grew as the American presence in the Middle East grew. Fifty years after Ibn Saud's decision to permit the Dhahran airfield to be built and occupied by non-Muslim American military personnel and workers, Ibn Saud's fears came true when the base suffered an attack by Osama bin Laden. Nineteen Americans were

killed in the June 1996 attack along with four hundred Arab workers wounded. Dhahran was abandoned for another base, the Prince
Sultan, which was in turn surrendered to the Saudis after Gulf War
II. Success in Iraq, assistant secretary of defense Paul Wolfowitz argued, promised, among other advantages, to allow American forces
to withdraw to another country, Iraq, to establish bases in a safer
environment—thereby ensuring the security of America's oil for
the future and keeping the Middle East from exploding outward or
inward. The breakthrough at Dhahran, nevertheless, proved to be
the first significant post–World War II base of what a conservative
defense analyst, Thomas Donnelly, later described in 2004 as a pattern for American expansion throughout its history at the end of
each war:

> Accompanying this expansion of the American security perime-
> ter has been a growing network of military facilities, both along
> the frontier and internally. Installations like Forts Riley and Leav-
> enworth in Kansas were once outposts for Indian fighting, part of
> Andrew Jackson's "Permanent Indian Frontier" plan, then "hubs"
> for further force projection. In the 1880s, Fort Leavenworth be-
> came the home of the Army staff college; Fort Riley has for some
> decades been the home of the First Infantry Division, a unit with
> much service in Germany and in the Persian Gulf. In Germany,
> Ramstein Air Force base, near the front line during the Cold War,
> is now a key pillar in the American air "bridge" that makes the
> U.S. Air Force's boast of "global reach" a reality. The general
> pattern has been that, when one war ends, the United States for-
> tifies the furthest reaches of the final front lines and, when the
> next war begins, it builds new facilities to support still farther-
> flung operations.[41]

The Iranian Occupation

Just across the Persian Gulf from Saudi Arabia, the postwar fate of
Iran seemed to mark it as a likely place for an explosion, a place
where the United States and Great Britain jostled for supremacy

during the war but with a big showdown looming with the Soviets. Only weeks after Hitler's attack on the Soviet Union in June 1941, British and Russian troops invaded Iran, ostensibly to halt pro-German activities, and remove the shah (whose goodwill the Allies doubted). The Russians occupied northern regions of Iran, while the British did the same in the south—almost exactly according to an old 1907 line demarking a division of spheres of influence. Iran had long suffered at the hands of both powers, who now claimed yet again their right to interfere in the country. The old shah attempted to call on Roosevelt to rescue him from this insult to Iranian nationalism. The timing of his appeal was interesting, as it came just after FDR returned from a mid-August meeting with Churchill where the two leaders had proclaimed their determination to build a better world with the Atlantic Charter as a guide. The document they signed on board a warship off Nova Scotia declared that they would support the "right of all peoples to choose the form of government under which they will live."

Designed as a response to German boasts of a new Europe led by the Third Reich, the charter was controversial and constantly subject to new interpretations. As noted, Churchill apparently had not realized that someone—Roosevelt, of all people, his ally!—might look at the Atlantic Charter and say that it applied to all the world, including the utterly ridiculous assertion, to him, that it included the colonial empires. Such suggestions shocked and infuriated him. Imperial affairs were London's business and no one else's. He had not become the king's first minister, he proclaimed to anyone and everyone, to preside over the breakup of the British Empire. Nevertheless, for the rest of the war (and to Roosevelt's amusement) Churchill was constantly on the defensive.

Churchill's adamancy actually helped the Americans reassure the world that *their* war aims were universal—and *were* destined to triumph. The president was left free, it seemed, to promote the war as a struggle for the rights of all peoples, led, of course, by the United States, with its anticolonial record. The Iranians were among the first to try to take advantage of this opening in the Anglo-American front and they continued throughout the war—

and, indeed, until the 1951 oil nationalization crisis proved that Washington would recoil from supporting a radical change in the original patterns of ownership of the oil wells. Much as they were displeased by British stubbornness during that crisis, when push came to shove, it proved easier to overthrow the Iranian government than countenance such a challenge to property rights. That episode marked the first encounter between the Truman Doctrine protectorate and revolutionary nationalism and will be discussed in chapter 4.

Churchill's interest in the country he continued to call Persia had originated when he was first lord of the admiralty just before World War I. As first lord, he had authorized the purchase of a majority interest in the Anglo-Persian Oil Company to safeguard the Royal Navy's fuel supply. Since that time, control of Iran's oil resources and the huge refinery at Abadan was the highest priority for all his successors. The Russians were equally determined, meanwhile, to keep northern Iran under their influence. To challenge the imperialists, Iranian officials had long sought a "third power" presence. In 1939 Tehran encouraged Standard Oil of New Jersey to open negotiations for a concession, but drew back when Moscow protested against allowing the American company into areas bordering the Soviet Union.[42]

The shah's 1941 appeal to Roosevelt brought little immediate response beyond a patronizing letter informing him that "we must view the situation in its full perspective of present world events and developments." Soon thereafter the Allies forced the uncooperative shah to abdicate in favor of his young son. Though the attack on Pearl Harbor was still three months away, Roosevelt excused the invasion and joint occupation of Iran as necessary to the "great common effort" to prevent Hitler from engulfing countries one by one from Europe to Asia, Africa, and even the Americas. All this was standard wartime boilerplate. But there was something else of interest near the end of the letter. He informed the shah that he had requested both the Soviet Union and Great Britain to issue a public statement disavowing any designs "on the independence or territorial integrity of Iran."[43]

What Roosevelt proposed here sounded—even to the words themselves—like secretary of state John Hay's "Open Door" notes to the powers at the turn of the century, calling on them to respect China's territorial integrity. So while Roosevelt would not "intervene" in 1941, as the war went on both American policy makers and the president's special emissaries crisscrossing Iran and other Middle East countries repeatedly invoked the Atlantic Charter as laying down the law against any postwar "imperialist" designs, and insisting that in the future there must be equal opportunities for all in regard to oil concessions. Moreover, Washington did soon provide a "third power" presence. Iran was declared eligible for Lend-Lease in 1942, and with the aid came American troops—a goodly number of them. Washington created its first Persian Gulf Command to help with the shipment of Lend-Lease supplies to the Soviet Union. Eventually American forces numbered thirty thousand and engaged in all sorts of building projects, including an airfield near Abadan that raised eyebrows in British military circles. Along with the troops, moreover, came several "special" missions to aid the Iranian government with its finances and to train the national police or gendarmerie.

Personal Diplomacy

Roosevelt's early message about Iran's territorial integrity was meant as a reassurance to others as well that granting Americans the right to build air bases would not initiate a parceling out of spheres of influence (thereby anticipating Ibn Saud's concerns about Dhahran). The best way for Americans to dispel such suspicions, insisted FDR's special emissary Pat Hurley and others, would be to take a strong line with the British. Roosevelt took delight in listening to Hurley's ranting about "Perfidious Albion." The British behaved like conquerors, not allies, in the common effort in Iran, Hurley thundered, commandeering the railroad, seizing all the trucks, taking food from the people, and even insisting that the Iranians print currency to pay the British troops.

Their presence was a scourge on the land, he charged: "He had seen the corpses in the streets and had heard the women and children wailing over their dead." All this was going on while the Anglo-Persian Oil Company continued to extend its operations and had declared a 20 percent dividend. Too many Americans out there, he charged, were "pole sitters," who sat around looking out of their office windows while Iranians suffered on the ground below. Someone should be appointed to take charge of it all, a "first-rate two-fisted man, preferably in uniform," who would have the president's mandate.[44]

Roosevelt knew better than to put Hurley in charge of American interests in Iran. He was most useful to the president moving around and stirring things up throughout the whole area. From New Delhi in early November 1943, the general returned to a favorite theme: "The British are using American lend lease and American troops not for the purpose of creating a brave new world based on the Atlantic Charter and the four freedoms but for British conquest, British imperialist rule, and British trade monopoly."[45]

While for Hurley an imperialist was an imperialist under either a lion's mane or a bear's snout, Cordell Hull saw the Russians as the greater threat, especially in Iran, which bordered the Soviet Union. When the Anglo-Russian occupation began, the State Department appealed to American missionary schools throughout the country to add to their good works by countering bad influences at work in Iran. Wallace Murray, chief of the Near Eastern Division, suggested to the Presbyterian Board of Foreign Missions that its school at Tabriz could restrain "Soviet separatist and ideological activities in that area, of which much has already been heard."[46]

Murray and his colleagues, who conferred with American oil interests during the war about Iranian concessions, agreed that there must not be a repeat of the situation after World War I, when the United States had to force its way into the Middle East oil fields. In anticipation of Russian foreign minister V.M. Molotov's spring 1942 visit to Washington to discuss military strategy, Hull asked the president to put the Russians on notice that the United States expected "trustful cooperation" in Iran, and more than this, that

Moscow should be made aware of U.S. interest in helping Iran. The secretary of state also pressed secretary of war Henry Stimson to send more personnel to the military mission. He could not spare more troops, Stimson replied, but he would send more experts and advisers. "It is to our interest," Hull urged the president in mid-August 1943, "that no great power be established on the Persian Gulf opposite the important American petroleum development in Saudi Arabia."[47]

Despite warnings from the American minister in Tehran that too much overt support for American enterprise could provoke the British and Soviets to increase their pressure for additional oil concessions, the State Department encouraged Standard Oil to resume negotiations for a concession.[48] Hurley, meanwhile, got behind another concession seeker, his old company, the Sinclair Oil Corporation. While the British were willing enough to put in a bid alongside the American companies, the Russians were becoming more and more disturbed at Iranian maneuvers, especially when—at State Department urging—Tehran hired an American consulting firm to help it sort out the offers.[49]

No one talked about oil concessions at the November 1943 Tehran Conference; rather, the main subject was the date of the long-delayed "second front" in Europe. Roosevelt had at last achieved his meeting with Stalin. His immediate objective was to get the second front decision nailed down so that even Churchill could not rip it up with some clever crowbar, such as a proposed strike at the "soft underbelly" in the Balkans. But in addition to settling on a date for the invasion of Europe, FDR did hope to sound out Stalin in a preliminary way on a variety of important postwar issues. He talked privately with the Russian leader about Indochina, for example, telling him that he did not want to see the French return. He also tossed out a bold plan for Iran's future that shocked both everyone present and those who heard about it afterward. FDR suggested privately to Stalin that he should think about an international trusteeship to operate the Iranian state railroad and to create a free port on the Persian Gulf. Was this a serious proposal, Stalin

asked? It was, confirmed the president, whereupon the Russian dic-
tator excused himself for a few moments to talk to an aide. When he
returned, he said he was agreeable to the proposal.[50]

Largely forgotten after Roosevelt's death and the onset of Russian-American tensions, the "plan" grew out of a casual remark
about trusteeships for "immature" nations that the president had
made a few days earlier to the Soviet delegate to the Allied advisory
council on the Mediterranean, Andrei Vishinsky. Without much
further thought, Roosevelt had elevated it to a full-blown overture
for Russian cooperation by channeling age-old Tsarist desires for a
warm-water port on the Persian Gulf into a three-power consortium. The State Department was aghast at the notion of inviting
the Soviet Union to crowd in on the coast of Iran, let alone to come
ashore and help run the railroads! Acting secretary of state Joseph
Grew sent Roosevelt a two-page memo before Yalta that began
by giving the president credit for thinking creatively about a way
to damp down inter-Allied rivalries and push matters toward three-
power cooperation. But, of course, it was really a terrible idea in
practice. It smacked of the worst of old-world imperialism, said
Grew. The Iranians would never let foreign powers take over the
railroads without a fight. The Russians would suspect it was just another way for the United States to gain control of the northern regions, where they were particularly sensitive. And the British would
have fits. Their whole policy, and now that of the United States, he
wanted to remind Roosevelt in a passage of greater candor, was to
prevent any other power, especially Russia, from securing a foothold
in the Persian Gulf.[51]

Chastened, the president did not bring it up again. But there was
something to celebrate about the outcome of other negotiations at
Tehran. The idea for a self-denying pledge by the Big Three had
been Roosevelt's in the first place. It was in his letter to the old shah
in 1941; but now he told Hurley to pursue Churchill and Stalin
until he got their signatures on the bottom line. He succeeded, and
thus came about the Tehran Declaration on Iran that pledged the
three powers to honor all their commitments to Iran's independence and to provide economic aid to postwar Iran. Naturally, the

main source of that aid would come from the United States. Roosevelt thus put the United States into Iranian politics on an equal footing with his colleagues, and in a position to demand that the British and Russians evacuate their troops by six months after the war. Indeed, the Declaration of Tehran became a key reference point in the first Cold War crisis over Russia's efforts to coerce an oil concession out of the Iranians by leaving its troops in the country after the war ended.

Roosevelt was "dee-lighted" with Hurley's achievement. Reading the draft three-power statement, he nodded his head, and looked up at his favorite Oklahoman with a twinkle in his eye.

"By the way, Pat," he said, "where's your other star?"

"Sir?" asked Hurley, surprised.

"Your other star. You've been promoted."[52]

Big Ideas

Hurley's second star portended greater things to come in the Middle East. At Tehran Roosevelt also appointed Colonel Norman Schwarzkopf Sr., former commander of the New Jersey State Police, to take charge of training an Iranian gendarmerie. To increase his stature with the Iranians and others he dealt with, Schwarzkopf was also promoted, to brigadier general. Schwarzkopf built the police force to forty thousand men, and even boasted at one point of controlling the Iranian parliament, the Majlis. In 1946 he led this new force north to make sure Russian troops did not linger or return to stir up separatist activities, thereby gaining the young shah's confidence—so much so, indeed, that he became the perfect "bag man" for doling out money to save the Peacock Throne and the oil wells in the 1951–53 nationalization crisis.[53]

Roosevelt also chatted with Arthur C. Millspaugh, head of the American Financial Mission, and encouraged him to write personally to Harry Hopkins about a proposition "the President apparently had in mind" to make Iran into something like a "clinic"—or, as Millspaugh remembered it, into "an experiment station for the President's post-war policies and his desire to develop and stabilize backward areas."[54] Iran had requested the financial mission, and Millspaugh was determined to make something special out of it to pave the way for postwar American interests to grow and prosper. "Our control of revenues and expenditures," he would note, "not only served as a stabilizing influence but also was indispensable to the full effectiveness of Americans in other fields."[55]

The trouble was, Millspaugh explained to Roosevelt, no one had really stuck with past efforts to do things along that line. It would take at least twenty years to do the job right. The other interested powers would have to agree not to interfere, he warned, a prerequisite perhaps assured by the just-signed Declaration of the Three Powers. As the president had remarked, Millspaugh went on, the proposed arrangement could not be called a "mandate." Neither trusteeship nor receivership was the right term, he mused, while "protectorate" was simply out of the question. Why not call the plan a "partnership pact"? That "would sound well and mean well." Let it be put into operation with an American high commissioner, whose first responsibility would be to appoint experts to guide all the key ministries, including finance, agriculture, commerce, education, interior (gendarmerie), and war. Described this way, of course, Millspaugh's plan sounded like something the British Foreign Office might propose for Egypt in the days of Lord Curzon.

FDR had returned from Tehran, meanwhile, "rather thrilled with the idea of using Iran as an example of what we could do by an unselfish American policy." "Iran," he wrote Secretary Hull, "is definitely a very, very backward nation." It consisted of tribes with 99 percent of the population in bondage to the other 1 percent. "The real difficulty," the president continued, "is to get the right kind of American experts who would be loyal to their ideals, not fight among themselves and be absolutely honest financially."[56]

As it happened, the Persian Gulf commander, Major General Donald H. Connolly, was an old friend of Harry Hopkins. He wrote the president's close adviser a long memorandum, describing how an expanded American role could be modeled on the Pax Britannica. The general was nothing if not blunt about what the American "mission" should be. All this sunny rhetoric about the Atlantic Charter, he wrote Hopkins, was just that—words. Had anyone thought out where that would end up? When it came down to it, the Atlantic Charter promised to cause serious problems. Did we really want to promote an absolute right to self-determination quite so blithely? American rhetoric put too much emphasis on "the moral side of relationships with various countries and it is filled with a great deal of high idealism." [57]

Looked at squarely, Connolly went on, Iran presented a situation where Russia and Great Britain had concrete objectives in oil wells and buffer zones, while U.S. interests depended on breaking the European hammerlock on trade and mineral resources. It was as simple as that, but more than moralistic rhetoric was going to be required to achieve that end. That being so, self-denying pledges like the one just signed at Tehran provided nice-sounding headings but left the pages of the future blank—until they were filled in with an American script, or someone else's. If the United States wished to supply the text, it could not do so without abandoning the idea that all countries had a right to absolute self-determination. The British had been the most successful at "empire building," he went on, and they had accomplished quite a lot in some places to create conditions where local people could assume certain functions. But make no mistake, it was done with tight control, not only to see that local conditions in each of the colonies or areas remained stable, but also that the pieces all fit together.

Just how far was the United States willing to go, how much money was it willing to spend, and was it prepared, finally, to override the promises of national sovereignty, he wondered, "to achieve the ideal of peaceful relationship of nations"? According to Connolly, "It would mean to a certain extent, that American policy would have to follow the lines of former English policy to assume the white man's burden with regard to backward races, and this would be a difficult task." It would take two generations to help Iran achieve a strong enough government to resist outside pressure— and even then there would have to be a permanent presence. At the end of this long, and, one must say, prophetic, disquisition, Connolly offered two policy recommendations, neither of which could be found in the Atlantic Charter:

The American government should endeavor to obtain for American capital the opportunity for the acquisition of concessions to exploit the oil fields or other mineral resources throughout Persia, if not exclusively, at least on the same terms as the British or any other government.

The American government should acquire the rights to the landing fields for airplanes and the rights to maintain and operate them in the postwar period.

In a supplementary memorandum some months later, Connolly added a third recommendation. Because Iran was in a period of "colonial exploitation," the United States would have to think about exporting its businesspeople to take up the task of development. Many of the officers in his command had seen the opportunities, he wrote, and were toying with the idea that they might return to set up in business. The Iranians would contribute the local knowledge and the Americans the know-how of starting trade with the United States. The British had been very successful in tying political and economic interests together, and the United States could do just as well or better.[58]

In the aftermath of Gulf War II, the Green Zone in Baghdad, with its corps of idealistic Americans struggling to export the free market to a nation while living behind layers of protective shields with an American high commissioner writing the rules for economic behavior, may not seem such a far distance from Connally's era and his caveats about the Atlantic Charter. Connolly understood American ambitions and made his recommendations accordingly, without flinching at a vision of the United States as the new hegemonic power to replace the old imperialism. While the formal colonial era might be coming to an end, even though much blood was yet to be shed, the neo-imperial era was just beginning in the

Middle East. Indeed, by the time of Connolly's first memorandum, in February 1944, the scramble for oil concessions had already reached levels of intervention that presaged both Cold War antagonisms and the nationalist uprising that culminated in the Iranian revolution. When the Americans and British opened negotiations for oil concessions, the Soviets promptly demanded they be given a concession over nearly all the territory of northern Iran that bordered on the Soviet Union. Moscow immediately sent a high-level minister to Tehran in an attempt to bully the government into granting the concession. When matters stalled, he denounced the Iranians as unfriendly and in violation of an old 1916 agreement granting Russia such privileges. It was ironic, of course, that the Russians fell back on a pre-Bolshevik, "capitalist" agreement, one never ratified by the Iranians, to justify their claims. But oil was oil, no matter what the Tehran Declaration said.

As Connolly foresaw, the first question became how much involvement were Americans willing to accept to "defend the interests of Iran" against Russian pressures in the north and Great Britain in the south? "As complicated as matters seemed in February 1944," writes historian Mark Lytle, "they soon got worse. Over the next year the oil negotiations became entangled with at least four separate conflicts: political factionalism in Iran, competing American interests, the great power rivalries over foreign oil policy, and nascent Soviet-American cold war tensions."[59]

With American support, indeed encouragement, the Iranian government suspended all negotiations for oil concessions until after the war, when, according to Allied commitments, all foreign troops were to be withdrawn. At the Yalta Conference, Roosevelt had urged on Stalin and Churchill the necessity for postwar cooperation in Iran. His appeal did not quiet Foreign Minister Molotov, who challenged his British and American counterparts to reverse their stand on postponement and the proposed Russian concession. British foreign secretary Anthony Eden and U.S. secretary of state Edward Stettinius hastened to reassure him that they thought Russia should have a concession—but not before foreign troops had been withdrawn. Getting nowhere, Molotov decided to let the question ride, closing the discussion by remarking, "The situation [is] not acute at the present time."[60]

Washington increased its pressure on the troop withdrawal question, but as Connolly had urged, the United States sought to keep the airfields that the Persian Gulf Command had built near Abadan, the refinery site of Anglo-Iranian Oil. It was desirable to keep them, wrote secretary of war Robert Patterson, to assure the Air Transport Command routes across North Africa to India. Perhaps, he said, Trans World Airlines, an American commercial company, could operate it under a contract with the War Department. Trans World was already the chosen instrument for expanding American airlines into Saudi Arabia.[61]

The air base at Abadan was evacuated but the Americans had nevertheless come to stay. Over the next five years, the "American Century" was truly launched in the Middle East, as Washington took charge of managing the fallout from the creation of the state of Israel, allotting military weapons to friends, keeping the Russians out, and containing Arab nationalism. Had he lived, Truman said to American diplomats stationed in the Middle East, Roosevelt had planned to send him to "visit all these countries of the Middle East and other countries on an extended tour." Well aware that the Middle East would never be the same again at the end of World War II, a French diplomat commented dourly to an American counterpart that he had observed in "recent graduating exercises at Annapolis the candidates had dipped their rings in a vase of water from the seven seas, whereas previously the water for this ritual had come from the Atlantic, the Pacific, and the Caribbean."[62]

With the Truman Doctrine in 1947 the Americans repeated the assurances that the Athenian representative Euphemus gave to Sicilians at Camarina in 415 b.c.: "We are forced to intervene in many directions simply because we have to be on our guard in many directions; now, as previously, we have come as allies to those of you here who are being oppressed; our help was asked for, and we have not arrived uninvited." Euphemus added, however, that "it is not for you to constitute yourselves judges of our behaviour or to act like schoolmasters and try to make us change our ways. That is not an easy thing to do now."[63]

In 1947 Dean Acheson would put it this way. The United States had undertaken to send military aid to Greece and Turkey because "we are willing to help people who believe the way we do, to continue to live the way they want to live."[64]

3

THE TRUMAN DOCTRINE PROTECTORATE

*Great Britain had within the hour handed the job of world leadership,
with all its burdens and all its glory, to the United States.*
— Joseph M. Jones, *The Fifteen Weeks*

*It may be wise to point out that American interest in the Mediter-
ranean is not a new thing. The earliest history of the American Navy
dealt with the Mediterranean. In fact, we were more active there than
we have ever been anywhere since we have had merchant shipping.
The actions of the pirates of the Barbary Coast in connection with that
shipping brought it home to us very sharply.*
— Navy secretary James V. Forrestal, 1947

As his profile edged out from behind Roosevelt's long shadow at
Potsdam, Harry Truman considered what places worried him most.
FDR was the "New Deal" president who had restored the nation's
confidence in itself during the Great Depression, and he was the
man who called on "Dr. Win the War" to defeat the Axis powers.
Now Truman had to find the way to win the peace. Despite common beliefs in the Cold War, Eastern Europe was not at the top of
the list, and besides, getting the Red Army out of those countries by
force was not something the public would support. Truman was determined, however, to prevent Japan from being divvied up into occupation zones. Seeing Stalin as a wily and determined foe in the
pattern of other would-be conquerors out of the East, he focused as
well on protecting the Mediterranean. Thus, when the Soviet khan
scorned his proposals for internationalizing the Black Sea Straits,
he felt sure he knew his man. "I had proposed the internationaliza-

tion of all the principal waterways," Truman would claim later. "Stalin did not want this. What Stalin wanted was control of the Black Sea Straits and the Danube." The handwriting was on the wall for all the world to see: *The Russians were planning world conquest.*[1]

There was actually much more to that exchange, as we will see, but the episode aroused in Truman visions of ancient battles and a sense of personal destiny at being put in the White House to stop the Russian advance at the historical crossroads of empire in the Middle East. This was not going to be easy, he told Congress nearly two years later, on March 12, 1947, but now it could not be avoided. Greece and Turkey needed American help, immediately, or they would succumb to outside pressures. The stakes had never been higher. It "must be the policy of the United States to support free peoples who are resisting attempted subjugation by armed minorities or by outside pressures." Failure to respond would have wide-scale repercussions. But while vivid images of Russian legions poised to strike down at Greece and encircle Turkey in giant pincers raced through newspaper columns in the next few days, the Truman Doctrine was not about stopping Russian tanks rumbling along ancient paths of conquest.

And despite the deliberate war-scare rhetoric, Truman's speech was about propping up a shaky regime in Greece and establishing a military presence in the eastern Mediterranean. If those governments lost their mandate, "confusion and disorder might well spread throughout the entire Middle East."[2] It was about the projection of American power into the Mediterranean and the creation of a system of Cold War protectorates that would make up the "Free World." In other words, the American quest was little different in purpose from that of previous powers seeking to dominate the area. Historian William Roger Louis quotes the American minister to Egypt, Alexander Kirk, for example, who hailed the coming era in the Middle East as one of liberation from British "dependence in perpetuity" and induction into the "American system" for their own good: "The American system . . . is based on the intent to help backward countries to help themselves in order that they may lay the foundation for real self dependence. *Needless to say a stable world order can be achieved only under the American system.*"[3]

Truman and his aides saw the July 1945 Potsdam Conference as an opportunity to clear the decks of World War II issues and to begin the quest for a stable world order with a series of tests for Stalin. None was closer to Truman's heart than a proposal to bring an international regime into being to supervise European waterways—especially, as it turned out, those running through Eastern Europe. Where Roosevelt had liked to drag out discussions, the new president had little patience with extended consideration of details. Roosevelt had believed that answers would eventually present themselves during debate—not so Truman, who believed that was a waste of time as matters only got worse.

Truman and the Dire Straits

Old barriers to transnational trade on European rivers, Truman asserted, had been a major cause of strife and war. Because the rivers under consideration ran through territory controlled now by the Red Army, he thought it would be a good test of whether Stalin was willing to go along with an Open Door policy in Eastern Europe.

Before he could really get into details, however, Stalin made the first move, laying on the table *his* proposal to revise the 1936 Montreux Convention that governed access to the Mediterranean through the Black Seas Straits. As matters stood, Turkey was the appointed guardian under that convention. Looking ahead to such a Russian gambit, the British had sought to persuade Ankara to enter the war against Germany as a means of protecting its postwar interests by lessening the opportunity for Moscow to make any claims against an ally. But Stalin set forth at Potsdam a plea for justice and equity as one of the victors, asserting that under the prevailing Straits regime his country had no more say than Japan, an enemy country and never a Mediterranean power. The convention should be revised to assign Russia and Turkey joint responsibility for transit through the Straits, including the right to maintain the fortifications that protected the strategic waterway.

Truman countered with the American proposal to internationalize inland European waterways. His plan, he suggested, would also be a good model for the Straits. In Truman's memoirs the ensuing exchange was boiled down to a "gotcha" exposé of Stalin's ultimate planning for "world conquest." But the actual response was not so sinister. Well, said Russian foreign minister V.M. Molotov, if this was such a good model, why stop with European rivers and the Straits? Why not apply it to Suez and Panama? Molotov's rejoinder did not appear in the history Truman would write as an account of the Potsdam conference.

And then the debate continued between British prime minister Winston Churchill and Molotov:

CHURCHILL said that the guarantee they [the United States and Great Britain] proposed would be more than a substitute for the fortification of the Straits.

MOLOTOV inquired if the Suez Canal were under the same principle?

CHURCHILL rejoined that it was open in war and peace to all.

MOLOTOV inquired if it were under the same international control as was proposed for the Black Sea Straits?

CHURCHILL said that this question had not been raised.

MOLOTOV said that he was asking. If it was such a good rule why not apply it to the Suez.

Truman interrupted at this point to say that his idea for the Straits did not contemplate fortifications of any kind, which effectively brought the discussion to an end. The president tried a new tack near the end of the conference, when he asked, as a favor to him, if the proposal could be put in the final document as unfinished business? Stalin broke in with, "Nyet." "Then very deliberately," recalled ambassador Robert Murphy, "he repeated in English, 'No. I say no!'" It was the only time Murphy heard him speak English. "Truman could not mistake the rebuff. His face flushed and he turned to the American delegation and exclaimed, 'I cannot understand that man.'"[4]

At Yalta, Secretary of State Stettinius had spoken with Molotov about Moscow's "eligibility" for a trusteeship over an Italian colony. But these various soundings and ruminations led to no specific proposals. There never really had been a Roosevelt "plan" to deal with such situations, only dreamy musings, and his successor was of a different mind altogether. Two days after Japan announced it would accept Allied surrender terms, the fate of the Italian colonies was discussed in the State Department. The policy makers quickly concluded the United States should oppose Russian efforts to control an area near vital oil reserves. That ended the Italian colony question—at least for Washington.[5]

By the time of the London Conference in mid-September, therefore, Truman's aides had primed Jimmy Byrnes to step in if the Russians resurrected the Yalta "promise." Outside the London Conference, the Russians had now sent bullying notes to Turkey insisting on bilateral talks about territories lost at the end of World War I, and proposing their Potsdam plan for securing the Straits by Soviet-Turkish military cooperation. Elsewhere in the Middle East, Russian troops remained in northern Iran after VE Day and were suspected of encouraging separatists in Azerbaijan, an area straddling the Russo-Iranian border, with separate ethnic roots from both countries, and near where the Russians were trying to secure an oil concession. To complete the picture, a civil war loomed in Greece pitting British-supported royalist forces against Communist-led guerrillas, who were supplied by Yugoslavia's Marshal Tito, then a Moscow ally.

When the London conference opened, Byrnes at once seized the initiative on the Italian colonies, proposing they be put under international trusteeships for ten years. After that time, he said, as the Atlantic Charter and subsequent declarations had promised, they would have the opportunity, like all other peoples of the world, "to choose the form of government under which they wished to live." Not surprisingly, Molotov protested that Russia had been promised it could administer one of the North African territories taken from Italy. He then asserted his country's "moral claim" to administer Tripolitania. Russia's role in the war had earned it the right, he said, to play a more active part in the fate of the Italian colonies than rank-and-file members of the United Nations.

No, Byrnes argued, there was a still higher moral issue at stake! Molotov's position, he warned, replayed the scenario after World War I, when the victors parceled out among them the choice parts of the Ottoman Empire. He would have none of it. World War II had ended such crass dealings once and for all. The Allies could not betray the Arab peoples, who "had supported us during this war because they had faith in the declaration of principles which we had all made during the war, and particularly with respect to the right of all peoples to choose the form of government under which they were to live."[6]

North of today's Libya and west of Suez, Tripolitania is directly south of Greece across the Mediterranean. Anything that came that close to Suez was sure to trigger a British outcry. When British foreign secretary Ernest Bevin and Molotov met privately to go over the question, the discussion would have brought smiles to the ghosts of Lord Curzon and his Russian counterparts as their successors turned the room into a nineteenth-century echo chamber, with old accusations and complaints bouncing off the walls. Molotov began the shouting match by accusing Bevin of losing interest in Russia now that the war was over and the Red Army was no longer needed to do Britain's dirty work in preserving the empire. During the last war, he said, the British had offered Constantinople to the tsar. This time Russia was being denied even "a little corner in the Mediterranean" to prevent the Turks from holding them by the throat. Bevin shot back that if Russia worried about being strangled, Britain feared being cut in half across its lifeline to Suez. He did not mention, however, that London had it in mind to establish new military bases in Libya to coordinate with other strongpoints to protect British control of the Suez Canal.[7]

Near the end of the London Conference—where little progress was made on any issue—Molotov offered a compromise of sorts.

While still suggesting that Russia should be allowed to administer Tripolitania, he joked, "If you won't give us one of the Italian colonies, we should be quite content to have the Belgian Congo." Byrnes was not amused by this clever reference to the uranium ore–rich colony. Whether Molotov was at all serious, Byrnes took him at face value. The real objective of the Russian demand for Tripolitania, he warned Truman's cabinet on his return, "was so they might have access over land to sources of uranium in the Belgian Congo."[8]

The First Cold War Crisis

Washington was no longer interested in any revisions of the Montreux Convention, neither Truman's Potsdam proposal for internationalization of the Straits nor anything that might increase in the slightest Russian leverage.[9] The president even fretted that he did not have the "divisions" if the Russians pushed matters to an extreme in the Middle East. At the end of 1945 it appeared possible there could be a clash over Iran, where Russian troops continued their occupation in areas close to the border. According to the 1943 Tehran Declaration, the two occupying powers, Britain and Russia, had agreed—after American urging—to evacuate their forces within ninety days of the end of the war. But Moscow now came forth to claim that a prior agreement between the two countries, signed in 1921, gave it the right to intervene to preserve order. Stalin insisted his troops were there for that mission and to protect Russian oil wells in the nearby Caucasus from someone with a book of matches. At the December foreign ministers' conference in Moscow, Byrnes "threatened" that he would present the Iranian case to the first full session of the United Nations in the spring of 1946. Stalin quipped that he would not do anything to embarrass his erstwhile allies, and left Byrnes to figure out his next step.[10]

That was not enough for Truman. When Byrnes got home the president complained he had not been kept properly informed of the negotiations—a reference to a *New York Times* article about the "ominous silence" on Iran in the conference protocol. "I think that we ought to protest with all the vigor of which we are capable against the Russian program in Iran," he wrote in a letter to his secretary of state—which he probably did not send. "There isn't a doubt in my mind that Russia intends an invasion of Turkey and the seizure of the Black Sea Straits to the Mediterranean. Unless Russia is faced with an iron fist and strong language another war is in the making."[11]

The president's fixation on the Black Sea Straits always came to the fore whenever he discussed Middle East questions. On Iran there was really little more for the moment that could be done except what Byrnes had attempted in threatening Moscow with public exposure. The Iranians themselves—with American support—did bring the issue to the United Nations. The matter was finally resolved, however ambiguously, when the Iranian prime minister promised Moscow it could bid for an oil concession. The Russians then backed off from support of a separatist movement and withdrew their troops.

Like the debates at London, the Iranian episode foreshadowed later Cold War issues, but it also highlighted ancient traditional rivalries over spheres of influence and oil concessions. The really radical moves in Iran and other Middle East countries, moreover, had less to do with the penetration of Communist influence than with new nationalist feelings stirring local governments. The Iranians played their cards well, dragging out the negotiations with Moscow for over a year as East-West tensions grew. Against the background of Winston Churchill's March 5, 1946, "Iron Curtain" speech at Westminster College in Fulton, Missouri—with President Truman sitting behind him on the stage—British diplomats had continued to encourage alarmist sentiments in the United States about Russian ambitions in the Middle East. But then a strange thing happened. The British suddenly dropped their opposition to the Russian bid for a concession, and indeed urged Tehran to conclude the negotiations. The American ambassador, George Allen, continued to encourage opponents of prime minister Ahmad Qavam's Moscow "deal" by asserting the right of the Majlis (parliament) to make its own choice on the disposal of oil resources. The Foreign

Office was not happy about Allen's interference or what he might be stirring up. For the British it had become a question of the lesser of two evils. London newspapers reported fears "that if the Iranian Government were encouraged to resist Soviet demands for oil concessions in the north it might later decide to cancel British oil concessions in the south."[12]

And that was indeed the way things started to shape up. No less interested than the British in securing oil concessions, the Americans—by playing the role FDR had essayed in his post-Yalta meetings with the "three kings," and Byrnes, by championing the rights of Arab countries to self-determination at the London Conference against Russian claims to administer territory in North Africa—had indeed stirred things up with promises of a new order. In Iran the Russians had been stopped, true, but the nationalist fervor aroused by the debate over the Russian concession bubbled up around all foreign concessions. The Majlis defeated the Russian contract 102–2, but then immediately passed Qavam's five-point oil bill stipulating that the Anglo-Iranian Oil Company (AIOC) "must" negotiate to give "a higher share of its profits" to Iran. In a stiff-necked fashion more suited to the previous century's imperial hauteur, London shrugged off the Iranian demand. No provision existed in the concession for revision of its terms, sniffed the Labour government, and, besides that, there were no grounds to complain that the arrangement was "unduly onerous" for Iran. Perhaps, after consideration, some minor changes could be considered, but nothing more.

Last updated in 1933, the AIOC concession was supposed to remain in force for sixty years. With new gusts of nationalist winds blowing across the Middle East, it strained the imagination to believe that the British concession would last that long basically unchanged. Eventually foreign oil companies would have to compete for new concessions and pay higher royalties to hold on to old ones. The challenge of doing so came sooner rather than later when the American company ARAMCO made a new contract with Saudi Arabia on better terms than had ever been seen in the Middle East.[13]

Too Many Promises

Thus it was ARAMCO that delivered a body blow to the old order, not the Russians, something the British had foreseen. All this would play out during the 1951–53 oil nationalization crisis, which ended with an American CIA coup to restore a nervous and frightened young shah to the Peacock Throne. Meanwhile, the scene shifted again to even noisier Anglo-American differences over the fate of Palestine. Britain had held the mandate over Palestine since the end of World War I when the victors parceled out the Ottoman Empire. But maintaining friendly relations with Middle Eastern governments had become problematic for the British because of the 1917 Balfour Declaration pledging support for a Jewish homeland in Palestine. In 1939, as war loomed with Germany, London had to deal with Arab unrest and rioting. After a conference with various Arab leaders while Zionist leaders fretted in the background, the British government issued a "White Paper." It called for the creation of a fully independent, binational state in Palestine after ten years. During that period, Jewish immigration to Palestine would be held to 75,000, and future immigration would depend on Arab consent. Zionist leaders were also upset about restrictions put on the sale of Arab property to Jews.[14]

Clearly, the British White Paper was unsatisfactory, and no one thought it was at all relevant to realities on the ground. The British high commissioner in Palestine warned that even a million soldiers could not prevent the coming struggle and its accompanying terrorism on both sides. During the war, Roosevelt stepped into the dispute, trying to find some "compromise" with Zionist demands for a national homeland and the adamant Arab resistance—without success. His efforts to finesse the Palestine question were overtaken at war's end by revelations of the Holocaust and the refugee problem in Europe.[15]

With concern already growing about Egyptian nationalism, London desperately wanted to maintain military strongpoints near the Suez Canal. Libya to the west and Palestine on the east offered the best possibilities. British forces could reach the canal within an hour or two from a naval base at Haifa and air bases in the Negev desert. Colonial secretary George Hall told the House of Commons, however, that over and above military bases, Britain's "great strategic safeguard in the Middle East was the friendship of its governments and people."[16]

London feared that large-scale Jewish immigration would wreck those friendships. Truman was also well aware that Palestine could play out in terrible ways, but he feared more than anything else being called on to send thousands of troops to enforce some unworkable plan like the White Paper. Otherwise, what weighed on his mind was the fate of the refugees. Originally he was not anxious to see the creation of a Zionist state. It was becoming painfully clear, however, that he could not separate the two, especially as the political pressure from pro-Zionist groups grew and the Democrats attempted to win elections with a candidate who lacked Roosevelt's charisma. "However much Truman may have been agitated by the public pressure and criticism aimed at him by the Zionist lobby," writes Israeli historian Michael Cohen, "he was still in need of Jewish finance, especially in election years."[17]

On his return from Potsdam, a reporter asked, "What was the American view on Palestine at Berlin?" He answered: "We want to let as many of the Jews into Palestine as it is possible to let into that country. Then the matter will have to be worked out diplomatically with the British and the Arabs, so that if a state can be set up there they may be able to set it up on a peaceful basis. I have no desire to send 500,000 American soldiers there to make peace in Palestine."[18]

Over the next several weeks and months Truman dueled publicly and acrimoniously with foreign secretary Ernest Bevin over the president's insistence that one hundred thousand refugees be admitted to Palestine as soon as possible. On one occasion a reporter asked if perhaps we would "get along better with England if we made some gesture toward welcoming a few of these immigrants to the United States?" Irritated, Truman tried to dismiss the matter with a brusque reply: the reporter knew what the immigration laws were, didn't he? "We have to comply with them." But that opened the way for a follow-up question. Did the president intend recommending any change in the laws? "I do not."[19]

Bevin—frustrated and angry at worldwide criticism of the British refusal to allow shiploads of Jewish immigrants to land—lashed out at a Labour Party Conference: "I hope I will not be misunderstood in America if I say that this [hundred thousand] was proposed with the purest of motives. They do not want too many Jews in New York." Bevin's Labour colleagues were embarrassed by this ugly display, but Truman somewhat surprisingly told a correspondent he understood the pressure on the foreign secretary, because he was often tempted to blow up himself at the pressure and agitation from New York, a remark it was not possible to misinterpret.[20]

Even so, Truman did not back down from his demand that one hundred thousand refugees be admitted to Palestine. And he knew what the game was. Bevin's objective, the president always believed, was simply to draw the United States into joint responsibility for whatever happened, so that the Arabs would have someone else to blame. The Americans had used World War II to gain the upper hand and were now all over the Middle East, but they could ruin things for everyone. Truman's affirmative statements about the refugees, however, were picked up by the Saudi Arabian government, which promptly demanded that the letters exchanged by Roosevelt and Ibn Saud be made public. The request left Secretary Byrnes in a quandary, forcing him to tell the British ambassador, on the one hand, that FDR was really too ill at that time to be transacting such important business, and to reconfirm to the representatives of Middle Eastern countries, on the other hand, that American policy had not changed since Roosevelt's letters. It was still the intention of the United States to "consult" with both Arabs and Jews before anything was done about Palestine's future. "Consult" was obviously a weaker expression than the impression conveyed in FDR's correspondence, especially his letter of April 5, 1945, which said that "no decision" would be taken without "full consultation" with both Arabs and Jews, and that he would "take no action . . . which might prove hostile to the Arab people."[21]

Even though Roosevelt's letters contained no binding commitment—as Truman rightly said—Arab leaders complained of being nuanced to death. It was not an unfair accusation. Secretary Byrnes tried to explain to British ambassador Lord Halifax how Truman understood the situation. "The problem now," he informed a non-plussed Halifax, "is . . . to determine the number that could be absorbed into the population. He could not join in a plan to divert from that." While Byrnes had given no commitment to a Jewish state, State Department specialists on the Middle East were deeply alarmed at the course the president was now steering, almost as if he had made himself captain of the lead ship filled with refugees steering toward Palestine.[22]

The career diplomats' concerns were a lot like those voiced by Bevin. William Eddy had returned home from Saudi Arabia in the fall of 1945 for a chiefs-of-mission conference hoping to head off any action that would commit Washington to the Zionist cause. Ibn Saud had made it clear to him before he left, Eddy said, that promises of "consultation" were not enough. He expected that the publication of Roosevelt's letter would put an end to Zionist demands for unilateral action. If it did not, there would be serious implications for American policy in the Middle East. The independence and survival of the Arab state of Palestine, he said, was a question for the nations of the region to determine, not a matter for Americans, Jew or Gentile, living five thousand miles away. Saud had not said he would take action against ARAMCO to retaliate against Washington if it went ahead with plans to put Jewish refugees into Palestine, but there were other dangers, specifically to the future of the Dhahran air base. "The more fanatic" Arabs, reported Eddy, had already called Dhahran a "base for political aggression and foreign occupation."[23]

Eddy's reminder that oil was not the only question involved draws attention to an issue that has persisted from this immediate postwar moment down to the time of the Gulf Wars. American plans and prospects for the Middle East required military bases, not just oil derricks. While the White House effectively responded to the State Department's concerns about oil—that the Arabs had no place else to sell their crude no matter what policy Truman pursued about Palestine—questions of stability and the American military presence were bound to be exacerbated by a pro-Zionist stance. The president did agree to meet with the diplomats to hear their arguments—for half an hour on November 10, 1945. They made the case the Arab world deserved the central place in foreign policy thinking, not only as a "counterpoise" to Zionist ambitions, or because it was at the center of British strategic concerns, or athwart the great air routes of the future, or even because it happens to contain both "the two cradles of civilization and the greatest known undeveloped oil reserves of the world." It deserved attention because of the revolutionary ferment spreading across the area, which posed the greatest challenge: "If the United States fails them, they will turn to Russia and will be lost to our civilization; of that we feel certain." Above all, the diplomats asked, what could they tell these governments about American policy toward "political Zionism"? Truman smiled at his own nascent Cold War rhetoric being thrown back at him: "That *is* the sixty-four-dollar question." It had caused him more trouble already, he admitted, than almost any issue facing the United States. He latched on to their phrase "political Zionism," however, to fashion his answer. He hoped that admitting "some refugees from Europe" would "alleviate" the situation at least long enough to work on a compromise with "'humanitarian' Zionists," but confessed he was not at all confident, because Palestine was and would continue to be a "burning issue" in domestic politics.[24]

A Churchill Argument for a Joint Protectorate

Truman was a good prophet. Palestinians and the Arab-Israeli conflict flared up from time to time over the next four decades until it burned with a white-hot flame on a permanent basis. The diplomats thought of Iran, Turkey, and Greece as a "piecrust guarding the anomalous Middle East," but it was a dangerously thin layer covering the nation's "strategic oil reserve" in Saudi Arabia. Palestine, they argued, changing Truman's metaphor, was a sharp knife cutting through that crust. Supporting Zionism would drive the Arabs to

Russia and create a pro-Soviet base on the Mediterranean, as the Jewish refugees brought with them old allegiances from Eastern Europe. But former prime minister Winston Churchill, a pro-Zionist, turned the argument on its head and gave Truman other counter-arguments. Churchill's main concern in the debate over Palestine's future, however, was not to forfeit the momentum of Anglo-American cooperation established during the war. His Iron Curtain speech offered a good view down the path leading to the Truman Doctrine. "Far from the Russian frontiers and throughout the world," he intoned, "Communist fifth columns are established and work in complete unity and absolute obedience to the directions they receive from the Communist center." These secret cadres constituted "a growing challenge and peril to Christian civilization."

"Turkey and Persia are both profoundly alarmed and disturbed at the claims which are being made upon them and at the pressure being exerted by the Moscow government," the speech went on. Confronted by these challenges, general and specific, the United States and Britain must develop a common strategy. "Would a special relationship between the United States and the British Commonwealth be inconsistent with our overriding loyalties to the World Organization? I reply that, on the contrary, it is probably the only means by which that organization will achieve its full stature and strength." The British Empire had much to offer, including bases all over the world: "This would perhaps double the mobility of the American navy and air force. It would greatly expand that of the British Empire forces and it might well lead, if and as the world calms down, to important financial savings. Already we use together a large number of islands; more may well be entrusted to our joint care in the near future."

Churchill's pro-Zionist stance, so out of tune with Labour, helped Truman with critics. He put his own government on the defensive on that issue by implying that a united Anglo-American front would check the Arab "fanatics" so many talked about (who were, in any event, less of a problem than keeping the Russians out). While it was certainly possible that the Palestine issue could unravel the "special relationship" into separate threads, building up the Soviet threat as a way of encouraging Americans to take seriously the general situation in the Middle East had become a central concern of British policy makers. The British purpose all along, writes historian John Keay, was to draw the United States into defending the periphery, Greece and Turkey, as vital to their common purposes.[25]

The Iron Curtain speech marked the first instance of a British statesman—in this instance, a past and future prime minister—essaying the role of advocate of an Anglo-American empire to replace the Pax Britannica. As Eddy had argued, one key for holding sway in the Middle East was the expansion of military facilities. Churchill's references to those advantages of joint Anglo-American dominion have not been much noted compared to the dramatic nature of his description of Soviet expansion from the Baltic to Trieste. But his meaning was clear. The United States needed Great Britain's experience and access to its strategic outposts. Truman's March 12, 1947, speech a year later was in some ways a response to the Iron Curtain speech, saying that the United States appreciated the offer but had a different idea about how to go about the project. Tony Blair's courtier role at the outset of a later president's initiative was in line with Churchill's offer, if largely limited to providing moral support.

Talking Tough

Churchill delivered the Iron Curtain speech at a tense moment in the Iranian "crisis." Instead of starting a war, Stalin settled for a promise of an oil concession (which never materialized) and verbal denunciations of Churchill as a racial theorist like Hitler: "Mr. Churchill and his friends . . . present nations not speaking the English language with something like an ultimatum: 'Recognize our lordship voluntarily and then all well be well. In the contrary case, war is inevitable.'" But the majority of the world's people did not speak English, he said, and would not consent to go into a new slavery.[26]

Tensions rose and fell, first over Iran, and then again when

Moscow renewed its effort to hustle Turkey into an agreement that would allow the Soviets to establish military bases near the Black Sea Straits. Talking with reporters onboard the presidential yacht, USS *Williamsburg*, as he stirred a bourbon highball, President Truman shrugged off the possibility of war in the near future. "No," he said, "I don't think we'll ever have any real trouble with Russia— not for a long time to come anyway. Russia is afraid to death of having to fight anybody right now and they know it would be over pretty quickly if they got into war with us. We's [*sic*] got too much stuff for them, too many thing[s] that they haven't got."[27]

When the Soviets renewed their campaign to persuade Turkey to yield to their demands on the Straits, Truman decided to demonstrate his toughness. Here was a golden opportunity to cast all these questions—the Straits, Greece, Turkey, and Iran—into an East-West framework. Navy secretary James Forrestal, always an ardent proponent of a "get tough" policy, led the charge, asserting that Moscow hoped to push out into the Mediterranean as far as five hundred miles, to be able to cut British lifelines to India. Dean Acheson, the under secretary of state, previously a moderate, joined him, saying that the demands foretold efforts to infiltrate and dominate Greece—with all that meant for the area. But, he added, Truman should be aware he could wind up in an armed conflict. The president seemed pleased at the prospect of showing he was tough enough for the job, and almost blasé about calling Moscow's bluff: "We might as well find out whether the Russians were bent on world conquest now as in five or ten years."[28]

The only dissenter appeared to be General Dwight Eisenhower. He thought Russian actions did not demonstrate that they were aiming at world conquest. Much to his surprise, Forrestal wrote in his diary, the general could not conceive of a Russian occupation of a part of Dardanelles Straits as "being an occasion for war." Forrestal quickly dismissed the World War II commander's opinion. It displayed the army's inability, he said, to "grasp the importance of control of the seas and their lack of appreciation of strategy in the broadest geographic terms." The navy was better at this, going back to the famous Admiral Arthur Thayer Mahan, the founder of

American geopolitics. Yet if Ike was not sure, others in important positions might not be either. And that could become a real problem. He recommended a press campaign to alert the nation to what was at stake.[29]

The press campaign proceeded apace, but it was still too soon after the war to persuade key figures that the Soviet Union had any intention of starting a war over the Dardanelles. C.L. Sulzberger wrote in the New York Times that from conversations he had with two high-ranking staff officers (Eisenhower, for one?) he had learned that the Soviet Union would be in no position to launch a war for "a minimum of two decades: it has no strategic air force, it has no navy, and, as far as is known, it has no atomic weapons." In fact, with the ability to send navy flotillas anywhere, the situation was pretty much the reverse; the American frontier was now, as one article put it, on the Dardanelles.[30]

Truman's advisers had become desperate to find a winning hand domestically to go with the A-bomb in foreign policy. With crucial midterm elections looming ahead, the president had problems holding together the New Deal coalition. Defections on the left did not bother him very much—in fact, he had always looked askance at FDR's liberal advisers. But he needed something to appeal to the middle range of voters. A clear electoral strategy using the Cold War had yet to be worked out, but it was not absent from White House thinking, especially not when the carrier *Franklin D. Roosevelt* was available to lead the way around the Mediterranean. On October 5, 1946, Secretary Forrestal announced that the carrier and several cruisers would remain on station to support allied occupation policies in Europe and "to protect United States interests and support United States policies in the area."[31]

A month later, further details emerged about American "courtesy calls" at various ports in the Mediterranean, Alexandria, Port Said, Izmir, Maramas, Crete, Lebanon, and on to Jiddah, Saudi Arabia. At the request of the State Department, however, the War Department had postponed a flight of B-29s to the area. "Some officials speculated," read a wonderfully puckish newspaper account, "that ultimately the bomber flight also would be carried out, if for no other reason than that the State Department would not want to discriminate between the War and Navy Departments." A British Foreign Office note caught the mood, even if it overstressed the element of "unconsciousness" in American policy: "The Americans, without necessarily knowing it, are bound to continue to see the world through the British window. Furthermore, their strategic power depends obviously and inevitably on both the resources and the geographical distribution of the British Commonwealth. If we can make shrewd use of these two main ways in which the United States depend on us, we may yet be able to turn their immensely superior power to our benefit as well as to that of the world as a whole."[32]

The Romans had called the Mediterranean mare nostrum, and now the claim belonged to Washington. As 1947 began, prime minister Clement Attlee felt concerned about what he had learned of American military plans, especially Operation Pincher, that posited attacks on the Soviet Union from bases in Turkey. It had been decided in Washington, he wrote to Foreign Secretary Bevin, that the only way to attack the Soviet Union was from the Middle East: "This needs very careful consideration." Such a strategy meant relying on the "congeries of weak, backward and reactionary states" to make it work: "We shall constantly appear to be supporting vested interests and reaction against reform and revolution in the interests of the poor. We have already that difficulty in Greece." Obviously, Moscow's pressure on the Turks to change the regime in the Straits could be a trigger to that plan. But by the time the United States had organized its "courtesy" visits to ports in the Mediterranean, the Soviets had already softened their demands— just as they had in Iran. As historian Arnold Offner writes, "Expansion of U.S. power into the Mediterranean had just begun."[33] The weeks and months from the time of Churchill's famous speech were filled with events and initiatives that knitted together the Truman administration's domestic and foreign policies. These included the arrest of Russian atomic spies in Canada in February, paired with U.S. tests of atomic bombs at Bikini Atoll in July that kept popular attention focused on the possibility of a World War III. The Republican victory in the 1946 congressional elections alerted Truman's advisers that the White House needed to focus on sustaining momentum on all fronts and could not be perceived as simply following a British lead. That is one way of understanding the rhetorical coating of the Truman Doctrine. But domestic party politics do not explain an expansionist agenda, or the perceived need for asserting specific objectives in an ideological doctrine. The "Russian" threat, as Truman understood, presented the opportunity to seize the moment to secure what American arms and their technological breakthrough with the atomic bomb seemed to offer: the tempting vision of omnipotence.

Carpe Diem

American military power was already present in the Mediterranean area and growing when the British ambassador presented his famous note to the State Department at the end of February, explaining the plight of His Majesty's government. It could no longer support the Greek government or provide military supplies to Turkey at a level sufficient to ensure their survival as allies. Afraid that a Republican-controlled Congress would not support the president, Truman's advisers arranged for him to meet with key leaders in the White House. At the meeting, Under Secretary Acheson described a vast Kremlin-directed Communist movement spreading out of southeastern Europe and spreading down across Africa. It was a bravura performance. After a stunned pause, senator Arthur Vandenberg allegedly burst out that Truman must go before Congress and "scare hell out of the country."[34]

Before the Truman Doctrine speech on March 12, 1947, asking for $500 million in military and economic aid to Greece and Turkey, favored journalists received leaks of what was brewing to build up support for administration positions. They became, in effect, part of the campaign, a tradition that would hold up especially well in Gulf Wars I and II and even Afghanistan I and II. Thus the *Times* columnist James Reston dutifully reported that there had been a top secret meeting at the White House where Truman revealed that the British were unable to continue bearing the costs of aiding Greece:

> The primary short-term objective of United States foreign policy in the past two years has been to halt the expansion of Soviet influence into western Europe and the Mediterranean. To attain this objective the United States has taken a firm position vis-à-vis the Soviet Union along a line running from Stettin on the Baltic down through Germany and Austria to Trieste. . . . The British have in effect asked whether the United States was prepared to assume a great part of the responsibility for world peace and stability assumed by Britain in the nineteenth century. That is what is at issue rather than the appropriation of a loan to a small Mediterranean country.[35]

Two things stand out here: First, Reston notes that the "short-term objective" of American policy is to halt Soviet expansion; second, that future policy will not be limited to the appropriation of a loan to a small Mediterranean country.

Those were almost the exact words Acheson had used at the White House meeting, as well as the words of Churchill's Iron Curtain speech. Reston's "help" did not end there. The day after the speech, he and navy secretary James Forrestal discussed the reaction on "the Hill," and how to manipulate the situation to make sure the proposed aid bill passed. The immediate reaction, Reston told Forrestal, was "very disturbing." "I think you're going to pull it through on the argument that a situation has been created to repudiate the President," with disastrous consequences. "The really deeply disturbing thing is that the Congress of the United States is simply not ready to have this country take over the leadership which it was obviously intended to take over."[36]

Inside and outside Congress there were serious questions raised about an ideological war without boundaries, and the consequences of circumventing the United Nations. The conservative *Times* pundit Arthur Krock mused about where following the "Doctrine," with its key word, "must," might ultimately take the United States.

"What is the President's definition of 'free peoples'?" he asked readers. "The Palestine Arabs insist they are, but we are exerting 'outside pressure' there."[37] This oblique reference to the conflict over
the fallout from Roosevelt's encounter with Ibn Saud and a promise to consult Arab countries over the fate of Palestine was prescient about future difficulties. Herblock, the liberal *Washington
Post* political cartoonist, drew Uncle Sam with packed bags leaving
home with tickets for Greece and Turkey. As he paused on the
doorstep to kiss his anxious young wife, whose skirt bore the letters
UN, she commented, "You're sure you'll send for me as soon as possible?"[38]

Truman's speech on the Communist threat portrayed the danger
as so urgent there was no time to lose. But specific American interests in Middle East oil reserves and other "crude" matters were all
but eliminated from the speech, elevating old-style imperial rivalries out of the dusty arena to higher levels of statecraft where the
most powerful became the most principled. For example, in an early
draft a White House aide had highlighted oil reserves that needed
protection: "Confusion and disorder might well spread throughout
the entire Middle East . . . an area in which the United States has a
vital interest in the maintenance of peace and good order. *This is an
area of great natural resources which must be accessible to all nations and
must not be under the exclusive control or domination of any single nation. The weakening of Turkey, or the further weakening of Greece,
would invite such control.*" State Department reviewers frowned on
those sentences. We can't make the speech sound too much like an
investment prospectus, they warned. Extracting all references to oil
or the need for American dominance in the area ensured the public
got the proper instruction on American motives, such as James Reston supplied his readers: "The president has challenged the Soviet
Union in one of the most direct public statements ever issued by the
head of a major state."[39]

The message was that it had become time to go head-to-head
with the Soviets—no more "babying" Moscow. Now doubting liberals as well as conservatives could believe in what was already
called the Truman Doctrine because it seemed to follow on so logi-

cally from the successful "crusade in Europe." It was hardly surprising after the momentous struggle against fascism, and the proven wonders of American technological prowess culminating in the atomic bomb, that Americans conceived of themselves as beyond old-world definitions of imperial behavior.

Near the end of Executive Session (secret) hearings on the bill in the Senate Foreign Relations Committee, senator Walter F. George made his key point that once the United States acted unilaterally, there would be no incentive for the United Nations to take up the question. As he saw it, the administration wanted to have it both ways: it wanted to claim not only that its aid was essentially nonpartisan in terms of the internal politics of Greece and Turkey but also that the aid (most of it military) was to prevent outside forces from causing the collapse of the governments.

Acheson continued his preemptive effort to stop the George movement from gaining steam by pointing out that the United Nations simply did not have funds to appropriate for the purpose, and even if it did agree to take action, the only source was still the United States. By then it would be too late. In his prepared statement on March 24, 1947, he predicted dire happenings in the short term: "The armed bands in the north [of Greece], under Communist leadership, are already fighting. In the event of economic collapse and Government paralysis, these bands would undoubtedly increase in strength until they took over Greece and instituted a totalitarian government similar to those prevailing in countries to the north of Greece."[40]

Maintaining a sense of urgency, building on the momentum of the president's speech, was the key. Thus Acheson and other administration officials must have winced a bit at Winston Churchill's unsolicited help with an article in the New York Times on April 12, 1947, in which he got back at some early critics—including Roosevelt himself—who had raised polite questions (and some not so polite) about British military intervention to restore a reactionary monarchy in Athens during the winter of 1944–45, an action that triggered the civil strife: "On Greek affairs in 1944–45 I seemed to find myself out of step. But today it seems I was pursuing the exact policy which, little more than two years later, the United States has adopted with strong conviction. This is to me a very intense satisfaction."[41]

When senator Claude Pepper of Florida, a liberal critic of the Truman administration, warned that the State Department refused to talk about the number of people that would be killed by American military equipment, or the number of soldiers trained by American personnel, for the "Fascist-minded King" who ruled Greece, he was countered by a Republican freshman senator from Montana, Zales N. Ecton, who offered an amendment to the Truman Doctrine to give control of the atomic bomb to a commission headed by secretary of state George C. Marshall. "Many of us," he said, "feel that it will take more than American dollars to stop totalitarianism and we feel we should strengthen the hand of General Marshall."[42]

The Ecton amendment failed, but there could be little doubt most Americans understood that the military component of foreign policy now stood in control as the incipient Cold War overrode traditional ways of thinking about international competition and cooperation. Given traditional American impatience at diplomacy as just so much palaver and avoiding the facts, it was not surprising that many wished Ecton would get his way. And while Churchill might feel a strong sense of vindication, Americans defined their responsibility in the Middle East and elsewhere as much more encompassing than replacing John Bull's pomp-and-circumstance version of imperial splendor.

During the executive hearings, Acheson made it plain that there was no immediate way to get into Eastern Europe, and that the Truman Doctrine did not presage an assault on Russian positions there: "It is true that there are parts of the world to which we have no access. It would be silly to believe that we can do anything effective in Rumania, Bulgaria, or Poland. You cannot do that. That is within the Russian area of physical force. We are excluded from that. There are other places where we can be effective. *One of them is Korea, and I think that is another place where the line has been clearly drawn between the Russians and ourselves.*"[43]

Perhaps it was this reference to Korea, perhaps his general worry about where this was all leading, but Walter George expressed a cri de coeur when the senators deliberated among themselves—not made public until 1973—that sends a shock to readers even today:

> Once the fact is accomplished and we are into it, the United Nations of course will have no incentive and it will have no proper motive, at least, to make any inquiry about it. They will say, "The United States has taken this burden. Let them carry it." And they will let it run, and that will be the situation. And we will have it on our hands.
>
> I do not know that we will have to go anywhere else in this world, and I do not say that at the moment. I do not see how we are going to escape going into Manchuria, North China, and Korea and doing things in that area of the world. But at the same time that is another question, and we have got the right to exercise common sense. But I know that when we make a policy of this kind we are irrevocably committing ourselves to a course of action, and there is no way to get out of it next week or next year. *You go down to the end of the road.*[44]

The Pentagon sent General George A. Lincoln to present the case for military aid to Greece and Turkey, and he more than confirmed that the Truman Doctrine was the first signpost on a one-way road to "Far Away Places with Strange Sounding Names," as the new ballad sung by World War II songstress Jo Safford began. Those places were calling me, she sang, "Goin' to China, or maybe Siam." Lincoln put it a little differently. Greece and Turkey, he said, "are just one of the keys on the keyboard of this world piano that is being played at the present time":

> This situation we face at the present time we in the War Department, the military people, consider is what you might call subversive war. We are in an ideological struggle, apparently. The stakes of the struggle are such that they may possibly come out so the opposition attain all their ends by means short of war, and we are left

in a position where we will be unable to fight even if we wanted to or desired to.

In the broad, the big picture, we feel that Greece, Turkey, even the Middle East, have got to be viewed always in the light of the global situation. It happens that we are having a little trouble about Greece and Turkey at the present time, but they are just one of the keys on the keyboard of this world piano that is being played at the present time. Anything that happens in Greece and Turkey inevitably has an effect on the rest of the Middle East, on western Europe, and clear around the Pacific, because all these peoples are watching what the United States is doing; they are watching which ways the peoples move, and we recognize that if the countries of the world lose confidence in us they may in effect pass under the Iron Curtain without any pressure other than sub-versive pressure being put on them.

This thing that I have said is approximately what Mr. Acheson said the other day. He pointed out that we ended this war with two nations and only two great nations left in the world, and *we face a situation that we have not seen since the days of Rome and Carthage—and we all know what happened to Carthage.*[45]

The clinching argument that secured the passage of the Greek-Turkish bill, the initial down payment on the Truman Doctrine, however, was the argument that Congress could not leave the president out on a limb. And as such, it signified the presidential "revolution" in American politics. From that moment onward, the United States really had one political party: the presidential party. In July 1947 the Truman Doctrine appeared in theoretical form in an article signed "X," "The Sources of Soviet Conduct," published in *Foreign Affairs*, an elite journal read by important people in all countries. The real name of "X" was George Frost Kennan. A Foreign Service officer in the Moscow embassy at war's end, Kennan would become famous after his article appeared and its authorship was leaked to the press. The article enlarged on an earlier cable he had sent to the State Department explaining why there was no chance the Soviet Union would cooperate with American plans to rehabilitate the world economy.

Forrestal brought Kennan home after his cable received a warm welcome in Washington, and installed him at the National War College, where the office in which he then wrote the "X" article has now been enshrined with a plaque. From there he went back to the State Department to head secretary of state George C. Marshall's new Policy Planning Staff. Although the *Foreign Affairs* article had been signed "X," supposedly to protect his identity, everyone soon knew it was by the cerebral Russian expert who, while stationed in the Soviet capital, would venture out into the countryside to give readings from nineteenth-century Russian masters like Tolstoy. Kennan warned in the "X" article that the Soviet Union would seek to fill every "nook and cranny available to it in the basin of world power." Yet it would not be difficult to turn back the Russians wherever they sought to creep over or around the barriers: "If it finds unassailable barriers in its path, it accepts these philosophically and accommodates itself to them." The only real question, he believed, was whether Americans could summon the will to oppose the Soviets at every location where they threatened the nation's vital interests. If they did so, he believed, Soviet power would collapse in on itself because of its own inherent contradictions.[46]

Once the Truman Doctrine was put in place and the Marshall Plan announced for rehabilitating European economies under American direction, "containment" became the general rubric under which all American policies were shaped so as to define the Cold War as a struggle between the Free World and the Soviet Bloc.

Palestine Quarrels

Even as the ideological foundations of the American side in the Cold War were being driven deep into the nation's political consciousness, there was still the disturbing argument with London over Palestine and Zionist aspirations. The biggest problem remained the Anglo-American difference over the fates of Palestinians and the Jewish refugees. Nothing London said could change

Truman's insistence on the early admission of one hundred thousand Jews to Palestine. Finally, foreign secretary Ernest Bevin threw up his hands and tossed the question to the United Nations, as if to say to Washington, "You made the crisis, now you solve it."

The United Nations actually tried pretty hard. It created a special committee, UNSCOP, to review all the proposals. As might be expected, it came back with a divided report. The majority favored partition, the division of Palestine into an Arab and a Jewish state, and making Jerusalem a protected international city. Truman had privately favored this approach, and when the report came before the General Assembly in the fall of 1947, the United States voted for partition. Behind the scenes, however, the White House brought pressure on several governments to fall in line. It was no secret the State Department opposed these maneuvers, seeing them as a too-clever-by-half attempt by pro-Zionist aides in the presidential mansion to avoid sole responsibility for an imposed "solution" sure to alienate the Arab countries.

Meanwhile, the British continued to suffer the blame for keeping the refugees from landing, without really gaining very much sympathy from the Arab countries. Contributing to the final decision of the UNSCOP to favor partition was the infamous *Exodus* affair in the summer of 1947, when British authorities turned back a ship carrying refugees from Germany. Had the British understood the power of this image better, writes historian Ilan Pappé, they would never have made this highly symbolic journey from the land of the Holocaust into a terrible postscript to the horror of the concentration camps. But they did not, while the Americans remained aloof from any responsibility. The upshot was that the insensitive British decision "prompted UNSCOP to discuss the fate of European Jewish survivors instead of the Arab demand to determine the future of Palestine according to the demographic reality of 1947."[47]

As early as 1946, however, Truman had acknowledged the inevitable—that a Jewish homeland in Palestine "would command the support of public opinion in the United States." And that was the way he played it from that time to the creation of Israel in 1948, hoping that the one hundred thousand refugees could be settled, thereby allowing for more time to work out the way the immigrants and Palestinians could somehow live together in a divided state. American maneuvering room was curtailed, however, by a surprising development: the Soviet Union, which had shown no interest in supporting a Jewish state, turned around during the partition debate in the fall of 1947 to declare its support for such a solution. State Department experts, already in despair about the White House's pro-Zionist bent, thought the Russians had devised a clever move to penetrate the Middle East by cultivating relations with Israel after being blocked elsewhere by the Truman Doctrine. Over the long term, even if Israel did not become a political outpost for the Soviet Union, American-Arab relations would suffer as a result of the creation of a Jewish state.

The British, meanwhile, abruptly announced that they would end the mandate on May 15, 1948. With nearly one hundred thousand troops and police stationed in Palestine, not even the prospect of losing military bases could change the raw economics of the situation. The only alternative—a last-ditch one—was to support King Abdullah of what was then known as Transjordan, who lusted after the area of Palestine known as the West Bank, and imagined himself the ruler of vast territories that would include the "realms" of Syria and Lebanon. Abdullah had good contacts with the Jewish Agency, the forerunner of an Israeli provisional government. In a secret meeting with some of its leaders at the time of the partition vote, the king assured them he would not attack a Jewish state, but "he would annex Arab Palestine."[48]

What gave Dean Rusk, director of the Office of United Nations Affairs, sleepless nights was the thought that if a war broke out, the same pro-Zionist influences would accuse the Arab countries of "aggression" and go to the Security Council for redress "and will use every means to obscure the fact that it is their own armed aggression against the Arabs inside Palestine which is the cause of Arab counter-attack." The ensuing debate could be devastating: "From the aspects of our relations with the Middle East and of our broad security aspects in that region, it would be almost fatal to put forces of the United States and possibly Russia against the governments of the Arab world."[49]

The Abdullah "solution" briefly appealed to Washington. Anything was better than a political "vacuum," which could only lead to a conflict with contending forces seeking favorable borders. The UN partition resolution envisaged two future states that looked like a Picasso painting, complained policy makers, and Abdullah's "pragmatism" offered the way out of a serious impasse. The State Department, led by secretary George C. Marshall, continued to oppose the White House's "haste" in being willing to extend de facto recognition to Israel before there was a real state with internationally recognized borders. More than anything, Marshall feared a conflict that could spread out, involve the entire Arab world, and jeopardize American oil interests and the internal stability of the nearby governments. But when Truman's White House advisers, led by Clark Clifford, pointed out that the creation of a Jewish state could only be halted by American military intervention, and that the Soviet Union would be ready to grant almost immediate recognition, Marshall and his chief aide, Robert Lovett, were thrown on the defensive. In a White House meeting, Lovett produced a file of intelligence telegrams detailing Soviet activity "in sending Jews and Communist agents from Black Sea areas to Palestine." It was shortly after this display that Marshall made his famous statement that if Truman followed Clifford's advice, and if he were to vote, "I would vote against the President."[50]

Marshall and Lovett had been fighting a rearguard action. As Clifford said, a separate Jewish state was inevitable. The effectiveness of the Jewish paramilitary forces in Palestine had already determined the outcome, along with divisions in the Arab forces and, especially, Abdullah's "bargain." The very day the mandate ended, the provisional government of Israel was announced. Truman granted immediate de facto recognition, followed some months later by de jure recognition, and the first of the almost constant loans and aid grants that have become a given. On November 29, 1948, Truman wrote a warm letter to Israeli president Chaim

Weizmann acknowledging the latter's letter of congratulations on Truman's election. They both had much to celebrate, he said, but "it does not take long for bitter and resourceful opponents to re-group their forces after they have been shattered." Truman went on to say that he had interpreted his own election as a mandate on the Democratic platform, including the plank on support for Israel. Still more, he assured Weizmann that the United States would "oppose any territorial changes in the November 29th Resolution which are not acceptable to the State of Israel." It would be hard to improve on such an oath.[51]

Trying to make the shock to Arab sensibilities a little less devas-tating, Clifford drafted a statement for the president saying that he recognized Israel, expressing the hope that "when the peoples in the portion of Palestine assigned for an Arab state have set up a State in accordance with the provisions of the Resolution of the Assembly on November 29, 1947, similar recognition will be granted to that State by the United States and by the other members of the United Nations."[52] It was never used. As Dean Rusk had feared, the vio-lence accompanying the birth of Israel seemed to settle once and for all that those "bitter and resourceful opponents" of the new state were on the wrong side of history. And it would be more than a half century until an American president seriously spoke of such a Pales-tinian state. Abdullah collected on his bargain, moreover, annexing the West Bank, which made another Palestinian state moot. He seemed to be on the verge of bringing Syria and Lebanon under his sway as well when a Palestinian extremist shot and killed him at the Dome of the Rock in Jerusalem on July 21, 1951.

At the conclusion of the first Arab-Israeli War (actually a series of short wars) in 1949, the odd people out were the Palestinians. Historian Ritchie Ovendale notes that the Anglo-American Com-mission on Palestine estimated that there were 226,000 Jewish refu-gees in Europe when Germany surrendered. By 1949 the wars in Palestine had created almost one million Arab refugees, living in various countries. Their numbers would double in the next two decades. Still, the war had not united the Arab world—far from it. It led instead to upheavals in individual Arab countries, "often fomented by a new, young and disillusioned generation which had been nurtured on what was considered the injustice of Zionist dispossession of Arab land with the assistance of the Western powers."[53]

The new state's military prowess came as something of a surprise in Washington, as Secretary Marshall had tried to discourage an Israeli diplomat by warning him not to bank on early military success as an indication of ultimate victory. Marshall's bias led him astray here. The new Central Intelligence Agency provided an estimate of future events, however, that was pretty close to the mark. The Israelis had won the first battle, but the Arab-Israeli War promised to be a long one. The Arab supply lines were insufficient to support a full-scale conflict, but "they can be expected to support guerilla activities indefinitely." With the boycotts and blockades Arabs planned to construct, Israel's "security will be continuously threatened, its economy stifled, and its future existence consequently will be entirely dependent on the continuing good will of some outside power or power."[54]

The situation evolved pretty much the way the director, Admiral R.H. Hillenkoetter, predicted it would. The United States became the "outside power" that ensured Israel's survival, not only through direct aid but also by making it clear that Congress and the White House stood foursquare behind all its declarations.

Robert McClintlock, of the Office of United Nations Affairs in the State Department, struck a realist note. Abdullah's reasons for wishing to expand into the West Bank, he said, were "pragmatic," by which he really meant they might serve American interests by hastening a settlement. As for the Arab reaction to the injustice of Israel's actions, McClintlock was unimpressed: "As for the emotion of the Arabs, I do not care a dried camel's hump. It is, however, important to the interests of this country that these fanatical and overwrought people do not injure our strategic interests through reprisals against our oil investments and through the recision of our air base rights in that area."[55]

In mid-May 1950, the United States, France, and Great Britain signed a tripartite declaration by which they pledged to one another not to supply arms to any country in the Middle East unless the purchaser promised not to "undertake any act of aggression against any other state in the Middle East." It recognized that Israel and the Arab countries had legitimate needs of self-defense and internal security; but the three signatory powers pledged to one another that if they found any state was "preparing to violate existing frontiers or armistice lines," they would take immediate action both within and outside the United Nations to prevent such violations.[56]

Though it referred to the Arab-Israeli question specifically, it ought to be noted that the Tripartite Declaration marked a considerable advance on the Truman Doctrine as it asserted that a big power had the right to determine questions of war and peace in the Middle East. The biggest power, of course, was the United States. The Truman Doctrine's ostensible target was the Soviet Union, or, in the Dulles years to come, "International Communism," but Washington had in the process created a protectorate and made itself the nation of last resort for all sorts of grievances. As British Prime Minister Atlee had feared even as Britain prepared to turn over its burden, "We shall constantly appear to be supporting vested interests and reaction against reform and revolution in the interests of the poor."

The Importuning Clients

From the time of the Truman Doctrine, Middle Eastern countries began importuning Washington for benefits equal to those Greece and Turkey received. When the Egyptian ambassador pressed his country's case for arms aid, for example, secretary of state Dean Acheson queried him about why Cairo would not follow King Abdullah's example and seek a peace treaty with Israel. It was the wrong approach, the ambassador replied. He then launched into a long discussion of the situation, first acknowledging that the future was in the hands of the Western democracies and asserting Egypt's desire to work side by side with them. But then he pointed out that certain groups in the United States opposed arms aid that Egypt needed for self-protection; as for Abdullah's path, Cairo did not believe that peace could be achieved except through an agreement with all the Arab countries, which Israel resisted. He closed his re-marks with an appeal that Washington accept the burden of getting the British to withdraw from Suez as the garrison there was a con-stant provocation and inducement to insurrectionary behavior.[57]

Assistant secretary George McGhee, on a mission to Saudi Ara-bia to secure a more permanent arrangement for the Dhahran Air Base, found that Ibn Saud had similar ideas about grants in military aid like those given to Greece and Turkey, and that he wished as well for a bilateral treaty of alliance because the British were back-ing his enemy, Abdullah. McGhee fended off these appeals, offering instead a treaty of friendship and commerce, and an oral commit-ment that the United States would protect Saudi Arabia's territo-rial integrity. When Saudi officials questioned whether McGhee's offer of a "loan" for arms aid was really any more generous than what could be obtained from other countries, and not the equal cer-tainly of the Truman Doctrine's support of Greece and Turkey, McGhee stiffened up, saying that he doubted if such a loan would be obtainable from "ordinary banking sources" elsewhere; more-over, he did not know "of any other government which was in a po-sition to make a loan to Saudi Arabia."[58]

These conversations in Washington and Jiddah, Saudi Arabia, give a good indication of the Truman Doctrine protectorate's vari-ous Middle Eastern permutations. As the successor to the Pax Britannica, the United States hoped to avoid direct rule and over-militarization of its allies. The initial complications that had re-sulted from support for the creation of Israel were under control for the time being, though there could be little doubt about the poten-tial for upheavals triggered by disillusionment with American in-ability to achieve more for the refugees. From Washington's viewpoint, the Arab-Israeli struggle diverted attention from the "Communist threat," which policy makers hoped would unify the region, and which supplied the necessary rationale for the Ameri-can public. While the governments in the region happily acknowl-edged their need for American aid, ostensibly to combat the Soviet threat, the real danger they feared was American indifference. They concentrated their efforts on seeking military aid from the United States so as to reassure themselves and Washington that they needed a protector against the old imperial powers and the threat of the new state of Israel. The first serious challenge to this new order arose quickly in Iran, which sought American aid in its struggle with the very symbol of British power, the Anglo-Iranian Oil Company. It was a situation, lamented Dean Acheson, made to order for Communist exploitation.

When Truman delivered his farewell address on January 15, 1953, he said this about the Middle East:

> There is no end to what can be done.
> I can't help but dream out loud just a little here.
> The Tigris and Euphrates Valley can be made to bloom as it did in the times of Babylon and Nineveh. Israel can be made the country of milk and honey as it was in the time of Joshua.[59]

Full realization of such possibilities had not yet been achieved, the president averred, only because of Cold War necessities. The struggle with Moscow had diverted limited resources, he claimed, and required defense spending on foreign military bases instead of other types of foreign aid. After the Russians got the A-bomb, Truman added in his January 15, 1953, message, "what we needed was not just a central force that could strike back against aggression. We also needed strength along the outer edges of the free world, defenses for our allies as well as for ourselves, strength to hold the line against attack as well as to retaliate."[60]

The Russian A-bomb certainly helped provide a rationale for foreign military bases, but the Truman Doctrine's momentum would have proved strong in any eventuality. Truman's legacy, as defined in this speech, was "strength along the outer edges of the free world," and, one should add, strength to hold the lines inside the free world.

The Trouble with "Containment"?

Between the Truman Doctrine and Truman's farewell message much had happened in the Middle East. The United States had supported the creation of Israel, and there were the beginnings of an alliance that would thereafter define the American approach to the Arab world. But besides the Arab-Israeli question, the Middle East was stirring anew, especially in oil-rich areas. There was a question about whether the "containment" policy and the Truman Doctrine approach would suffice to meet that challenge. Indeed, the celebrated author of containment, George F. Kennan, would argue in 1952 that there was a fateful misunderstanding involved in the U.S. "approach to the peoples of Asia and the Middle East."

The reason Kennan deplored the expansion of containment to the world outside Europe and the area surrounding Japan was because those parts of the globe were beyond understanding and suffered "various forms of neuroses." At the heart of U.S. troubles in what would be called the "Third World," he wrote later in a policy recommendation, was a fateful misunderstanding of "our inability to understand how profound, how irrational, and how erratic has been the reaction generally of the respective peoples to the ideas and impulses that have come to them from the West in recent decades." Intellectuals in those countries were chiefly to blame: "To ascertain the reasons for the intensely anti-American attitudes manifested by these people would be to delve deeply into psychological reactions and the origins of various forms of neuroses."[61]

The belief in the essentially irrational characteristic of people outside the world's temperate zones presented a difficult conundrum for policy makers, beginning with the Iranian crisis of 1951–53, continuing through the years of Vietnam, 1954–75, and into the next century in the Middle East. While professing to be missionaries of democracy to the world, and championing self-determination for all peoples, when elections went the wrong way for supposed American interests, they were simply disavowed as evidence of "various forms of neuroses," or, a little more generously, as mistakes

resulting from the pressure of outside forces on people as yet too immature to govern themselves.

   This new Kennan was not listened to by his superiors, for very
good reasons—alas, not because of the inherent cultural bias in his
remarks, but because they wreaked havoc with the whole idea of a
"Free World" sheltered under American bases from pole to pole and
longitude to longitude. If, as he had said, the Soviet Union sought
to fill every nook and cranny in the basin of world power, how was it
possible to neglect a challenge anywhere, especially in the Middle
East? The task before them was to turn the world into a battlefield
of ideas—the American Revolution against the false Leninist
Revolution—and in that way mobilize opinion at home (and
abroad) for the long haul. Kennan deplored efforts to project the
American Revolution on those incapable of understanding their
best interests, as he saw it, but even if he were right, it was argued,
and even if leaders outside the "rational" West were hard to manage, that was a question of tactics and what would one day come
under the general heading of counterinsurgency. In the case of the
Iranian oil crisis, the task fell to the Central Intelligence Agency.
And within the "Company," as it would become known by insiders
and fiction writers alike, there was the grandson of Theodore Roosevelt, Kermit Roosevelt, who looked nothing like the Rough Rider
type, and carried out his mission of overthrow in an entirely different manner than a ride up San Juan Hill. According to historian
Stephen Kinzer, "Roosevelt slipped into Iran at a remote border
crossing on July 19, 1953, and immediately set about his subversive
work. It took him just a few days to set Iran aflame."[62]

4

THE IRAN OIL CRISIS

The U.S., with its increasing stake in the area, wishes to play a commensurate role in the development of plans and policies toward the Middle East.
—Paper prepared for Truman-Churchill talks, December 31, 1951

So this is how we get rid of that madman Mossadegh!
—John Foster Dulles, June 1953

On his very first visit to Washington in November 1949, Shah Reza Pahlavi complained about being neglected. Iran been left out of the Truman Doctrine and Marshall Plan, he said. Why was that? President Truman assured him he understood Iran's concerns. But our friends must understand as well that United States had many responsibilities worldwide. Consequently, some things had to be left undone for a time to use available funds in the wisest way.[1]

Not satisfied, the shah continued to enumerate grievances and propose remedies. Why couldn't the United States adapt wartime Lend-Lease to take care of Iran's urgent needs besides military weaponry, such as wheat and railroad locomotives? Because the Lend-Lease Act had expired some time ago, said Truman. Well, what about the Marshall Plan? It only applied to Europe, said Truman. He did not think Turkey was a European country, said the shah. Turkey had been included because of "special circumstances," the president replied. This half-hour "conversation" ended with Truman's promise to give Iran's requests careful consideration, within the limits of current laws; this ploy would be used over and over in the future.

But the shah was not finished pleading his case. In Secretary of

State Acheson's office he brought up the NATO treaty. European countries enjoyed a favored position in the new treaty, he began, and Turkish officials had just told him that a bilateral pact between Ankara and Tehran was useless without an American connection. How could Iran feel secure if that situation continued? Oh, well, NATO was just an experiment, replied Acheson, crossing his fingers behind his back. We were not at all sure the pact was going to meet security needs, he went on in this bogus fashion, or how long it would take for those nations to stand on their own. Until we knew the results, the United States had to be wary of extending any more commitments. "I added, however," Acheson wrote later, "that our interest was not limited to the area of our formal treaty obligations. I was sure that our interest in Iran would be great indeed if trouble should come."[2]

Fire Burn, Cauldron Bubble

Thus began an unsatisfactory thirty-year dialogue. It is important to understand from the beginning that most Iranians, and not just the shah, felt cheated by the failure of the Allies to extend serious help when the war ended. The Anglo-Russian occupation had set back Iranian economic development, and the country felt it had a moral claim to treatment at least equal to that granted the war-ravaged European countries. Iran had served as a Lend-Lease lifeline to Russia during the war, but, as detailed in chapter 2, had suffered both economic hardship and military occupation. Revenue from oil royalties, the shah warned American officials, was insufficient to provide for Iran's seven-year development plan without leaving his military requirements "unprovided for." The shah's references to Lend-Lease, of course, recalled both Roosevelt's flirtation with Arthur Millspaugh's schemes for some sort of "partnership" and the promises of the 1943 Declaration of Teheran, engineered by FDR, in which the United States, Britain, and Russia solemnly pledged not only to end the occupation at war's end but also to provide compensation for the sacrifices Iran had made. "With respect to the post-war period, the Governments of the United States, the

U.S.S.R., and the United Kingdom," it read, "are in accord with the Government of Iran that any economic problems confronting Iran at the close of hostilities should receive full consideration, along with those of other members of the United Nations, by conferences or international agencies held or created to deal with international economic matters."

The pledge went unredeemed, but not forgotten in Tehran. The Iranians made no bones about their desire to take on the whole issue of foreign oil concessions as a way to both make up for the neglect and assert national aspirations to control its one major natural resource. The Majlis (parliament) had set in motion a process for reconsideration of the long-standing terms of the Anglo-Iranian Oil Company's (AIOC) concession. Any shadow passing across Abadan Island always sent a chill through Whitehall and straight into the House of Commons. AIOC royalties and taxes dating from the age of imperialism now supported Labour's welfare state agenda, and helped fund military budgets at a time when sterling balances remained low and the Exchequer was as needy as in the days of Elizabeth I.

In 1913 Abadan was a small port city of a few hundred located on an island off the southwestern corner of Iran. Twenty-five years later it "hosted" the largest oil refinery in the world, a completely self-contained imperial enclave, where British managers resided in comfort and the thousands of Iranian workers lived lives not unlike those of Welsh coal miners from an earlier time. Averell Harriman, sent to Iran by Truman in 1951, reported that workers' homes in Abadan were little better than slums, "shocking for housing of employees of a large Western oil company."[3]

Negotiations between the AIOC and Iranian officials over a Supplementary Agreement to the 1932 concession had stalled on the key issue of Iranian access to company books. When the shah returned from Washington in 1949, prospects for a resolution of the dispute had dimmed. Had he come home with an aid package, it might have made some difference, but very likely not. He did not hide his disappointment. "American aid stops at Iran's frontier," he announced to an already-agitated Iranian audience. His words, however, did have some effect in Washington. State Department aides now took notice of Iran for the first time, and a few expressed fears the government would look north to the Soviet Union. The "lack of American aid" has to some extent replaced "British intrigue" as the whipping boy of Iranian politics, read one policy paper. If this situation went uncorrected, it seemed certain Iranians would reach out to the Soviet Union to relieve its sense of isolation—no matter the consequences. Unfortunately, these were the thoughts of "many responsible Iranians" who believed that when the shah returned "empty-handed" they had been left alone to face the Soviets.[4]

Facing the shah now were two dedicated and skillful nationalists, Mohammed Mossadeq and the religious leader Ayatollah Kashani, who both held seats in the Iranian parliament. Getting that body to approve the Supplemental Agreement, or any other arrangement that did not fundamentally alter Iran's share of the oil profits, was not possible. One question was how far would the shah go to risk his throne on the outcome. The State Department feared that the British were dug into impossible positions and willing to risk a breakdown that would jeopardize oil investments around the globe. As matters stood, it was a bad situation all round. Given the danger of an ill wind sweeping out of Iran across Middle Eastern oil fields, the State Department advocated an aid program for the shah, but only if he named a prime minister "willing to and capable of using this assistance to strengthen Iran's internal defenses against communism"—the magic words that would untie congressional purse strings. This was not the first instance of Washington seeking to impose such restrictions, or the last as the Truman Doctrine protectorate spread across the Middle East. The first order of business was always "internal defenses against communism." External protection was up to the United States, with its atomic bombs and Strategic Air Command. Everyone had to understand that. Those that did and agreed to accept military advisory missions would get aid; those that did not, well, they would have to understand that American resources were limited, and make do with less.

Iranian ambassador Hussein Ala knew how to play that game. He appealed once again for large-scale economic aid as a remedy to cool off nationalist fevers, recalling for his American hosts those heroic days of 1945 and 1946 "when his country was directly threatened by Soviet aggression." But now the threat was an internal economic crisis, not the Russian military. Iran had suffered crop failures, a shortage of money, rising unemployment, and an unfavorable balance of trade. Local communists were exploiting the situation, and the "danger of a Communist-inspired disturbance of major proportions was very real." Acheson assured him that America's Iranian policy was by no means frozen, but that foreign aid could be useful only where the recipient country had the internal organization to make good use of the assistance. He was confident Ambassador Ala would use his influence to head the shah "in the proper direction." Ala knew what direction that was: toward reforms of his government. But there was trouble ahead, he warned, because "Iran had not received fair treatment" from the AIOC.[5]

American policy makers actually agreed with that statement—in private, of course—and were irritated at British negotiating tactics (or, better put, the absence of any negotiating tactics). "The annual income to Iran from the company was currently only some $30 million a year," wrote George McGhee, the assistant secretary whose lot it became to seek a way to avoid nationalization, "which the Iranians said was less than their expenses in providing security for AIOC installations."[6] Royalties were an especially hot question, particularly when the American company ARAMCO announced a new deal for Saudi Arabia that boosted royalty payments to a fifty-fifty basis. ARAMCO's action upset many competitors, especially AIOC, since it wouldn't cost the U.S. firms a penny! Overseas royalties, the U.S. Treasury ruled, would be considered tax payments at home. Thus American oil companies now enjoyed a multimillion-dollar subsidy and a competitive edge to boot. But the Treasury ruling had another long-term effect—it became more profitable to explore for oil abroad than at home, thereby deepening the American stake in Middle Eastern politics.

Little wonder that AIOC officials and the British government resented McGhee's pleas for flexibility. In January 1950, nevertheless, McGhee lectured the company's executives, asserting that the only thing holding up agreement was the matter of "reserves allocated in the company's books before profits." Not so, they protested. Iran's demands would end by leaving "nothing in the till." Well, said McGhee, he had taken the time to read the company's annual report and, "as one oil man to another, profits were still far from disappearing." AIOC simply could not go on thinking Middle Eastern countries were unaware of the arrangements that were being negotiated in the Western Hemisphere and even elsewhere in the Gulf. He did not need to remind them about ARAMCO's new deal for Saudi Arabia; they knew only too well what the Americans had done.[7]

But McGhee was no softie when it came to the bottom line—not the profit line, but the bottom line of American tolerance for solutions outside the bounds of capitalism. As Acheson had said to the shah, the Truman Doctrine was still very new. But the developing oil crisis pushed Washington toward incorporating Iran within the borders of the protectorate—to make sure that nothing inside Iran pushed outward with an even greater force. At dinner in the Iranian embassy McGhee encountered General Ali Razmara, a favorite of British and American diplomats since the days of Norman Schwarzkopf and the Iranian gendarmerie. Now chief of staff of the Iranian army, he was thought to be the best man available to deal with Mossadeq and his dangerous National Front Party. "A slight wiry man with a deadpan face," McGhee wrote of their conversation, "he talked quietly and soberly. I was impressed and was prepared to recommend U.S. support when he was proposed for Prime Minister."[8]

On June 20, 1950, the Majlis created an eighteen-member committee to study the Supplemental Agreement. The British immediately demanded that the shah appoint Razmara prime minister. McGhee felt relieved, because he assumed the British felt happy about Razmara's elevation and would accord him a real opportunity to reach agreement by allowing access to AIOC bookkeeping records. No happy ending there, however, because opening the books was the last thing AIOC was willing to do. With American oil companies increasingly worried about the impasse and what it might portend, McGhee hastened to London to argue that having helped to put Razmara in office, pulling the rug out did not make good sense: "The AIOC Board, in effect, told me that I should mind my own business."[9]

While the shah opposed nationalization, he was in no position to force Razmara to accept terms that did not go at least part way toward meeting Iranian demands. Indeed, his complaints about the lack of American aid grew louder, and, as some had predicted, he undertook to negotiate a trade agreement with the Soviet Union. It is interesting, therefore, that the first move toward Moscow was the Shah's gambit, not Mossadeq's play. London saw the move as nothing more than a negotiating tactic, and dismissed the supposed threat of a Communist menace. Later, when things got really hot, the British would unleash the "Red scare" dogs to frighten Washington; but for the moment they worried more that the nervous Americans would promote some modified form of nationalization as the only way to keep Iran on the right side. When the Americans finally offered Iran a "subsistence"-level aid package of $30 million, there was much grumbling in Whitehall and complaints that McGhee's moves seemed less than impartial and designed to position American oil companies to take advantage of the dispute and displace AIOC. That was not the case, but tempers all around were growing short.[10]

At almost the same time that the Majlis set up its committee to study nationalization, North Korean troops began storming across the thirty-eighth parallel on June 25, 1950. Remarkably, as he considered the proper American response, Truman thought first of the deteriorating situation in Iran. Indeed, the president's obsession with a Russian advance into the Middle East only grew stronger with the Korean War. He eyed that conflict as a clever diversionary tactic—but one that could not be ignored. The last place anyone would want to fight was in Korea, but the Cold War struggle flattened out the world so that the last place seemed as important as the first place. In one sense, it could be argued, the Korean War was an unintended consequence of the Truman Doctrine, with its rhetorical excess, because it posited all the world as a single battlefield where Free World forces stood on guard against an enemy who gave orders to armies poised on borderlands, according to a specific Communist master plan that must exist somewhere in a Kremlin safe file. "The President walked over to the globe standing in front of the fireplace," remembered an aide, George Elsey, "and said he was more worried about other parts of the world." He seemed hesitant, Elsey remembered, about using air- and sea power except to evacuate Americans from the Korean peninsula. But then he saw a connection. He spun the globe and put his finger on Iran: "Here is where they will start trouble if we aren't careful." It was like Greece: "If we just stand by, they'll move into Iran and they'll take over the whole Middle East. There's no telling what they'll do, if we don't put up a fight now." [11]

The Shah Blinks

"There's no telling what they'll do" became the standard retort to any and all questions about American foreign policy and the expanding defense perimeter stretching around the globe. When Prime Minister Razmara attempted to halt the push toward nationalization, he was assassinated by a zealot on March 7, 1951, a sign, some leaped in to say, that foreign agitators were at work. The day after the assassination the oil committee reported out in favor of nationalization, and little more than a week later the Majlis acted. Razmira was followed by Hussein Ala, who lasted less than two months. At the Ayatollah Kashani's call more than fifteen thousand then rallied in Tehran in favor of nationalization. The leftist Tudeh Party—with supposed links to Moscow—had opposed nationalization, and even attacked one of its leading advocates, Mohammed Mossadeq, as a "hireling of the imperialists." While it was impossible to see nationalization simply as a Communist scheme, it soon became clear that the only way to stop the Iranians was to jam the dispute into a Cold War framework, and cease talking so loudly about property rights.

McGhee arrived in Tehran ready to lecture British ambassador Sir Francis Shepherd on the AIOC's stupidity in allowing things to come to such a pass. Shepherd's aloof indifference to the "temporary" setback amazed McGhee. It was all ARAMCO's fault, Shepherd insisted. They had "thrown a wrench into [the] Persian oil machinery." No, said McGhee, he had warned the AIOC board about the impending ARAMCO action, and despite owning a controlling interest in the company, the British government had done nothing to loosen its grip on a self-defeating strategy: "We provided more guidance to our companies even though they were privately owned."[12]

Leaving Shepherd to think over this scolding, McGhee went to see the shah. He had not seen him since the fall of 1949, and now he was shocked at the young monarch's appearance: "He had then been a proud, erect young man, insistent that his requests be taken seriously. As I saw him in the darkened audience chamber in which he received me, lounging on a sofa, he was a dejected, almost a broken man." He feared for his life. Razmara's assassination was a sign he would be assassinated, too. There had already been one attempt on his life: "The specter of death and impending chaos hung gloomily over Teheran like a dark cloud."[13]

McGhee asked if he thought nationalization could be avoided. Perhaps the ARAMCO solution would work even now to save the situation? No, it was too late, the shah said, and pleaded that he not be forced to try. McGhee reported to Washington that the shah was too much in shock "to consider such a strategy." Instead, to save his throne (and maybe his life) he moved to appoint Mohammed Mossadeq prime minister, even though he knew that the result would be a firm commitment to nationalization.[14]

Born in 1882, Mossadeq came from a wealthy family of landowners. He had studied in France, and spoke more elegant French than many Frenchmen. His time in Paris, however, also saw the beginnings of a lifetime of ailments neither purely medical nor purely psychosomatic. Historian Stephen Kinzer writes, "He was as dramatic a politican as his country had ever seen. At times he became so passionate while delivering speeches that tears streamed down his cheeks. Sometimes he fainted dead away, as much from emotion as any physical condition. When he became a world figure, his enemies in foreign capitals used this aspect of his personality to ridicule and belittle him. But in Iran, where centuries of Shiite religious practice had exposed everyone to depths of public emotion unknown in the West, it was not only accepted but celebrated."[15]

The British still could not believe that the Majlis had said its last words. Once the Iranians woke from their dream and realized they could not run the refinery or market the oil, they would reconsider such a foolhardy act. In the meantime, the great danger was that they might bring on an Iranian financial crisis that would destroy the country's "equilibrium" so that "Iran will easily fall prey to communism and Soviet domination." With the Korean War as backdrop, the campaign was on to blame the oil crisis on local Communists and the usual suspects in the Kremlin. The *New York Times*, for example, easily bought into the argument, and fulminated about the "violent storm of nationalism that has blown up in the quaking land between the Caspian Sea and Persian Gulf," and insisted Iran must not be allowed to get away with stealing property. Of course, it conceded, if a fifty-fifty offer had been made earlier the whole mess might have been avoided. But the trouble went deeper than the deepest oil well, the paper asserted, in code words that stood in for traditional attitudes about people who lived in countries with oil fields and deserts.

It was accepted as fact that the Iranians could not run the refinery or market the oil effectively. The situation had to be checked before the contamination spread. Expropriation, the pride of American newspapers declared, was not a step toward—but away from— independence. Could anything be clearer? Iran's action would provide the Russians with a Marx-sent opportunity to expand its power over and around the Truman Doctrine's borders. At one point the *Times* printed a cartoon of Prime Minister "Oily Baba" quaking in front of rows of ancient pottery jars holding his enemies. "I'll drown them in boiling oil," read the caption, "when I find out how to get some!"[16]

London spared no effort to insure that the Iranians could not sell oil, even including threatening military action—a step effectively vetoed by Washington. The cabinet split on military action, but, as William Roger Louis points out, "the unwavering American opposition to military intervention, which Acheson had persistently made clear, presented an insurmountable obstacle." As it happened, there was too much oil coming to market at this time, so British actions did not cause panic or a wave of price increases. Rather, London's measures did, as was intended, cause increasing pressure on the Iranian economy.[17]

The British feared that Iranian "fanaticism" would spread to Egypt and Iraq, a possibility that also occurred to policy makers in Washington, who, nevertheless, continued to blame London's bullheadedness for the emerging crisis. Recounting the rapid pace of events from Razmira's assassination to the formal proclamation of the nationalization law on May 2, 1951, secretary of state Dean Acheson quipped, "Never had so few lost so much so stupidly and so fast." The AIOC had brought this on themselves, Acheson told Sir Oliver Franks, just like American companies had in Mexico two decades earlier. The Mexican oil "crisis" of 1938, when that country nationalized its companies, was still fresh in everyone's mind. It had stirred deep feelings on all sides, but, eventually, with much pulling and hauling, Washington accommodated itself to that changed situation. The coming of World War II helped, because FDR and his aides could persuade the oil "hawks" of that day that no one should court a squabble with Mexico at such a tense time: "The Persians might be crazy enough to do the same thing the Mexicans did, which would profit no one." Surely there must be a way to satisfy Iranian nationalists while maintaining effective control of the oil through some sort of management arrangement. The ambassador complained in response that while Americans accused the British of appeasement in the Far East (the recognition of Communist China), London felt the Americans were guilty of appeasement in the Iranian situation. It seemed to him that the universities were the dangerous new element: "The universities are the acid in the situation. These chaps now have ideas. The same problem exists in Cairo." [18]

Another warning about "these chaps" with ideas came from old New Dealer Adolf Berle, who wrote to a friend in the State Department urging preparations for moving "a very moderate force into Iran. . . . I should guess that force was the only real solution since what Iran needs and wants is something capable of maintaining order and peace." Berle saw the problem exactly as had the shah, only from a different angle. Since there was no regional "defense group," it would take some ingenuity to work up the "appropriate formula" for intervention. While American attention was focused on the MacArthur situation—the "old soldier" had just been fired as commander in Korea—control of the Middle East was at stake, which, with its Persian Gulf oil, meant "substantial control of the world." [19]

In response to the furor, the State Department released a statement on May 18, 1951, expressing its "deep" concern about the dispute and explaining that it had made its position clear to both nations. What this came down to was a pro forma expression of sympathy with Iran's desire to receive "increased benefits" from the development of its petroleum resources, coupled with a stern warning that unilateral cancellation of clear contractual relationships would destroy "confidence in future commercial investments in Iran and, indeed, in the validity of contractual arrangements all over the world." ARAMCO had played softball in its offer to the Saudis and it really did not cost the company anything; but the thought of trying to settle affairs with Iranian nationalists raised the stakes to whole new levels. The American statement also repeated British assertions that the Iranians were not capable of marketing the oil—without noting that the British were making it impossible to do that, or to hire petroleum experts for the refinery. Then came the obligatory Cold War clincher, a warning to the Soviet Union: "The United States has repeatedly expressed its great interest in the continued independence and territorial integrity of Iran and has given and will continue to give concrete evidence of this interest."[20]

Throughout the summer of 1951 the United States continued efforts to find some way to reconcile what Truman called "the deeply felt desires of the Iranian people for nationalization of their petroleum resources" without disturbing the basic structure of old relationships between the resource countries and the metropolitan powers. Truman sent Averell Harriman to persuade the Iranian government to receive a special ambassador from the British—one, the United States hoped, who would now be prepared to offer a solution that recognized the nationalization law. In exchange, the Iranians would pull back from their insistence on controlling the production and marketing of the oil—in other words, that they would allow AIOC to run things under some new name. That gambit led nowhere. The British minister Sir Richard Stokes's offer of a fifty-fifty split fell short of what the Iranians demanded. That was no surprise, for he had assured London that the offer was a way to keep AIOC operating as before but "under a new name." Sir Richard lamented that he could not "disguise this hard fact" without being "too transparent for even the Persians to accept."[21]

Mossadeq twitted Sir Richard about his religion. Was he a Catholic, asked the prime minister? Yes, said Stokes. Well, he was probably unsuited for his mission, then, because Catholics did not believe in divorce, and Iran was in the process of divorcing AIOC. Sir Richard was not amused. The prime minister then said he was only willing to negotiate the terms of a final settlement: guaranteed sales to Britain, the employment of British technicians in the new Iranian oil company, and the amount of money Iran would pay for AIOC's nationalized assets. Harriman accompanied Stokes to Abadan and came away with the same impressions of British policy—or nonpolicy—that had exasperated McGhee. Stokes was no better than Sir Francis Sheperd. Instead of negotiating, the British gave themselves over to issuing rash statements about property theft, never hiding their "completely nineteenth-century colonial attitude toward Iran."[22]

When Acheson and McGhee met with a committee of American oil executives, however, they found the group not much interested in Harriman's opinion of British attitudes. They made it plain they were concerned about "the very grave consequences of giving the Iranians terms more favorable than those received by other countries." If that happened, the entire international oil industry would be "seriously threatened." Implicitly endorsing the British decision to shut down Abadan and boycott Iranian oil around the globe, they told the secretary that even the "loss of Iran would be preferable to the instability which would be created by making too favorable an agreement with Iran." Not just oil, "but indeed all American investment overseas" depended on "the concept of the sanctity of contractual relations."[23]

Acheson promised to keep in mind the points the oilmen had made, but reminded them he had to give consideration to the possible consequences of British policy leading to "the loss of Iran to the free world." Harry Truman could be candid in talking about such threats. In a long conversation with the venerated *New York Times* columnist Arthur Krock, he again downgraded the possibility of a general war with the Soviet Union, or even that the Russians would attempt a move into Iran: "He does not think the Soviets are in a condition to do it now and that this will be increasingly the fact." When Krock suggested there might come a time when the Russians achieved military parity, the president did not seem much disturbed. They would still need oil, he said: "The President believes the Russians are hundreds of thousands of barrels short of the daily million they would need. To get the oil of Iran into Russian centers . . . would call for a pipe-line to the Caspian which would take years to build. And to make this supply certain the Russians would be obliged to occupy Iran, which would mean war. Thus, he thinks, in a move to fit themselves for war by obtaining the essential oil supply, they would have to provoke war itself—an untenable program."

He was not very sympathetic to London's behavior: "The British, he said, have dealt ineptly and disastrously with the Iran oil matter. We told them how to avoid it but they did not follow our consul.

The head of the Anglo-Persian company (from his photographs) looks like a typical Nineteenth Century colonial exploiter. The contrast with the oil policies our people have followed in the Middle East is striking."

Truman did not mention the Treasury ruling essentially exempting the American companies from taxes on much of their income. Instead, he gave Krock a lesson in political economy and the way the American Century worked: "These foreign oil countries have a good case against some groups of foreign capital. The president said he thought Mexico's nationalization of oil [in 1938] was 'right'; he thought so at the time, but it was regarded as 'treason' to say so. If, however, the Iranians carry out their plans as stated, Venezuela and other countries on whose supply we depend will follow suit. That is the great danger in the Iranian controversy with the British."[24] Truman's occasional private insights into the true nature of the Truman Doctrine are always startling examples of a reality-based understanding of American Cold War policies.

A Stab at Personal Diplomacy

Truman wrote to Mossadeq in an effort to find a "compromise" solution, and received a reply that practically repeated the shah's complaint of two years earlier. It began with an assurance that Iranians regarded the United States as a "sincere and well-wishing friend and are relying upon that friendship." Perhaps, it went on, the United States did not know the history of the oil company's dealings with Iran? First of all, there were the "meager" royalties AIOC had given the Iranians over the years, which, coupled with the sacrifices forced on Iran during the war, left the laboring classes to face "an unbearable rise in prices and wide-spread unemployment. . . . Had we been given outside help like other countries which suffered from war, we could soon have revived our economy and even without that help, could have succeeded in our efforts had we not been hampered by the greed of the company and by the activities of its agents." The message ended with assurances that he was ready to negotiate a final settlement with the "former oil company," and further that he had no intention of disrupting oil supplies to the British or other world markets.[25]

The British closed down Abadan on July 1, 1951, in effect saying that they would wait out the crisis they had made for Iran, confident that internal pressures would lead to Mossadeq's demise and a new government that would reverse his policies. On September 21, 1951, a Cold War–sired agency of the American defense establishment, the Psychological Strategy Board, issued an interim report on the Iranian crisis. Iran was a "continuing objective" of Soviet expansionist desires, it argued, which was most likely to be achieved "through a Communist uprising." If Communists should attempt to seize power, read the report, the United States and Great Britain should support the "legal Iranian government." While the board did not say the United States would send military forces, it did warn that the country should be prepared to give full political support and at least consider sending its own forces if need be.[26]

The paper's authors feared the outcome if the British tried military force, and lamented that American ability to shape British decisions or to force terms for a settlement were limited. But the United States could not stand aside: "There is limited agreement that Mossadegh will have to be replaced before the chances for an oil agreement can improve. However, there appears to be some disagreement as to ——————————— the advisability of backing an alternate candidate." The words excised by the "weeders" apparently referred to CIA covert activities, for in the next paragraph the report talks about the complexity of the problem, American desires to be seen as a "friendly third party," and ends with "—————— is confined to anti-Tudeh (Iranian Communist Party) activities."[27]

That same day at a Truman cabinet meeting, defense secretary Robert Lovett issued a warning that the Soviets would not have to construct a pipeline into Iran to secure needed oil supplies; they could do it by reducing Iran to a "subservient" position and using tankers acquired on the open market. If the British were not going to settle the oil dispute, he went on, then the United States should consider supplying technicians to Iran to make sure the oil did not get sold to Moscow. Acting secretary of state James Webb, sitting in for Acheson, approached Lovett after the meeting to explain that it would "cause real difficulty . . . if any indication came from anyone in the Government that we were considering putting American technicians into Iran."[28]

Policy makers felt driven into a corner. Acheson discussed his frustrations with the Senate Foreign Relations Committee in executive session: "I don't think the idea which is talked about, if you replace the present Foreign [Prime?] Minister, will solve the problem. I don't think that is it at all. I doubt whether any government could take a very different attitude." If the British acted more reasonably, then maybe progress could be made or perhaps even a new Iranian government could make a compromise. "I have very grave doubt," Acheson continued, "as to whether they can operate the wells."

But the question was all tied up in emotional knots in both countries, said Acheson, as British elections approached: "Mr. Churchill is roaring like a lion and saying that nobody can shove him around, and that leads the [Labour] Government to say, 'Well, nobody can shove me around either,' and the fact is that they are both going to be shoved around, and the question is, by whom? They had better be shoved around in a friendly way than a hostile way." Mossadeq was coming soon to Washington, and Acheson hoped that maybe they could get him to hold back a little on some of his actions while the British moved up "a little bit."[29]

Mossadeq arrived in Washington after he had turned the tables on the British at a UN Security Council meeting that London had demanded to call Iran to accounts before the world body. Like the other strategies the British had devised, it proved a big mistake. The meeting gave the Iranian prime minister a perfect forum to indict the British for their past behavior and blindness to his country's needs. The idea that the Iranian action threatened world security, he began, was simply ludicrous. It required "a deficient sense of humor to suggest that a nation as weak as Iran can endanger world peace. . . . Whatever danger to peace there may be lies in actions of the United Kingdom Government. . . . Iran has stationed no gunboats on the Thames."[30]

He asked the council to remember that AIOC was a private company, however many of its stock shares were owned by the British government, and that no country would admit that a foreign government could negotiate for such an enterprise on nationalization matters: "No independent state would . . . subject itself to such degradation and slavery." The AIOC was a latter-day example of the East India Company, the chosen instrument of British imperialism that had once brought India under its sway in the long-ago days of imperial expansion; it behaved in the same way, interfering in internal affairs to secure the highest possible income, while the oil workers continued to live in hovels.[31]

By and large the American press agreed that Mossadeq had the better of the argument, and he came into Washington ready to renew the debate over American aid. The prime minister spent much of his time in the hospital (a not uncommon pattern for him), where American policy makers like George McGhee attempted to convince him that by themselves the Iranians could never manage production and marketing. The first conversation, however, was held in Truman's office in Blair House (where the president resided while the White House was under repair). Almost immediately the Iranian got onto the matter of aid. The United States, he said, had helped Iran "in some small matters," but there had been nothing big like the aid extended to other countries, and he wondered why that was. Just as he had replied earlier to the shah's arguments, Truman tried to deflect any blame by talking about his burden of global responsibilities: "We had been faced with the problem of helping almost the whole world." Mossadeq then responded with the sort of comment his enemies would seize on to use against him: "The present situation in Iran, if it were to continue for any length of time, would gravely endanger the independence of . . . [his] country and the preservation of peace."

He could have been reading from a CIA estimate, or a report like the one from the Psychological Strategy Board. Truman readily agreed with the prime minister. There were problems all around the area, extending to Suez and Kashmir: "Russia was sitting like a vulture on the fence waiting to pounce on the oil. That is why we were so anxious to get these problems solved. Our only interest was in

[the] wellbeing for all and preservation of peace. If the Russians secured this oil, they would then be in a position to wage a world war.
They are not in a position to do so now."[32]

Mossadeq then launched into a long discussion of how bad things
were in his country, and why not even expected oil revenues would
be enough to set things right. As Acheson recalled the scene,
Mossadeq leaned forward in a pleading manner and said, "Mr. President, I am speaking for a very poor country—a country all desert—
just sand, a few camels, a few sheep—" "Yes," interrupted the
secretary of state, "and with your oil, rather like Texas!" Mossadeq
exploded in a delighted laugh, "and the whole act broke up, finished." From then on, the secretary said, his case for large-scale aid
to fight the British was finished.[33]

Mossadeq's plea had indeed failed, but Acheson had failed, too, if
he thought the analogy really answered the challenge. The Iranian
leader now was sure that the United States had lined up with the
British, and that Truman and Acheson were telling him to settle for
much less than half a loaf. The conversation made it clear that the
administration would not consider large-scale aid so long as there
was no settlement of the oil question—on terms that would not dis-
rupt the fabric of the international oil production and marketing
structure. They took the prime minister's description of the possible
outcome quite seriously, but he was, in effect, asking them to choose
between Britain and Iran—between capital-exporting countries
and unsettling nationalist dreams that might spread to other lands.

Mossadeq's description of what was likely to happen if he went
home without either an oil settlement on Iranian terms or a significant aid package sounded like a threat. If he went home empty-
handed, he told Acheson in another meeting—this one in Walter
Reed hospital, where he was recuperating from one of his many
ailments—"the consequences for Iran would be disastrous, and
therefore equally disastrous for the preservation of peace. The
United States would then have to fight a war in Iran like the war
in Korea, equally without result."[34]

What a remarkable statement that was! Obviously determined to
paint the situation in dire terms, by such utterances the prime min-

ister only made it easier for hard-liners to demand a plan to remove him from power. Even so, Acheson had no desire to force the issue if there was another way. In the Walter Reed discussion, the secretary obtained the prime minister's agreement that there would be a seven-man board of directors, four from "neutral countries," appointed to run the new National Iranian Oil Company. At least he appeared to have such an agreement until the discussion turned to how the price for Iranian oil would be determined. Mossadeq protested that the price the Americans had put forward was far too low. That was the only way Iranian oil could compete on the world market, insisted George McGhee. Look at it this way, Acheson said: with this agreement the prime minister could claim credit for a solution that would provide more revenue than ever before. Mossadeq did not think so. As a result of the agitation against AIOC in recent years, the prime minister said, many people in his country had become oil experts and knew something about prices and such. American oil companies had suggested the price Acheson proposed, but they took oil from producing countries and sold it in bulk at much higher prices. What was left out of Acheson's explanation, he added, was that the distributors usually owned the producing companies, so that the higher price was essentially all profit for one entity. To accept the lower price meant that nationalization would have gained Iranians nothing. The discussion ended on that note.[35]

Efforts to persuade the British to consider a "compromise," albeit one the Iranians would probably reject, were equally unsuccessful. In Paris for talks with NATO leaders, Acheson reported that the British—with Churchill back in power—were adamant all down the line, through the ranks of the civil service. Allowing Iran to "despoil" the British company would surely destroy confidence in British power and the pound sterling, they told the secretary of state, and within months all British property abroad would disappear, and soon after all Western investments. "In my judgment," summarized Acheson, "the cardinal purpose of British policy is not to prevent Iran from going Commie; the cardinal point is to pre-

serve what they believe to be the last remaining bulwark of Brit solvency; that is their overseas investment and property position."[36]

Mossadeq at Large

"The circle is complete," Acheson sighed. "The only thing which is
added to the Labor party attitude is a certain truculent braggadocio.
They have not been returned to office to complete the dissolution
of the empire." What to do? There was no good choice, but rather
than allow Iran to slip into the Soviet orbit because of British bum-
bling, Washington would have to step in with an aid package—but
only after Mossadeq's situation had grown uncomfortable enough to
make him amenable to a reasonable offer. That was the trickiest
part. The same day Acheson dispatched his report from Paris,
Mossadeq wrote Truman a farewell letter. He related once more
British schemes to bring about economic distress in his country: the
technical staff at Abadan had refused to perform their duties for the
new company, leaving him no choice but to dismiss them.

If Iran's nationalization succeeded, he wrote, it was true that
other governments might desire similar privileges, "thereby causing
heavy losses to the revenue of concession owners." His answer was
that compared to the costs of military expenditures, such losses
were insignificant; hence, it would be advisable for investors "to
seek the satisfaction of the countries who have granted concessions,
and in this way help the furtherance of world peace and security."

This vague formula was not one that would commend itself to
capital-exporting nations. The prime minister apparently saw himself as an Iranian Gandhi, determined to lecture the great powers on
the need to abandon old ways. He also poked around in old, forgotten promises, coming up, not surprisingly, with the much-cited
1943 Declaration of Tehran: "We are in no way regretful for the sacrifices we have made; but we were both sorry and bewildered when
we found that none of the wartime promises materialized in the post
war era. On the contrary, the agents of old fashioned imperialism blocked Iran's chances to develop its own resources, the most

important of which is oil." The letter ended with a strange sort of threat: "It is obvious that a serious internal crisis in Iran could have repercussions that might place the government of the United States in a difficult world situation. We believe that in light of the great responsibility taken by the United States in world affairs it is only logical and right that your country would have a great interest in seeing the situation repaired before it reaches a critical point."[37]

Mossadeq had stopped off in Philadelphia on his way to Washington, where he visited Independence Hall and linked his nationalization policies with the "ideals that inspired the United States to wrest freedom and liberty from Britain in 1776." But what resonated more in Washington was his frequent insistence, repeated in his letter to Truman, that if "abandoned by the United States Iran will have no choice but to turn to the Soviet Union." Although the administration refused to comment on the prime minister's aid request, it was reported in the press he had asked for $120 million, while from Tehran there came word the Iranian Supreme Economic Council had signed a trade and barter agreement with the Soviet Union.[38]

From Washington the Iranian premier traveled on to Cairo, where a crowd of two thousand met his airplane, and ten times that many gathered at the square in front of the Abdin Palace. On placards he was greeted as the "Destroyer of Britain" and the "Enemy of Imperialism." "For good measure," said a newspaper account, "anti-American slogans were heard, apparently because the United States was charged with refusing Dr. Mossadegh a loan to get the oil fields and the Abadan refinery going." The prime minister's aides thanked the crowd, as he was not feeling well again and had to be carried into his hotel in a "bath chair," but he was well enough to send a message that Iranians would support Egypt's demands that Britain quit Egypt. In response the crowd shouted, "Revolution!" and "Give us arms!" His visit to King Farouk, it was reported, would be highlighted with a documentary film on "British atrocities."[39]

The next day Mossadeq and Egyptian prime minister Mustafa Nahas Pasha appeared together to talk about a joint declaration of their intention to conclude economic and cultural agreements, which, they said, would then be extended into a network of such agreements with other Middle Eastern states. Back in Tehran, Mossadeq's supporters were planning a triumphant reception for him upon his return. The people of Tehran, said the announcement, would "thwart the plans of the traitors who, aided and abetted by the English, are plotting the downfall of the Mossadegh Government."[40]

What Must Be Done

Back in Washington, meanwhile, the State Department prepared for a visit from Prime Minister Churchill, putting together its briefing papers for the president in anticipation of a showdown over how to meet the Iranian challenge. One of these papers went over all the differences and noted especially the ominous connections between the oil crisis and the burgeoning demands from Egyptian nationalists that the British quit Suez. Perhaps, American policy makers tried to convince themselves, these demands could be diverted with an offer of a Middle East Command, centered in Cairo. The United States would participate but would not provide military forces. The idea originated in response to the shah's complaint that Iran had been excluded from NATO. In Washington's pipe dreams, the proposed MEC would include both Israel and Iran along with Arab states; thus, just as NATO "contained" the German problem, the Cairo organization would resolve the Arab-Israeli dispute and overcome resentment over the supposed neocolonialism triggered by American support for Israel. MEC had no chance, but that did not deter Truman's successors from trying a similar approach.[41]

The real danger to American interests, as the MEC scheme revealed, was not the Red menace, but local arms races in part as a result of the fallout from the creation of the state of Israel. The United States at this point still very much wished to maintain Britain's role as the nation with primary military responsibility for the entire area. It was all very complicated, even without the Iranians stirring up nationalist feelings and the British behaving in such a difficult manner. It was also clear that the need to ensure "internal stability . . . must be done even if it necessitates dealing with governments competent to exercise power, but with whose policies the free world is not in full sympathy."[42]

Truman should stress to Churchill, preconference papers recommended, that the Middle East was developing from what had been a primary U.K political and military responsibility "toward an eventual multilateral responsibility which we hope ultimately will include the friendly local states if the Middle East area." That was the only "realistic" way to deal with the strong nationalist movements. He should say, "I am especially concerned over the present crises in Egypt and Iran. To prevent these from spreading we will provide political support and economic aid and also small amounts of military supplies and equipment when available to countries of the area if U.S. security interests make this necessary."[43]

But the "Negotiating Papers" could not get around the hard core of the problem: some resolution of the Iranian crisis had to be found to end the Anglo-American impasse. "At the present time," read one paper, "Iran seems to be narrowly balanced between the East and the West. In the world as it is today such a position is inherently unstable. Unless we are successful in moving Iran back toward the West, we fear events will force it to move more or less rapidly in the other direction." It is important to note here, once again, that the paper did not say the Soviets were planning to take over by military force, but rather that the actions of the British were creating a situation where Tehran's only choice would be to find outlets in Russia.[44]

There was no way it would be easy. Truman would have to tell Churchill that the United States had decided to negotiate a loan to support Iran's budget as a last-ditch effort to stave off a collapse of the Iranian economy. The State Department also faced an obstacle in Congress, which had imposed restrictions on aid recipients, banning them from exporting a proscribed list of materials to the Soviet Union. Besides that, there was an Export-Import Bank loan still pending since before the nationalization. There were bound to be awkward questions, and the Truman administration feared it did not have all the leverage it needed with the legislature—ironically, partly a result of its own Truman Doctrine hyperbole, adopted with additional zeal by Congress, and, of course, the Korean War. But the United States wanted to go ahead with some plan. It was not likely, however, that the prime minister would appreciate hearing about these plans—and he didn't. At their first meeting on January 5, 1952, on board the presidential yacht, the USS *Williamsburg*, Churchill responded to a Truman complaint about British ships carrying goods to the Chinese Communists with a rejoinder that the United States was letting down the side in the Middle East. "If we would put only a brigade of troops into Suez," Churchill said, "the British could withdraw a whole division or more. This one step would indicate such solidarity between us that the Egyptians would stop their unlawful conduct and get on with the four-power discussions [about the Middle East Command]. Similarly, in Iran, if we undertook to give financial support to the Iranians, the problem would never be solved. Whereas, if we would stand solidly with the British, the Iranians would come to terms in short order."[45]

Acheson disputed that point. Here was a situation, he said, that was right out of Karl Marx: "Vast masses of people in a state of poverty; practically no middle class—that is, small property owners or businessmen; a small owning and governing class, incompetent and corrupt; and foreign influences, against which agitators could arouse the population, which, after being aroused and destroying foreign influences, could be used to bring about a communist regime. I thought we must jointly devise some way of acting in this situation other than by merely sitting tight." As matters stood, the United States and the United Kingdom were like "two people locked in loving embrace in a rowboat which was about to go over Niagara Falls." We should break the embrace, he added, and take to the oars, which "amused the Prime Minister."[46]

The next evening, however, Churchill returned to the charge with a different analogy. The British had been kicked out of Abadan in a most humiliating fashion: "If he had been in office, it would not have occurred. There might have been a splutter of musquetry [sic], but they would not have been kicked out of Iran." He had been informed that the Labour government's failure to act had been because of American refusal to support strong measures. The oil company had made mistakes, certainly, but it was time to put those aside and stand together in the face of this challenge. Acheson did not yield the point. He did not think, he said, that one could dismiss the past quite so easily as the prime minister had done. The Iranians were undoubtedly difficult people, but the fact remained that it was only there where this trouble had arisen, out of all the places where the British and Americans were exploiting oil. What was the reason? He could think of only one. The British had been too late in offering a deal that had become standard elsewhere: "This had precipitated a national position in Iran which was far more serious and permanent than the mere personality of Mr. Mossadeq."[47]

Well, in a sense, that was precisely what worried Churchill—the possibilities of many more Mossadeqs lining up around the world to challenge the way oil companies and other powerful interests did their business in the nonindustrialized world. Acheson was still ruminating about British fecklessness after he left office. Talking with former colleagues, he remembered the British leader's call for an American cruiser and a brigade of marines and Churchill's insistence that it was the only way to turn things around in Egypt and Iran. Truman had tried to point out that the marines would be a lot more than symbolic in the sense that Churchill meant: "This was not just a little thing that you did and undid."[48]

The Odd Couple

The administration still blamed the British as much as they did Mossadeq, but Truman finally decided to reject Iranian appeals for a loan, telling the Iranian prime minister on February 11, 1952, that he could not justify additional aid because Tehran could obtain the revenues it needed by reaching an oil agreement.[49] As the stalemate dragged on, Mossadeq found himself checked on many corners: the British continued to refuse to recognize nationalization, and to "blockade" Iranian oil; their agents were stirring up the street and bazaar crowds; and the American "evenhanded" approach offered the prime minister no material aid. Yet his popularity continued to soar. In an attempt to break the impasse, he demanded still more power from the shah: the right to appoint a minister of war sympathetic to his policies. The shah refused, and Mossadeq resigned in protest, no doubt intending to make the appointment a showdown. In his place, the shah named Ahmad Qavam, who had successfully negotiated Tehran's way out of the Russian crisis in 1946—an appointment that once more gave the British fleeting hopes of a settlement on favorable terms. Qavam lasted just five days. Widespread riots and demonstrations instigated by the leftist Tudeh Party greeted his appointment, and when the shah attempted to deploy the army to quash the uprising, an outpouring of support for the deposed Mossadeq resulted. Badly shaken, the shah had to ask him to form a new government.[50]

In the brief moment of Qavam's premiership, Acheson had come up with a proposal for a $26 million loan to boost his chances for forming a government, but, he told Truman, "we had not proceeded upon this because Qavam fell before action could be taken." With Mossadeq back in power, he floated a new idea. The United States would make $10 million available to Iran, and the British would agree to purchase oil presently stored in Iran at a suitable discount. If things proceeded along, Mossadeq would then agree to international arbitration to determine compensation for the expropriation. The idea died at birth when Churchill complained that Washington's efforts to reach a settlement had now produced suspicions that American oil interests were out "to take our place in the Persian oil fields after we have been treated so ill there."[51]

The rest of Churchill's petulant letter argued that the British were helping all they could in Korea—as if this was a quid pro quo for American support of British "efforts" in Iran. "No country," he added, "is running voluntarily the risks which we are, should atomic warfare be started by Soviet Russia. . . . I hope you will do your best to prevent American help for Musaddiq [sic], either Governmental or commercial, from becoming a powerful argument in the mouths of those who care little for the great forward steps towards Anglo-American unity in the common cause which you and I have worked for so long."

Truman responded sharply that Iran's nationalization law had become as sacred as the Koran, and if Iran went down the Communist drain it would provide little satisfaction to anyone that legal positions were held out until the end.[52] Nevertheless, he accepted the prime minister's suggestion that they send the Iranian prime minister a joint letter offering some of the terms Acheson had devised as a proposal, including $10 million in financial aid. The president also accepted, however reluctantly, London's argument that any reference to arbitration over compensation should be based on "the legal position of the parties existing immediately prior to nationalization." In other words, as the Americans realized, the only joint proposal the British would offer after all this time still did not accept the legitimacy of the Iranian law. Mossadeq's response was no surprise. He dismissed the $10 million as nothing more than "charity." Instead, he said, Iran insisted on being paid a much larger sum, which—according to his lights—the old company still owed Iran. If the proposals were revised to meet his demands, then, and only then, could negotiations begin.[53]

The Iranian's rhetoric, Churchill shot back to Truman in another carping letter, demonstrated that only a continued Anglo-American stand would force him to back down. Iranian oil policy, he huffed, was costing Great Britain £60 million a year—losses that could not be sustained any longer without precipitating a solvency crisis. "It seems also to me," wrote Churchill, "if I may say so, that it would be a hard prospect for the American taxpayer to have to bribe Persians (and how many others?) not to become Communists; once this process started it might go a long time in a lot of places." Alarmist sentiments all mixed up with the old colonial bravado, Churchill's surprisingly frank dismissal of the possibility of a Cold War confrontation over Iran spoke volumes about the meaning of the crisis: "Naturally, I have thought a great deal about the danger of a revolution and Soviet infiltration or aggression. I may of course be wrong but as I at present see it, I do not feel that it will happen that way in the near future. Anyhow, it seems far more likely that Mossadeq will come to reasonable terms on being confronted with a continued Truman-Churchill accord."[54]

Churchill's stubbornness grated, and Acheson was fast losing patience with the wartime ally's obstructionist mentality as he sought a solution to the double impasse. With Dwight Eisenhower's victory in the 1952 election, however, time was running out. Using all his lawyerly talents, he put together a basket proposal for getting money into Mossadeq's hands in timely fashion, while tying him down to a long-term contract to deliver oil to a "distributing company" made up of companies from different nations, including the United States. It offered little to the British. Perhaps the only advantage of such a scheme, if they participated, was to obtain oil at a discount as "compensation" for the nationalized properties. Truman and Acheson explained the plan and their reasoning to President-elect Eisenhower on November 18, 1952. It now appeared that the only way to move forward, they told him, was for the United States to take unilateral action, even though this likely meant "violent competition and conflict with British distributors . . . , with some periods of considerable bitterness." Eisenhower said very little at this meeting, and certainly did not indicate what he thought about the situation.[55]

What American oilmen thought, however, was made clear to Acheson a few days later when he tried out his proposal on executives from the majors. His purpose, he began, was to find a solution "in order to avoid passing on the burden to the new Administration." Neither side was acting reasonably, and the main sticking point was compensation. It had to be high enough to provide the British with a reason for accepting—however reluctantly—a settlement, and yet not so high as to force Mossadeq to reject all negotiations. But the British still clung to the view, he went on, that continued economic pressure would bring the Iranians to heel, and believed there was no chance of a disintegration and Russian intervention. Acheson did not agree. There was a real revolution under way in Iran, he said, and we ignored the implications to our peril. Then he shifted ground to an alarmist scenario of Russian military intervention. Soviet control of Iran would provide oil resources needed for further military ventures. A Russian presence in Iran would add target problems for the Strategic Air Command, making it more difficult to prepare a defense for the Middle East. It was essential, therefore, that the British understand that the United States did not intend to throw in the sponge and see Iran go under. They had to realize that Washington would take action, even though this could mean a rather sharp break with London: "We feel that the people sitting at this table could reach a figure which would be a reasonably equitable settlement."[56]

The oilmen gave Acheson the cold shoulder. All his carefully arranged arguments were turned against him. Indeed, the men around the table all sided with Churchill, at least to the extent that they were not willing to see a settlement that jeopardized their current position in the Middle East or the world oil trade. Any variance from the fifty-fifty formula, they said, "would be fatal to the structure of the industry and to huge American investments overseas." The secretary interrupted to assure them the administration understood their concern, and would take the point fully into account in discussing any proposed solution. That did not seem to change anybody's mind across the table. Acheson fell back to the military concerns. The administration really could not hand General Eisenhower such an intolerable situation, he pleaded: "The stakes were too large for us not to force the situation." The response was the same as before: "If any arrangement with the Iranians resulted in an accrual to them of an amount above the income now earned by other countries under this formula, this would open a Pandora's box."

He understood their concern, Acheson said. But the oilmen had more to say. How could there be a settlement, they added, with oil in a buyers' market that would provide Iran with enough money or the companies with an assurance that the fifty-fifty formula would not be breached? Socony-Vacuum's Brewster Jennings predicted "a cataclysmic result." ARAMCO's representative declared that his company could not afford to hurt its standing in Saudi Arabia by moving Iranian oil. Any further cutbacks in royalties would cause great difficulties for the company at a most delicate moment with the oil glut depressing prices: "He could appreciate the national security viewpoint but that basically they felt this was a British problem." The meeting ended with an agreement only to talk again.

Acheson had learned he could not convince the oilmen that there was a Russian threat, even if the economy deteriorated to the point of chaos: "They felt this was a British problem." When the Eisenhower administration came into power, the new secretary of state, John Foster Dulles, laid out the situation as he saw it for the National Security Council. So long as Mossadeq was alive, there might be little danger, but if he were to be assassinated or "otherwise to disappear from power," a political vacuum would open the way for a Communist takeover. Defense secretary Charles Wilson lamented bygone days when other right-wing dictators replaced deteriorating right-wing dictatorships: "Nowadays, however, when a dictatorship of the right was replaced by a dictatorship of the left, a state would presently slide into Communism and was irrevocably lost to us." President Eisenhower felt unhappy that the situation in so many places was rife with demonstrators against the United States, and wished he could read instead about "mobs in these Middle Eastern states rioting and waving American flags." Trying to be helpful, his top psywar expert, C.D. Jackson, currently on loan from Henry Luce's Time-Life conglomerate, spoke up: "If the President wanted the mobs he was sure he could produce them."[57]

Enter the Spooks

Jackson did not get the assignment. But a plan for using the mobs to get rid of Mossadeq—so that he would no longer pose a danger to the stability of world oil markets—was well under way. The initiative was already passing to men whose craft belonged to what a later notable, future vice president Dick Cheney, would call the darker side of international relations in the wake of 9/11. The principal British actor in the drama to come was C.M. Woodhouse, who had served behind the lines with Greek partisans in World War II. He arrived in Tehran as the last of the AIOC personnel were departing in the late summer of 1951, and took up a "nominal post" in the British embassy. His real job was to organize the downfall of

Mossadeq by working with the mysterious "brothers," wealthy merchants who could influence opinion in the Majlis and the bazaars—"and more important they could mobilize street mobs, which were a powerful force in Iranian politics."[58]

Woodhouse found a congenial "partner" in the American embassy, which had anticipated that the new ambassador, Loy Henderson, would be more receptive to an overture from the cousins: "He was a second-generation American of French descent, so he was both bilingual and quick to grasp a European viewpoint." Woodhouse had made a special visit to Washington in mid-November 1952, just after Eisenhower's election. He went to see some old friends at the CIA, and found that they had also been in contact with his favorite nominee for a post-Mossadeq government, General Fazlollah Zahedi: "He was an ironic choice, for during World War II he had been regarded as a German agent. . . . Now we were all turning to him as the potential savior of Iran from the Soviet bloc."[59]

Of course the idea that Iran needed saving from the Soviet bloc was a contentious issue, and had been adopted by British policy makers—even though Churchill pooh-poohed it—as the best way to appeal to the Americans. On this trip, Woodhouse found CIA director Walter Bedell Smith skeptical and gloomy about Iranian prospects: "You may be able to throw out Musaddiq [sic], but you will never get your own man to stick in his place." Kermit Roosevelt, grandson of Teddy and then head of CIA operations in the Middle East, was convinced that Operation Ajax (the British preferred Operation Boot as more descriptive) could work.

"Kim" Roosevelt well understood what the plan required. The Americans did not balk at any of the conditions Woodhouse outlined, including a stipulation that the British would not make an oil deal with a new government on terms any more favorable than those offered to Mossadeq (to protect American interests like ARAMCO). Time would tell how good those promises would be, but there was no lack of enthusiasm for the plan when Allen Dulles became director of the agency. The early assessment of the

Eisenhower administration—as Allen's brother, secretary of state John Foster Dulles, had outlined—was that Mossadeq's alliance was splintering. But instead of attempting to restore a stable situation by pressuring the British and the oilmen, the new administration opted for a coup d'etat. On April 4, 1953, Allen Dulles authorized the expenditure of $1 million to be used "in any way that would bring about the fall of h [sic]."[60] As the plot moved forward, it turned out that the most reluctant participant was the shah himself—and he became Kim Roosevelt's responsibility. Reza Pahlavi was not one for bold actions at this point, having tried to oust Mossadeq once and failed. He was still only in his mid-thirties, and very unsure of his footing. It was one thing to talk back to Truman on a state visit, and quite another to risk dethronement in his own land.

There was no lack of public information about an impending effort to get rid of the troublesome prime minister. Nor was General Zahedi's presence at the head of the "opposition" any secret, for, being released from prison on conspiracy charges in late March, he immediately sought out the press to tell them all about his plans. He would restore constitutional order—wrecked by Mossadeq's rule by fiat—and then seek "to clarify Iran's foreign policy." By clarifying foreign policy, Zahedi meant that he would sort out the Communist Tudeh Party, which had become a supporter of the prime minister. Once these steps were accomplished, he said, "the oil question would be settled quickly."[61]

There was little doubt that Mossadeq was having difficulty holding his original coalition together. The most important "defector" was the Ayatollah Kashani, who now promised to restore constitutional rule as he offered himself as an opposition candidate for the premiership. In a violent attack on the prime minister delivered from his chair as speaker of the Majlis, Kashani declared that the prime minister had murdered the constitution: "Such men should be hanged by the people." Kashani overreached on this occasion. Instead of succeeding in bringing Mossadeq down, he himself was ousted from his position as speaker.[62]

Kashani's removal was a signal that the Iranians were probably not going to remove Mossadeq without some "help from their friends." The prime minister had made a new appeal for aid to Eisenhower, and Ike's reply came just at the moment of Kashani's dismissal. It was only the failure to reach an agreement on compensation, the president's reply stated, that "handicapped" the United States in its genuine desire to help Iran. There was a strong feeling, even among those most sympathetic to Iran's economic difficulties, he wrote, that it would not be fair to "American taxpayers" for the government to extend "any considerable amount of economic aid" when Iran could have access to funds derived from the sale of its oil if a "reasonable agreement" was reached regarding compensation, thus enabling "large-scale marketing of Iranian oil" to be resumed. All the factors Eisenhower listed were contentious matters, as was his insistence that "compensation merely for losses of the physical assets of a firm which has been nationalized would not be what might be called a reasonable settlement and . . . might tend to weaken mutual trust between free nations engaged in friendly economic intercourse." Given the emotions involved, he concluded, the fairest means of settling the question would be to refer it to some "neutral international body."[63]

Mossadeq played his last card. He immediately made the letter public, believing the rebuff would bolster his case as he planned other steps. American diplomats were not overly displeased by this act because "informed Iranians" thought it clarified the issues. Final approval for Operation Ajax had preceded Eisenhower's letter by five days. On June 25 Kim Roosevelt had presented the plan to an assemblage of top American leaders. The only one with doubts was ambassador Loy Henderson. "I don't like this kind of business at all," he said, as if he had just been informed of Elizabeth's decision to sentence Mary, Queen of Scots, to death. "But we are confronted by a desperate, dangerous situation and a madman who would ally himself with the Russians. We have no choice but to proceed with this undertaking. May God grant us success."[64]

The Ajax Caper

Ajax encompassed several different "operations," including the co-opting of British plans for using Tehran mobs, the stiffening of the Shah's spine, and various bribes to military figures and others. The "bag man" for these cash deliveries was none other than General H. Norman Schwarzkopf, who had headed the American military mission in Iran in the war, and who now appeared on the scene as a casual "tourist" ostensibly on a visit to Tehran to see his old friend—the shah. Roosevelt had recorded "You won't have any trouble in London" as under secretary of state "Beedle" Smith's bon voyage words as the CIA man left to engineer the plan. "They'll jump at anything we propose." Then he paused and said, "Ike will agree." Roosevelt noted the hesitation: "I felt he was about to say, 'with whatever we tell him,' but he bit that back."[65]

The prime minister used what he knew of American plans in order to stir up antiforeign sentiments, but he also began a dedicated campaign to find ways of escaping from the tightening economic stranglehold placed on the Iranian economy by British policy, now with greater moral support for London from the Eisenhower administration. Plans were announced to sell oil to Italian and Japanese companies willing to brave the British embargo, and for a new Iranian-Soviet trade deal. And it appeared he had new support at home—but of a kind that played into the hands of his enemies. A rally in Tehran led by the Tudeh Party turned out one hundred thousand demonstrators yelling, "Death to U.S. Imperialists." Party leaders told press reporters that the large numbers had surprised them. But the article by Kennett Love in the *New York Times* carried the sensational title "100,000 Reds Rally in Iranian Capital": "A large Broadway type balloon went up carrying in Iranian and English the phrase, 'Yankee Go Home,' which is crudely lettered on nearly every wall in certain parts of the city."[66]

On July 28 Secretary of State Dulles told a news conference that the United States was seriously concerned with the growing activities of the Tudeh Party, and with the Iranian government's toleration of such activities. This development, he said, certainly made it more difficult to "grant assistance to Iran." A decade later the Kennedy administration would signal its displeasure with Ngo Dinh Diem in almost the same language. And in both cases the signal was picked up by those for whom it was intended: the military, whose future was closely tied to Washington's goodwill and beneficences. Links between the American military and aid recipients— present and future—were at the heart of the Truman Doctrine, after all.

By mid-August, writes Stephen Kinzer, Iran had been pushed to the brink of chaos. The battle over removing Ayatollah Kashani had left Mossadeq weakened on one side, while the CIA shipped in money and propaganda to boost the morale of the dissidents. The prime minister had ordered the Majlis dissolved and was ruling by edict. Still, it took Kim Roosevelt considerable effort and several trips to the palace hidden under a rug in the backseat of a car to convince the shah to sign decrees dismissing the prime minister and appointing General Zahedi in his place. The first go at unseating Mossadeq failed, however, as the intended target learned of the plan and the military remained loyal for the time being. Facing arrest, Zahedi, aided by Roosevelt, snuck off into a hiding place near the American embassy, while the shah fled the country. In Washington, gloomy officials prepared to wash their hands of Ajax, but Roosevelt arranged for Kennett Love, the *New York Times* reporter friendly to the cause, to interview Zahedi. The American favorite of the moment indignantly denied that any coup had been intended. Instead, he asserted, the truth was that the shah had dismissed Mossadeq, but he had dodged the messenger! He, Zahedi, was now the rightful premier, and all of Mossadeq's acts were now illegal.[67]

Love's help with outside opinion might have had some influence in legitimizing the Zahedi cause, but it was Roosevelt's ad hoc maneuver of pitting street mobs against one another that won the second and final round. By sending supposedly pro-Mossadeq crowds into the streets to do mayhem, pulling them back, and then sending in military and police units to restore "order" and capture "old Mossy," Kim achieved a Kipling-era triumph. The mob had no ideology and was paid with American dollars. As soon as the streets were clear, Zahedi was fetched from his hiding place and brought to the Officers' Club in central Tehran, where he held court. Roosevelt knew he must not be seen with his protégé, but the CIA was ready with an immediate $5 million advance to get his government started—along with an extra million for General Zahedi, the man of the hour.[68]

The King's in His House—All's Well with the World

The shah returned and was greeted by a "crowd" of few hundred well-wishers trucked to the airport in time for his secret arrival. They were led in cheers by the most reliable of the hired mob chiefs, Shaban Jafari, called the Brainless One. His route from the airport was lined by soldiers with fixed bayonets, and was guarded as well by armored-car patrols. According to Kennett Love: "The crowds were kept fifty yards from the road to prevent the possibility of assassination." Zahedi's first official call, however, was on Ayatollah Kashani, to assure him that under "no circumstances" would he agree with the present British position on settlement of the dispute over the nationalization of the Iranian oil industry: "General Zahedi reportedly said he was unwilling even to pay the British for the property."[69]

It is hard to imagine that his American handlers did not know Zahedi held such an opinion, however well hidden it was from his original British supporters. Mossadeq was put on trial, sentenced to three years, then kept under house arrest the remainder of his life—"protected" by the shah's secret police, the SAVAK. The British, who had waved the Red flag of danger to secure American support for their plans to restore AIOC's control of the Iranian oil industry, had to be satisfied with Zahedi's zealous pursuit of communists—for there was no change from Mossadeq's determination not to pay compensation for the loss of future revenues. The immediate influx of American money, lamented the British Foreign Office, made it unlikely Zahedi would ever yield on that point, or others. Indeed, that proved to be the case. Churchill had been too clever by half, but he quickly grasped what had happened. He explained to the cabinet on August 25, 1953, "It would be easy for the Americans, by the expenditure of a small amount of money, to keep all the benefits of many years of British work in Persia." [70]

Washington agreed that AIOC was finished in Iran, and would have to be replaced with an international consortium. It also agreed that Zahedi was right: if Iran had to settle for the fifty-fifty deal, it should not have to pay compensation. And Washington agreed, finally, that in the consortium, AIOC (or whatever the British company was now called) could not have a majority status. When foreign secretary Anthony Eden protested that the British should have 51 percent, John Foster Dulles cut him off with a blunt statement that no U.S. company should be asked to join and run the risks in a consortium where majority shares were held by a British firm. [71]

Eventually a group of American "majors" agreed to join in an international consortium and accept a 40 percent share. AIOC would hold a 46 percent share, and the remainder went to Royal Dutch Shell and a French company. British negotiators then tried to insist that the companies should pay compensation to AIOC for this privilege. Sir William Fraser, the head of AIOC, who had been the original negotiator in the failed dealings with Iran preceding the nationalization legislation—and whose reputation as an old "imperialist" had not endeared him to Washington, either—worked it out so that the entrance fee would be absorbed by Iran providing compensation "for rupture of agreement" by supplying 110 million tons of oil for free, in effect a subsidy of $1.5 billion. The American companies would agree only to $800 million as an overall settlement. Eisenhower had told Mossadeq that a neutral body would have to work out all these arrangements, but it now appeared that the settlement would be dictated by the American companies. And so it was.

Irritated by Fraser's continued stubbornness, Dulles cabled the U.S. ambassador in London, Winthrop Aldrich, as Iranian diplomat and historian Mostafa Elm has written, that unless Fraser drastically changed his attitude, the American companies would pull out. "Such a development," said the secretary of state, "would undoubtedly . . . force us to reconsider our whole attitude toward the Iranian oil question since it would appear impossible ever to obtain a reasonable solution. . . . It might ultimately force us, with great reluctance, to review the whole scope of our Middle East relationships."[72]

Herbert Hoover Jr. carried on the negotiations for the American side, both with the British and the Iranians. He reported on progress to the National Security Council on May 27, 1954. The two most difficult issues remaining with the Iranians were the matter of management, because the Iranians were still seen as incapable of providing efficient management control, and military aid. On the first question, the situation had reverted back to the pre-Mossadeq days. Iran would not have management control or the right to examine the books. The other question was the shah's demand for military aid as his price for signing off on the consortium agreement. And on this issue, he now had a stronger hand than he had held back in 1949 when he first launched his efforts to gain military support. That story would play out tragically over the next quarter century. He owed the restoration of his throne to the Americans, and they now had an investment in his success that led down an ultimately disastrous path.[73]

For years American participation in the coup was hidden from view. Reporters sought out General Schwarzkopf on the day of the restoration to ask him about Russian comments that he had been involved in the "present turmoil." Speaking at his Maplewood, New Jersey, home, the general said he had been in Tehran to visit old friends from World War II days: "I conducted no business there." Inside the CIA, however, the Iranian caper was recorded in a secret history as the high point of the agency's Cold War achievements. "It was a day that should never have ended," the secret history said of the day the coup succeeded, August 19, 1953. "For it carried with it such a sense of excitement, of satisfaction and of jubilation that it is doubtful whether any other can come up to it."[74]

The Price of Success

For a time, indeed, the watch cry of the Eisenhower administration was, "the shah's on his throne, all's right with the world." Under secretary of state Walter Bedell Smith summarized the news from Iran as, "The Shah is a new man. For the first time he believes in himself because he feels that he is King by his people's choice and not by the arbitrary decision of a foreign power."[75]

How exactly the shah could believe that he was the "people's choice" challenges the imagination. Smith certainly knew better, as did Eisenhower and everyone over at Langley, the headquarters of the Central Intelligence Agency, where the coup had been organized. Believing the shah was the rightful ruler of Iran did not make things any easier for policy makers, who, over the next twenty-five years, struggled to find a proper "balance" in dealing with Tehran. Almost as soon as he was restored to power, the shah reverted to where he had left off during his 1949 visit to Harry Truman. Policy makers were convinced that his appeals had to be met—at least in part—to bolster his prestige at home, because, to start with, that was the only way a satisfactory settlement of the oil nationalization crisis could be achieved. Despite their doubts about what he could (or would) do with the weapons he desired, there seemed no alternative to providing him with some of the advanced weapons on his shopping lists. At first, therefore, the weapons were a sort of bribe to make sure that the shah supported a final settlement of the oil question according to the terms dictated by the new international consortium Washington organized to take over from AIOC. Later it became a matter of boosting his prestige and internal security.

There were tough negotiations ahead to bring the British to accept that they no longer called the shots, and it was essential that Washington could count on the shah to support a long-term contract with the oilmen. As in other dealings with Middle Eastern countries, moreover, the arrangement had to be carefully worked out so that the new oil regime in Iran did not offer a precedent to other would-be Mossadeqs waiting to see how they could profit from his example. But policy makers also believed that if the shah were to succeed over the long term, he would have to consolidate his position with a serious effort at land reform and other measures designed to create a middle class with a vested interest in supporting a pro-Western government. Franklin Roosevelt had reached that conclusion as early as the 1943 Big Three Conference, and had solicited plans from his aides to begin the modernization of Iran. These efforts came to naught, but a decade later Eisenhower's aides understood that the intervention they had launched to protect and preserve the Free World's investment in Iran would end in calamity if nothing were done to improve the economic and social foundations of a state that remained in a prerevolutionary condition.

A 1956 "Country Plan" developed by the United States Information Service (USIS) listed as a top objective "to direct nationalistic yearnings toward realistic evolution instead of impatient revolution as the way to build a lasting foundation for unlimited progress in Iran."[76] Well and good, but the prospects for directing Iranian nationalism along such lines were not great. The shah's new prime minister, who replaced the obstreperous Mossadeq, was General Fazlollah Zahedi, a man of many talents who had organized the Iranian end of the coup. A wealthy landowner, Zahedi had ridden with the Cossacks in the tsar's army, helped to put down rebellions in the northern regions, and had been known for pro-Nazi sentiments during the war. Exiled to Palestine in 1942, he returned after the war and served in Iranian governments as minister of the interior. At first he supported oil nationalization, then broke with Mossadeq and reemerged from political exile to lead the coup. The shah rewarded the general by naming him prime minister. Walter Bedell Smith assured Eisenhower that he had "behaved throughout this crisis with bravery and steadfastness." He seemed a good fit. "Zahedi has no love for the British," wrote Smith, but he recognized the need to have good relations with London, and desired "an oil settlement as soon as possible." What he was not, however, was a land reformer.

Aside from the need to get the Iranian "spill" cleaned up as soon as possible for political reasons, there were other matters needing attention. The United States was in effect paying a subsidy to keep the Iranian government up and running until the consortium started moving the oil into world markets. This was an unhealthy situation, as it delayed the time for getting reforms under way. No final settlement had been reached when Hoover reported on the situation in June 1954. It looked bad, he advised the National Security Council. The Iranians refused to accept anything that smacked of a "foreign concession," while the consortium demanded a contract that would provide it with "full and effective management" of operations and exports. The Iranians probably could be convinced to go along with such a plan, he said, but only if a "face-saving" device could be found. There was also the question of the length of the contract. The companies insisted that it be for the same duration as the now-defunct AIOC concession, lest other oil-producing companies seize on an Iranian settlement to change the terms of their contracts. That was hard for the Iranians to swallow, as it was a painful reminder of AIOC's intransigence in making changes. "In view of the dangers inherent in too prolonged negotiations," said Hoover, and "Iranian reluctance to reach distasteful decisions, . . . it may become necessary for the U.S. Government to apply the full weight of its influence on the Shah and the Iranian Government to accept a consortium offer which we consider reasonable for Iran and the irreducible minimum for the companies."[77]

Hoover feared a stalemate, and preferred to suspend negotiations if a danger point approached, thereby keeping the consortium always "available." The Iranians had to be warned, he said, that we were not prepared to keep on carrying them forever. A carrot-and-stick approach was needed to make sure the shah and his aides understood what was what. Once an agreement was reached and was ratified by the Majlis, it would still be necessary to send aid for an indeterminate period. Too much pressure on Tehran might backfire and collapse the still-fragile edifice of the monarchy. The shah was the key to obtaining the desired long-term contract, warned Hoover, "and making it stick": "If the Shah wobbles or fails to sever his connection with nationalist demagogues, an agreement will be worth nothing." The problem boiled down to doing what was necessary to get the shah to sign and keep an agreement, without completely acceding to his every demand.[78]

Inevitably, then, the discussion turned to what could be done to keep the shah in a good frame of mind. As matters stood, and would stand in the future, the shah had achieved a position where the United States had to pay for his loyalty. The cost would begin with a sweetened arms deal and in later years CIA guidance in setting up the shah's internal security system, known as SAVAK. There are several variations on neo-imperialism, and Iran under the shah's reign was certainly among the least appealing to Washington. Already it appeared that the only course open to policy makers was to offer the shah military aid, not only "within present concepts for the improvement of Iran's military forces but particularly designed to appeal to the Shah's prestige as well as his ideas on what Iran's military requirements are." That was a dangerously loose interpretation of how to use the carrot and the stick, in effect throwing the stick away and always hoping for the best.

Only three years after the coup a report on Iran's prospects lamented that the shah had failed to adjust his political position "so as to be in tune with and draw strength from constructive nationalist elements who reflect an increasing, though still inchoate, public opinion." Success or failure in Iran had implications for American relations with the entire area, especially when relations with Egypt soured after the Soviet arms deal with Cairo. According to the report, "Iran could be [a] considerable asset to the U.S. in an area where the U.S. is not surfeited with political assets."[79]

Another way of framing the situation was that as options for persuading Egypt or Iraq to become junior partners faded, the shah's leverage in Washington increased still more. As the Shah kept pressing for more military aid and advanced weapons systems, Washington tried to respond in two ways: it pushed for Iranian participation in a regional defense system, and then, to contend with its own skepticism about the likelihood that the Soviet Union would launch an attack on Iran, it developed the formula that such arms were needed to protect Iran from "International Communism" (a tactic that Dulles famously employed to conceal the real purpose of the "Eisenhower Doctrine" when it came before Congress in early 1957). The originator of this formula was actually Loy Henderson, the ambassador to Iran, who had helped to facilitate the coup from his post. He was a key advocate of meeting the shah's arms requests, and his reasoning was clear: if the shah was to remain in a position to ensure internal stability, he needed the prestige that American arms would give him with his people: "I make this recommendation partly for psychological reasons. It is my belief that unless the Shah, the Iranian Government, the members of the Iranian armed forces and the Iranian public are convinced that western powers expect Iran to defend itself if invaded by armed forces of international communism, and unless the U.S. indicates this expectation by assisting the Iranian armed forces to prepare to maintain a strong withdrawal-delaying action, *the determination of Iran to suppress internal communist activities and to resist external communist pressure will be seriously affected.*"[80]

One does well to pay close attention to what Henderson is saying here. It comes down to a contention that the shah's prestige with his own people was the deciding factor in supplying arms to Iran or, put another way, bribing Iranians to support the shah. It is a telling characteristic of American neocolonialism in many countries, not just Iran, and it has a poor record of anything other than temporary success.

The overall formula under the rubric "International Communism" evolved out of the concern to make sure that American arms were not used in local wars for individual ambitions, as well as a cover for supplying arms to friendly regimes. Like Egypt's Nasser, the shah did not buy into such limitations, and his requests continually exceeded what the Americans thought was good for him—and for the overall American position. Iran's strategic position bordering Russia and its oil gave the shah bargaining leverage that Nasser did not enjoy. In the Middle East, perhaps more than any other region, this was the tricky aspect of military aid, for it inevitably meant that strings were always a part of any "package," requiring in some instances participation in regional defense pacts, and always requiring the recipient to receive a MAAG (Military Advisory Assistance Group) to oversee training with the weapons. American relations with Nasser's Egypt would founder on that question.

Reporting on the dangers to the Iranian government at the end of 1955, the National Security Council warned that the threat to internal security once posed by the Tudeh Party had declined, but there were new dangers among dissident tribal organizations and "xenophobic religious elements." Although these elements lacked arms or the capacity for armed insurrection, they would "still be able to stir religious sentiments against almost any target—foreigners, religious minorities, or the government."[81]

It was a prescient warning. A year later, Secretary Dulles recommended to the president that he respond to the shah's latest plea for more military aid by making the point that Iran's true safety could only be found "in collective security and cooperation with the Free World." He should be reminded that the United States would take a grave view of any threat to Iran's territorial integrity. He did not need to worry on that score, in other words, or keep on making an argument that the Russians were coming. Eisenhower continued to fend off the shah's requests with warm letters of appreciation for the "spiritual" strength Iran had demonstrated in withstanding Soviet pressures. The shah took advantage of the formula the Americans had adopted, "International Communism," to urge his case that left-leaning Afghanistan and Iraq posed major military threats to his country.[82]

Eisenhower's advisers warned him that the shah was deliberately overstating the danger, but it was also true that Washington contributed to its own Iran dilemma by its public and private comments in regard to the Iraqi internal situation. The more the shah harped on his "vulnerabilities," nevertheless, the more worried policy makers became that he was neglecting everything that would make his situation more secure in terms of domestic reforms. There were fears that he was imperiling the monarchy by his actions, and hints that it might be necessary to look beyond the shah should matters reach a crisis.

The American position was that the shah's requests went beyond anything he could use effectively, and that piling up arms was now becoming a danger to Iranian internal security, as well as a burden on U.S. military aid programs. The shah had a counter for this last argument. Iran could pay its own way, he said, if the United States would take a strong position with the consortium, which was favoring Kuwaiti oil at the expense of Iran's economy. During Eisenhower's "farewell" tour around the world, he stopped in Tehran and was immediately subjected to the shah's assertions that his country was the center of the shield protecting the Free World in the Middle East: "God forbid, it should fall to Russia then the entire Middle East would collapse."[83]

During their conversation the shah pressed for medium-range bombers and help with constructing suitable airports for their use, as well as various sorts of missiles. Talking with the head of the MAAG, he elaborated on a need for "mobile forces with atomics." He repeated that he wished to locate "the atomic type in areas of greatest threat; that Afghanistan and Iraq be covered with highly mobile forces strongly supported by an effective air force; that a mobilization base be established for quick call up in conjunction with the establishment of highly mobile atomic forces."[84]

Here were early indications of an ambition that went beyond being only a junior partner, and a sobering reminder that the ultimate cost for restoring the shah had only begun to be paid. Once again Eisenhower responded with promises that Iran would not be abandoned, but he had doubts about the papers the shah had submitted to back up his requests: "I find that, as we see it, they overstate somewhat the threat to your country from Iraq and Afghanistan. I also find that your paper includes a number of complicated and advanced weapons which would involve a high initial cost, which would be very costly to maintain, and which would require an advanced level of technical training which could only be achieved over a considerable period in time."[85]

It was an ironic addendum of sorts to the earlier argument that the Iranians were incapable of managing the intricacies of refining crude oil, and would also be taken as just as insulting by the shah and his successors. In a message for the incoming Kennedy administration, an NSC staff officer outlined for McGeorge Bundy, the new national security adviser, the prospects for American relations with Tehran over the next several years. On the one hand, there was the danger that the shah might seek to get closer to the Soviet Union, either for self-protection or as a ploy to increase his leverage with Washington to get the weapons he had been denied; on the other hand, his promises to do something about political and social reforms seem as far off as ever from being realized. Elections he had scheduled "may well give rise to violent expressions of dissatisfaction over the rigging of results." It was entirely possible that once again the United States might be faced with a "nationalist-Communist collaboration."[86]

The shah's rule was very much that of a "hollow crown," haunted by the 1953 coup, and held in place over the Peacock Throne by the support of Americans who quickly came to fear his pseudodynastic ambitions, but feared more letting go. The shah's knowledge of American fears constituted his only real strength.

The End of the Affair

The full consequences of that 1953 day when the shah was ushered back from exile have, indeed, never ended either for Iranians or Americans. For a quarter century Reza Pahlavi controlled both his country and, it can be argued, American policy. He became one of the biggest customers ever for American military products, and when Richard Nixon was searching for a policy to replace the Vietnam model, he became the "answer" as a regional stabilizer. A famous turning point came in July 1972, when Nixon was on the way home from a Moscow summit meeting and stopped in Tehran to talk with the shah. After their conversation, the president ordered that the latest aircraft, F-14s and F-15s, along with the necessary training missions, should be made available to Iran just as soon as their effectiveness had been properly tested.

Nixon's successor, Gerald Ford, continued the policy, writes historian William Burr, for Iran now became not simply an oil-bearing state, but also an aid in redressing other Cold War dilemmas, especially the efforts to overcome Vietnam-induced economic problems:

> Just like the Nixon administration, the Ford White House saw the Shah and Iran as a critically important ally in the volatile Middle East, and not only as a source of oil, but as a major proxy in support of U.S. interests in the region. Despite the notoriety of the Shah's police state, the importance that Ford and Kissinger attached to a stable Iran made them willing to conciliate the Shah by keeping their eyes blind to the human rights abuses associated with the dictatorship. For his part, the Shah sought close relations with Washington to strengthen his domestic position as well as to counter the Soviet Union, such rivals as Iraq, and radical forces in the region generally. No puppet, the Shah was relatively impervious to U.S. importuning against oil price increases, although he recycled billions of petrodollars in arms purchases from the United States. Indeed, the White House maintained a "green light" for arms sales to improve the balance of payments. In light of the varied interests at stake, U.S. senior officials worked hard at cementing the relationship, to the point where Vice President Nelson Rockefeller compared "His Imperial Majesty" to Alexander the Great.[87]

The shah's desire for nuclear reactors set off some alarm bells in Washington, but there were plenty of counterarguments for meeting even this demand. His arms purchases did partially offset the high oil prices that OPEC mandated in the wake of the 1973 Arab-Israeli War. When Gerald Ford succeeded Nixon in the summer of 1974, secretary of state Henry Kissinger immediately reassured the Iranian ambassador that there were no "major problems" in the relationship: "Iran is for us a key country in the Middle East." But then he noted, a bit too casually, that when he visited Tehran he was interested in taking up the price of oil. He did not believe that the way to get lower prices was to concentrate on Iran, of course, but he did maintain that "there should be a discussion."[88]

Much of the Ford administration's effort in Iranian relations was directed toward persuading Iran to opt out of the OPEC pricing scheme, a lost cause before it began. As the State Department admitted, there was very little leverage that could be brought to bear, such as cutting off arms shipments, because that would only worsen balance-of-payments problems and deflate the shah's prestige throughout the area where he was viewed as a stabilizing force. "The Shah is a tough, mean guy," Kissinger warned the president. "But he is our real friend. We can't tackle him without breaking him."[89]

Kissinger's 1974 talks produced appeals for new weapons systems and a plea that the United States buy more oil from Iran. He also repeated old charges that the consortium favored other countries in terms of marketing. Kissinger persevered, nevertheless, and attempted to negotiate a bilateral deal with Iran that would have Tehran selling oil directly to the U.S. government, which would then resell it to American oil companies for refining. The scheme, he suggested to Ford, would undermine OPEC's challenge to Western dominance on oil questions, solidify relations with the closest U.S. ally in the region, and help to curb Soviet influence: "We can counter complains by Venezuela and possibly Saudi Arabia by asking them to make us a better offer."[90]

Fortunately, one supposes, Kissinger's reputation as a "realist" in international relations did not rest on this sort of fantasy. Kissinger's associates in the administration, Brent Scowcroft, the national security adviser, and defense secretary Donald Rumsfeld, took a very dim view of deal; they saw it as benefitting mostly the shah, rather than the United States, as he would gain a guaranteed price at the outset at a time when the market was falling. Frustrated by their inability to work with the shah, Kissinger and the administration turned to Saudi Arabia and succeeded in getting that country to increase production to lower prices. But then came the earthquake of 1979 with its aftershocks and the continuing dilemma of a nuclear Iran. Although the administration was never entirely comfortable at any time with Reza Pahlavi, the alternative always seemed worse. Even as waves of popular opposition swept higher and higher in the last months of the shah's regime, president Jimmy Carter in 1979 described the shah as a rock of stability in a greatly troubled region. That Washington had no other option was the almost inevitable result of the 1951–53 oil crisis, when the CIA rescued the shah from exile to turn back the challenge of a charismatic nationalist prime minister, Mohammed Mossadeq. The shah ruled for twenty-five more years after the "countercoup" until the 1979 revolution finally ended the American era in Iranian history. Incredible as it might seem, in 2006 there were efforts by "top American officials" to enlist remaining supporters of the shah living in exile around Los Angeles as the Bush administration sought regime change in Iran.[91]

But in the 1950s, the Iranian crisis slipped from memory as the scene shifted to Egypt, where, once again the initial struggle was about how to convince the British to go quietly so that the United States would have a free hand to deal with the nationalist threat.

5

DAMMING THE EGYPTIAN REVOLUTION

*The US cannot dictate to Egypt. Power must come from the people
themselves. Nevertheless, he would like the Prime Minister to know
when the new Administration had studied world strategy in the Department of State and in the National Security Council they had concluded that Egypt is the country in the Middle East which, under the
leadership and guidance of the Prime Minister contains the promise of
a great future.*
　　　　　　　　　　　—John Foster Dulles in Cairo, May 11, 1953

*The United States had tried its best to keep Egyptian friendship despite
the effects of its Israel policy on the domestic political situation. Nasser
had followed exactly the opposite course. Whenever he saw that popularity could be gained thereby, he had shown no restraint in leading the
mob against the West.*
　　　　　　　　—John Foster Dulles in Washington, May 17, 1956

At the height of the Iranian oil crisis premier Mohammed
Mossadeq received a tumultuous welcome in Cairo. He came to the
Egyptian capital after talks in Washington had once again failed to
produce a solution that would satisfy both British demands for
"compensation" for their lost property, the Anglo-Iranian Oil Company, and the Iranian demands for control over its only natural resource. It had been a hopeless mission, of course, for nothing short
of a reversal of the nationalism decree would have satisfied London.
Even as the oil imbroglio continued, moreover, the British were
faced with another crisis in Egypt. From the time of the construction of the Suez Canal in 1869, its value as the lifeline to India had
been paramount in British strategic thinking. British troops had

first occupied the Suez area in 1882 to put down a rebellion, promising to retire, said generations of foreign office secretaries, "as soon as the state of the country" permitted it. "Egyptian nationalists spent the next 72 years trying to get the British to act on their expressed desire to withdraw."[1]

Instead of withdrawing, however, the British tightened their grip around Suez as the years went by. In December 1914, the sixth month of World War I, London declared that the Ottoman suzerainty had been terminated, declared a protectorate over Egypt, and transferred all foreign policy functions to its chief representative in Cairo, now called the high commissioner. At that war's end, foreign secretary Lord Curzon declared, "The welfare and integrity of Egypt are necessary to the peace and safety of the British Empire, which will therefore always maintain as an essential British interest the special relations between itself and Egypt."[2]

Egyptian politicians refused to associate themselves with British ideas of conditional sovereignty, and the struggle for true independence began. At its heart was the huge British garrison located at Suez. A 1936 treaty imposed on Cairo permitted the British to house ten thousand troops and four hundred pilots there, along with all necessary support personnel, for twenty years. In 1942, as Field Marshal Erwin Rommel's Afrika Korps approached the Egyptian capital, student demonstrators cheered. Fearing rioting and insurrection, British high commissioner Sir Miles Lampson ordered three tanks and a company of soldiers to smash through the palace gates to King Farouk's chambers. Farouk had apparently been toying with the idea of appointing a pro-Axis premier in case the Germans actually reached Cairo. Either name pro-British Mustafa Nahas premier, Lampson demanded, or be thrown out of the palace. It took the king less than an hour to decide he wanted to stay. The episode marked Egypt's worst humiliation, said a young army officer, Gamal Abdel Nasser. "Hearts were full of fire and sorrow."[3]

Egypt and Israel: An American Dilemma

When President Roosevelt entertained King Farouk on an American battleship in the Great Bitter Lake area of the Suez Canal after the Yalta Conference in February 1945, it was not the same as Rommel coming to Egypt, of course, but it signified, in less dramatic ways, that the British monopoly was finally coming to an end. With Indian independence in 1947, however, the Suez base and canal took on a new importance. A vital connecting link to the old empire, the canal was now the main transit route for Middle Eastern oil. And instead of a German menace, it was now the Russians who posed a potential threat. To protect the oil, and block a supposed Russian advance, the British had sent eighty thousand troops to Suez—eight times the number permitted under the 1936 treaty.

With the creation of the state of Israel and the first Arab-Israeli War, the political situation in Egypt deteriorated. Egypt's sorry military performance in the war shifted the focus to the incompetence of the regime itself. Morale in the officer corps plummeted. Corruption had grown to fantastic proportions, wrote Nasser's confidant Mohamed Heikal: "Farouk was in his palace and one half per cent of the population was getting 50 per cent of the national income. . . . The political parties had collapsed with no sense of direction and no sense of purpose. There was nothing to be proud of and there was no dignity."[4]

An American diplomat in London reported a common feeling that the "Palestine War" had been the last straw for Farouk. It was only a question of how much longer the "have-not donkey" would tolerate the weight of the unenlightened "haves" before it kicked them off. Farouk was likely to go out of Egypt feetfirst. Revolution in Egypt would imperil the Suez base, but if things continued as they were it would hardly be any better. For the time being, it was a British problem. The truce that ended the Arab-Israeli War had resolved no major issues, especially the matters of refugees and territorial boundaries. President Truman's successors would face the same issues over the decades and into the next century. And like them he had no solution to offer for the eight hundred thousand or more Palestinian refugees who fled or were driven from their homes. "I told the President of Israel in the presence of his Ambassador just exactly what I thought about it," Truman wrote to a special emissary. "It may have some effect, I hope so."[5]

Truman hoped in vain. No question bedeviled American policy makers more than the Palestinian refugee issue. Egypt was always considered the key to finding an answer to that conundrum as well as to the question of a Middle Eastern "defense system." Egypt would not attack Israel, ambassador Jefferson Caffery was told by the foreign minister, but neither would it make peace nor collaborate in any regional plan. To do so, he said, would destroy Arab morale as other countries looked to Cairo to uphold the right of return.[6]

The Arab countries declared it impossible to absorb the refugees for several reasons, but none more important than the fear that Israel's ultimate aims included annexation of other pieces of Arab lands. Israel's announced policy of encouraging Jews everywhere to immigrate, and not just the survivors of the Holocaust, offered the proof. The open door that Israel offered to Jewish immigration, said Arab leaders, meant the newcomers would have to go somewhere—and somewhere meant Arab lands. Yet even without added territory, Israel limited the Arab future, it was argued, as a new outpost of Western imperialism. The refugees were only the first victims.

The Israelis argued for their part that the refugees were being kept homeless to serve as the ultimate rationale for a final campaign to eradicate their country. As for any move toward offering large numbers of Palestinians an opportunity to return to lands they had vacated, that was impossible. They would constitute a "fifth column" loyal to those dedicated to Israel's destruction. Besides, given the very limited territory of the new state, such a demand on Israel was tantamount to calling for it to commit economic suicide.

Under such conditions the shaky truce was unlikely to last very long. An arms race of sorts had already begun. Israel complained to Washington that Britain was supplying weapons to the Arabs intended for use in a renewed war. The ambassador argued that the weapons the Arabs acquired were not meant to repel an attack by the Soviet Union, but for the purpose of attacking his country. "I completely agreed with the Ambassador," Secretary Acheson noted in a memorandum, "that the arms being supplied to the Arab States would not enable them to stand off an attack by the Soviet Union. For that matter, the arms we were furnishing the Western European states would not enable them to do this either. But I thought that I could understand the desire on the part of the Arab states to restore their self-confidence by strengthening their arms, and the necessity from the British point of view of having this self-confidence restored to strategic nations in the Near East."[7]

Always one who saw to the heart of the matter, Acheson here made a classic statement about managing the world. Israel had no choice, then, said the Israeli ambassador, but to buy weapons from Czechoslovakia: "My government has no alternative but to take all steps necessary for its protection." Five years later, ironically, an Egyptian arms deal with Czechoslovakia would set in motion a series of events leading to the Suez crisis; but for the moment there still seemed ways to control the situation. Acheson hoped, for example, that it might be possible to start a peace process in some other country besides Egypt—for example, in Saudi Arabia, where American influence might be greater because of the oil concession run by ARAMCO. Acheson went so far as to have George McGhee broach the question of a possible treaty in Riyadh, only to have the Saudi foreign minister take the opportunity to warn against any move by Israel to annex Jordanian territory. Jordan was within the wall separating the Arab countries from Israel, he said, and any attempt to expand beyond that barrier would be met by force: "We shall never admit a Jew in Saudi Arabia and we shall never admit anyone traveling with an Israeli visa."[8]

Since there was no way to halt arms shipments to the Middle East, and, in fact, no desire to give up such an avenue to increased political influence, the answer had to be to incorporate the arms within some larger scheme, as Acheson had implied in his statements to the Israeli ambassador about American arms for NATO. At a cabinet meeting on April 14, 1950, the secretary of state said the United States was not doing what it could to see that the Arab countries and Israel were both "properly armed," an intriguing euphemism for "controlled." The solution might be to get the British and French, as the primary suppliers for the Arab countries, to join with the United States in a nonaggression statement, committing the three to send only "defensive" arms to their Middle Eastern customers, and pledging they would come to the aid of any country attacked in violation of the armistice agreements that had ended the 1948 Arab-Israeli War.[9]

Truman thought that was a grand idea, and such a tripartite declaration was duly made on May 25, 1950. Israeli efforts to obtain arms in the United States continued, of course, as much to elicit political support as for the weaponry itself. Its staunch supporters, such as vice president Alben Barkley, argued that Israel was "an oasis of liberty in the desert of despotism," and therefore the only Middle Eastern country worthy of full American sympathy and support. Such arguments would continue to have an immense impact on American policy over the next half century. It was certainly true that Israel was the only democracy in the Middle East, and that made everything seem different about the Arab countries, news stories, cultural doings, manner of dress—all of it.

From the time Israel first appeared with such gale-like political force in the 1948 election, the split between the White House and the State Department had never fully mended. Acheson, more circumspect than George C. Marshall (who had once threatened to resign), tried to work around Truman. In late 1951, according to one of those who participated in the planning, the secretary of state "borrowed" Kermit Roosevelt from the Central Intelligence Agency to head up a highly secret committee of specialists to study the Arab world, with special emphasis on the Arab-Israeli conflict, and to "work out solutions, *any* solutions, whether or not they fitted orthodox notions of proper governmental behavior." Among the ideas put forward was one for promoting a "Moslem Billy Graham," who would be used to mobilize religious fervor in a great move against communism.[10]

Acheson's concerns about the Arab-Israeli conflict were not lessened by the visit of Israeli prime minister David Ben-Gurion in May 1951. Ben-Gurion began his appeal for aid with an assertion that Israel had the capacity to defend itself and was ready to take part in the defense of the Middle East. Manpower of military age, he said, was growing rapidly and was now twice what it had been since the establishment of the state: "Israel has followed, and will continue to follow, a policy of unlimited immigration. It is the ideal on which the State is based." Aside from Turkey, he went on, Israel had more military potential than any other Middle Eastern country: "The other countries are not of much use in any plans for the defense of the area." [11]

Acheson's special committee had come to pretty much the opposite conclusion. It was Egypt, it asserted, whose potential offered the most to American interests in the region: "Egypt was a country worth high priority on its own merit, and its influence on other Arab states was such that a turn for the better there would be felt throughout the Arab world." The defense of the Middle East, as Acheson had already insisted in earlier talks with the Israeli ambassador, was not a matter of large armies or big air forces, but rather of bases and political positions. American arms were for internal security, Washington insisted, not for taking part in strategic missions against Russia. Ben-Gurion continued along in his presentation of Israel's military potential, nevertheless, and presented a shopping list of needed items to make it the arsenal of democracy for the area. Acheson interrupted the recital to suggest that "we had given a great deal of thought to what could be done in the Middle East. The first essential, however, was to get peace in the area." But, countered Ben-Gurion, American military aid to Israel would demonstrate to the Arab nations that "Israel could not be destroyed." The Arab states would then be prepared to make peace. He acknowledged that Egypt was the key. An Israeli agreement with Cairo would go a long way to bring about peace agreements with the rest. "There were no problems between Israel and Egypt," he asserted, "and only desert lay between the two countries." It was probably the most remarkable of all the statements he made that day. [12]

Ben-Gurion ended by stating that the West might find that

Israel's cooperation was "the decisive factor in the successful defense of the Middle East." Acheson hardly thought that was the case. The American plan centered on Cairo. The idea was to channel Egyptian ambitions to lead the Arab world by making their capital city the home of a Middle East Defense Organization (MEDO), complete with Egyptian staff officers who would bustle around in offices and on the parade ground to give the appearance of real decision makers. MEDO never got off the ground. The Egyptians weren't interested, at least not until matters were settled with the British about the evacuation of Suez and—even more problematically—an answer was found to the far more complex and no less emotional refugee problem.

Good-Bye to All That: Farouk's Final Days

In Egypt, the supposedly pro-British premier, Mustafa Nahas, announced that Egypt was abrogating the 1936 treaty that had guaranteed the British base for twenty years. Things began to fall apart after Nahas kept his promise: terrorists kidnapped and killed British soldiers, threw grenades into officers' clubs, and generally raised hell all over the canal area and in Cairo. Mossadeq's famous visit occurred amid all this turmoil, and added fuel to the nationalist flames already burning high. On January 25, 1952, at Ismalia, the halfway point on the canal, a fight broke out between British troops sent to quell recurring troubles and a battalion of Egyptian auxiliary police. In the ensuing gunfire exchange forty-one police were killed and another seventy-two wounded. The next day mobs surged through downtown Cairo, setting fires and attacking the symbols of British power and prestige, such as Shepherd's Hotel, the St. James restaurant, and the British Turf Club. Nine British civilians were killed in gruesome fashion, four of them disemboweled and another trampled to death. Additional troops were sent into Cairo from the Suez garrison and succeeded in bringing the rioting to an end on what became known as "Black Saturday," January 26, 1952.[13]

The British felt they had made their point—not only in Egypt but also in dealing with Mossadeq—but Truman rejected London's appeal for American forces to present a united front. Churchill had pled with Truman that such a demonstration would "divide the difficulties by ten." In Washington, however, "Black Saturday" was seen as only the beginning of real difficulties unless a new approach was adopted. "It did not impress him," Acheson told the British ambassador, "that the operation of Ismalia had been carried out with 'unusual skill,'" as Eden had put it in a telegram to Washington. "The 'splutter of musketry' apparently does not stop things as we had been told from time to time that it would."[14]

On July 23, 1952, a group of senior army officials disenchanted with the regime mounted a successful revolt. Farouk appealed to the British and American embassies for help. Neither would lift a finger, fearing the consequences for the Suez base if they did. But no physical harm came to Farouk. He sailed off into exile to continue his sybaritic lifestyle elsewhere without the troublesome business of ruling. A few hours after the takeover, one of the plotters met with a U.S. military attaché to assure him of the revolutionary council's pro-Western sentiments, and to ask for his help in persuading the British not to intervene.[15]

In Egypt, as in other places in the Third World, the military was destined to play a leading role—but to do so required a guaranteed source from which to obtain weapons. As that source, the United States could exert considerable leverage (and even more so, it would later become clear, as the final authority approving weapons transfers from NATO members). The expected appeals from the Egyptian military were not long in coming. Ambassador Caffery cabled Washington that he had received word from General Muhammad Naguib that he would be willing to give secret assurances to the United States about the long-term objectives of the new regime, including MEDO or partnership with the United States. But before he could do more in the way of public statements, the regime's first job was to sell the Egyptian public on the United States. And to accomplish that would require military supplies and financial assistance.[16]

For Acheson, that was a good beginning. The United States would accept secret assurances, but only with the understanding

that they were preliminary to open commitments. Adherence to
MEDO was only one of three issues of interest to the United States.
There was the question of a long-term arrangement over Suez guar-
anteeing ready access to the base; *and* there was still the most pressing matter of all—peace with Israel. In the meantime, however, the
new regime could signal its intentions with "certain gestures," such
as a public vow of support for the UN actions in Korea, and an offer
of compensation to victims of the rioting on "Black Saturday."
These should not be too difficult for Cairo and would offer evidence
of the new regime's orientation in the Cold War.[17]

But a strictly bilateral program of military cooperation, Acheson
cautioned, was not in the cards. The NATO model, with its mutual
obligations and safeguards against the use of American weapons,
was what Washington had on offer. Yet he did suggest that Cairo
"look to its habitual sources of supply." In other words, until Egypt
had cleared the hurdles Washington had set, it was welcome to try
the British, who had doled out some surplus materials over the years
(although nothing too modern). No one expected Egypt to send
troops to Korea, but a public expression of support would be
counted as both a contribution and commitment to the right side in
the Cold War.

No one understood better than Acheson the various techniques
a dominant power could use to make a "coalition of the willing."
Two months later, Mohamed Heikal, a newspaper editor and confidant of Colonel Nasser, the strongman behind Naguib, arrived in
Washington ostensibly to cover the presidential election. His real
mission was to provide Nasser with information about likely attitudes of the new administration, Democrat or Republican. Heikal
received a warm welcome in the Pentagon. His host was a general
who entertained him with a special map show. The general pushed
a button and behind him, Dr. Strangelove fashion, descended a
huge map of the world covered with buttons and flags, each repre-
senting an American garrison or base. Pointing to the display, the
general looked meaningfully at Heikal. The Middle East was largely
bare, he said. "Don't you think we could do with some buttons and
flags in your part of the world?"

Heikal protested that the real issue was the hopes and aspirations of the people. The general seemed surprised, and not quite aware of Heikal's point, so he elaborated a different line. An alternative to buttons and flags, the general suggested, was an Islamic pact. Because of its heavy religious content, such a pact would provide a natural bulwark against communism. Turkey, the general carried on, was the strongest military power, Pakistan the most populous, Saudi Arabia the custodian of the Holy Places, and Egypt would have a special role—it could supply the cultural focus. An Islamic pact might even cause uprisings in the Muslim populations of the Soviet Union and China and have a chastening effect in India. Heikal learned later that the idea did not have State Department backing, but thought it revealed a troubling lack of comprehension about Middle Eastern politics in the postcolonial era.[18]

Dulles and the New Look at the Middle East

When the Republicans swept to power on Eisenhower's World War II reputation and promise to go to Korea, secretary of state John Foster Dulles announced he was taking a "new look" not only at what had gone wrong with the Truman/Acheson containment policy in Eastern Europe and Asia, but especially at the Middle East. American policy there had been less than even-handed, he contended. The challenge was to divert Middle Eastern attention from the Arab-Israeli conflict and channel the emotions into a worldwide anticommunist crusade. An evenhanded approach would make it easier to convince the Arabs to make peace with Israel, he hoped, and, with the security threat removed, easier to convince Israel to offer permanent borders.

When he made the Middle East his first extended tour only a few months after coming into office, Dulles chose an odd gift for General Naguib—a .38-caliber pistol with a silver plate on the butt inscribed: "To General Mohammed Naguib from his friend Dwight D. Eisenhower." It was supposed to be a private affair but one photographer caught the scene, and his picture caused uproar in the British press. Prime Minister Churchill appealed to his old friend and wartime colleague for an explanation. It had no larger significance, Eisenhower reassured Churchill: one pistol did not "presage a flow of planes, tanks, and guns to arm that nation."[19]

Had the British known more about Dulles's game than the pistol picture revealed, London's reaction would have a whole lot louder—an outcry probably—for when Dulles talked with General Naguib he all but promised to provide arms to Egypt. If such aid was *justified*, he said, "the US would be prepared to consider making the Egyptian Army a real force in the world." Washington had neglected the Middle East for too long. It was the area from which the great religions and much culture had sprung. At this point Dulles implied that more than military aid could be Egypt's reward for accepting these obligations: "In the past the US has perhaps centered too much of its interest on Israel as a result of pressure groups in the US. The new Administration is seeking a balanced view of the Middle East directed against neither the Arabs nor the Jews."[20]

General Naguib's reply seemed responsive to these hints. Yes, the British should have access to the base on short notice; and yes, once the dispute with the British was settled there might be progress toward making peace with Israel. Well, Dulles pressed for specifics, would Naguib promise that the British could oversee the maintenance of the base? Egypt will have won a great political victory when the British troops evacuated Suez. Think of that, he said, and the dismal alternative: "Could it be that the great vision of a new Egypt could collapse over the problems of a few inventory-keepers?"

The dialogue continued when he met Col. Nasser, the key man in the revolutionary council. A real solution to the Suez base problem and the general defense issue could arise naturally as British troops left the area, said Dulles, in his best Wall Street lawyer tones: "The US hopes Egypt will lead the Arab States into a new area defense system (not MEDO since this was out of date) which, when it is achieved, will find the material in the depots available to it." But Nasser seemed less agreeable than Naguib had been. Egypt by itself would maintain the base depots and determine access. That was his position. What Dulles proposed was a lightly disguised ploy to sustain British influence in a new multination alliance. Well, the situation was dangerous, replied Dulles, and the base must remain a living organism. "How can we get the talks going again?" Simple, Nasser said: "By getting the British to agree to the Egyptian point of view."[21]

Whatever he thought of Nasser at this moment, it was clear to Dulles that the British were a handicap to increasing American influence in the new Middle East, however unready the United States was to take charge at every weak point. Eventually an Anglo-Egyptian agreement was reached on the future of the Suez base, but Dulles returned from his first encounter with Nasser and Naguib filled with foreboding and ambiguous about the next steps. Eisenhower had told congressional leaders the big problem was how to organize the Middle East into some kind of NATO defense system, including an arrangement that guaranteed the Suez base would always be available. But Israel complicated the problem. On his return, Dulles painted a much darker picture. The Middle East was in the grip of a "fanatical revolutionary spirit." It was not just a temporary problem: "The Israeli factor, and the association of the U.S. in the minds of the people of the area with French and British colonial and imperialistic policies, are millstones around our neck."[22]

In a television report to the nation, Dulles declared that the United States must pursue an impartial approach to Israeli-Arab disputes, so as to win the support of both sides against the common threat of communism. At present the Arabs were "more fearful of Zionism than of Communism," he lamented, while the Israelis feared that the ultimate aim of the Arabs was to push them into the sea. Then he went out on a very narrow limb: "The leaders of Israel themselves agreed with us that United States policies should be impartial so as to win not only the respect and regard of the Israeli, but also of the Arab peoples." He juxtaposed that comment with praise for Naguib as a popular hero, who deserved the adulation because he was determined to provide Egypt with a government that will "truly serve the people." Israel, Dulles said, needed to "cease to look upon itself or be looked upon by others, as alien to this [Middle Eastern] community."[23]

Egyptian reactions were muted. "The speech is friendly," said one high official, "but we should not be too optimistic." Meeting with reporters after seeing assistant secretary Henry Byroade, Israeli ambassador Abba Eban said he had sought clarifications of some points. Asked which points, he replied, "Well, if you read the speech practically every point." A few weeks later, *Times* reporter Dana Adams Schmidt reported from Tel Aviv that the Israelis had sensed in Dulles's remarks an ominous shift in American opinion, to which they were extremely sensitive "for there is no country in the world so completely dependent on outside—especially United States—economic support." [24]

Israelis feared they were beginning to lose the "pathos" argument, Schmidt added, and that it was being transferred to the eight hundred thousand Arab refugees. Following Ben-Gurion's example in talks with Acheson, they had hoped stressing Israel's strategic importance as an all-out American ally would keep attention focused elsewhere. For Dulles's recent visit Israel had organized an exhibit of locally produced new weapons, including a submachine gun it claimed was the best in the world. The secretary declined the opportunity to tour the fair, pleading time constraints.

Mission: Impossible

While Americans pondered sending arms, the political clock in Egypt sped up as Naguib was formally deposed in February 1954 in favor of Nasser, who had already emerged as the real force in the revolutionary council and made no secret of his desires to move Egypt forward on all fronts. Washington dispatched "Kim" Roosevelt to Cairo, hoping he would act as Nasser's tutor, somewhat like those the Europeans used to send to Oriental potentates. Although his great adventure had been overthrowing Mossadeq in Iran and restoring the shah to the Peacock Throne, Roosevelt's new mission was to shape the Egyptian into a positive influence on postcolonial leaders in Africa and Asia. At first Nasser seemed a good pupil, indeed an eager one. Policy statements prepared by Roosevelt for Nasser to deliver were often reprinted on Egyptian presidential letterhead with scarcely any changes. Surely he was destined for big things. But appearances were deceptive. Little real progress was being made on the conditions Washington had set down for welcoming Egypt into full membership in the "Free World." Matters approached a stalemate as Cairo continued pressing for arms aid. Nasser asked for $40 million, then $20 million, and finally just $3 million for parade items—helmets, pistol holsters, and various kinds of shiny equipment that would look good when the army paraded through the streets of Cairo. There was no question about using this equipment in a war with Israel, wrote one of Roosevelt's CIA compatriots, Miles Copeland, who agreed with ambassador Jefferson Caffery that Nasser was right, a "shabby army [w]as a potentially disloyal army."[25]

Nasser talked a good game, Washington policy makers insisted, but Egypt had yet to toe the line. Cairo must first accept a Military Assistance Advisory Group (MAAG), like other "allies" had done, before any significant grants could be made. Even if the colonels cleared this hurdle, there remained the other requirements, above all a peace treaty between Egypt and Israel. Congress would never allow the executive branch to go ahead with arms sales without such a treaty. At one point the State Department considered a one-time $10 million packet funneled through the economic aid programs so as to avoid complaints that Egypt was receiving special treatment. Nothing came of it.[26]

Events outside Egypt in the Arab world had also created a new situation for Nasser. Despite his warnings against overweening Western influence in any military pact with Washington-imposed conditions attached, Iraq's ruler, Nuri al-Said, was eager to join an alliance with Turkey and Pakistan, sponsored by Great Britain. This "Baghdad Pact," formally announced on February 24, 1955, infuriated Nasser, not least because it made Iraq a rival for leadership of the Arab world. Secretary Dulles thought the United States could well profit from such a rivalry, but had no desire to join the alliance as a signatory. Dulles had been most favorably impressed with Pakistan's potential as a Muslim state for a military alliance, especially if it were allied with Iraq as the anchors of a "Northern Tier." Add Syria and Turkey, and this tier would be too high for the Soviets to climb, and too much for Egypt to overcome in any quest to unite

Arabs behind its leadership and create an autonomous, all-Arab army.

The back-and-forth in public and behind the scenes between Cairo and Washington was still going on in February 28, 1955, when an Israeli raid on an Egyptian military post in the Gaza Strip pushed the question to the forefront. Nasser immediately surmised a connection between the raid, which left thirty-seven dead and another thirty wounded, and the appearance of the Baghdad Pact. Both, he believed, were designed to diminish his standing as the putative leader of the Arab world. Ben-Gurion, now Israel's defense minister, launched the attack for a variety of reasons. The ostensible cause was retaliation for raids from Gaza carried out by displaced Palestinians, but Ben-Gurion's larger objective was to demonstrate that Israel could not be strangled by Arab economic or military policies. Since the 1948 War, Egypt had kept the Suez Canal closed to Israeli shipping, under a disputed interpretation of the original protocol governing international shipping through the canal. The protocol stipulated that it was to be kept open in time of war and peace; only if Egypt's security was endangered could ships be denied passage. Because there was no peace treaty, Egypt had asserted the right to keep Israeli shipping from passing through the canal. In his 1951 conversation with Dean Acheson, Ben-Gurion, then prime minister, had stressed the urgency of demonstrating that Israel could not be destroyed by war or by slow strangulation. American economic and military aid to Israel, he had said, would prove to the Arab nations that "Israel could not be destroyed." A dramatic move like the raid on Gaza, Ben-Gurion hoped, would force Egypt to reconsider all its policies.

Instead of the result Ben-Gurion hoped for, the Gaza raid made it easy for Nasser to promote himself as the one Arab leader most deserving of support and military aid, and to denounce his competitors as not true nationalists. Dulles had not imagined that Nasser would react so strongly to the proposed Baghdad Pact, but he knew there was a "danger that the Israeli [sic] might be deliberately trying to break the armistice open on the theory that that was the only way to get a better arrangement."[27] His new ambassador, Henry Byroade, had arrived in Cairo just before the Gaza raid. Known as a champion of "evenhandedness," Byroade had given speeches urging Israel to behave as a "normal" state, which brought angry retorts from American Jewish groups. Byroade did not define "normal," but his antagonists believed they knew his meaning only too well. At the June 1954 convention of the Zionist Organization of America, Dr. Emmanuel Neumann denounced "Byroadeism" as an effort to separate world Jewry from Israel: "Byroadeism would isolate Israel, sever her vital connection with the Jewish people, block out her cultural hinterland, foreshorten her world horizons and reduce her in the end to an enclave buried away in a corner of the Arab world."[28]

Byroade's coming to Cairo may well have been one of the triggers of Ben-Gurion's decision to launch the Gaza raid. However that may be, when Nasser summoned the new ambassador to a private meeting the very evening of the raid, the Egyptian leader spent most of the interview denouncing the new Baghdad Pact, especially its open admissions policy. It was clear, Nasser exploded, that the United States had cast him aside for Nuri al-Said. Nasser disliked Nuri intensely, but that was only part of the problem: "The injection of an actual new treaty arrangement of one Arab State with Turkey (i.e. West) he interprets as a great setback to his own plans of bringing into being a genuine pro-Western sentiment among the people." Byroade did not argue the specific point, but told Nasser he should be "under no illusions that we can support a unified Arab Army under present circumstances in the Middle East."[29]

A Chess Game

No one was naive about the purposes of the Baghdad Pact. Just as Dean Acheson had envisioned NATO as a way to contain both Russia and Germany, Dulles had eagerly sought to create a Northern Tier not primarily as a way of blocking Soviet military advances but of containing Arab nationalism. Whether it was Acheson or Dulles, the purpose of the military pacts was the same. The formal colonial era was almost over. In its place the United States had started assembling a new structure that would substitute military connections for the old sinews of empire. The Soviet Union played a key role, obviously, by offering a "threat," so that the organization of the "Free World" could be rationalized as "empire by invitation." He was ready, he told British prime minister Anthony Eden, to help Nuri al-Said get tanks for an armored division and weapons for other members of the group, but still refused formal membership because of strong opposition from Israel's supporters. Eden suspected the real reason was a desire to take credit in Cairo for opposing "colonial" attitudes.

Nasser had lectured Nuri al-Said on British strategy, insisting that its only purpose was to drive a wedge in Arab nationalism. Nuri appeared to agree, but late in 1954 he accepted what Egypt had refused, American conditions for obtaining military aid, and thereby paved the way for the Baghdad Pact. When all was said and done, Nasser concluded, the United States still preferred the old colonial style of divide and conquer. After the Gaza raid, he pressed anew his case for arms, but the Baghdad Pact threatened his long-term ambitions. In April 1955 Nasser agreed to damp down criticism of Nuri and the pact if the British ceased trolling for additional members, especially Jordan, where British influence had been paramount since the end of World War I, but where the Egyptian leader now hoped to create an Arab alliance. Churchill's successor, Anthony Eden, had promised him, Nasser told an American journalist, "that they will freeze the Baghdad Pact" and make no efforts to enlist other Arab countries. Meanwhile, Nasser negotiated a military pact with Saudi Arabia and Syria, a fateful step that—theoretically at least—would bring all of Israel's close neighbors under one military command. And if Jordan joined such an alliance, the prospects for checking Nasser's ambitions would pretty much disappear. Nasser blamed Arab defeat in the 1948 war on a lack of cooperation and coordination. If his plans bore fruit, he vowed, that would not happen again. The Baghdad Pact, however, stood in the way.[30]

Whatever assurances Nasser thought he had from Anthony Eden, the question of British pressure on Jordan to join the Baghdad Pact was very far from a settled matter. King Hussein obviously enjoyed being courted so assiduously by all the parties. Returning from a Cairo meeting, he assured the American ambassador that he had not committed himself to join Nasser's proposed pan-Arab group. He then said that his country was "prepared to listen to any request" from the United States and was keen to know "the conditions involved." He was especially interested in the sort of air force aid that Pakistan—a traditional British ally—had received from the United States. Later in the year, however, the ambassador reported that the apparent reorientation in Jordan's foreign policy was at serious risk over continuing developments in the Arab-Israeli impasse. He concluded, "Political situation in Jordan is disintegrating and resulting instability is playing into [the] hands of anti-western nationalists and Communists. Unless something is done . . . this former strong point in the Near East will become [a] source of weakness to [the] west." [31]

The Gaza raid fallout had also focused Arab attention on Nasser's inability to obtain arms. If he was to be the leader of an Arab alliance he would have to offer more than the rhetoric of Pan-Arabism. In March 1955 Nasser submitted a new list of wanted items so modest that Eisenhower even called it "peanuts." But that still didn't improve his chances in Washington. The administration held up Iraq as the model client, a nation that had accepted American conditions, especially a MAAG to oversee how the aid was used. In addition, Washington insisted on cash payment. Nasser responded in a radio speech at the Cairo Officers' Club, publicly vowing to organize the defense of the Middle East "without any link or partnership with the West . . . I think it would be a miracle if we ever obtained any arms from this direction." [32]

It was still assumed in the United States, nevertheless, that he had little option but to capitulate. But there were other levers the Egyptian leader could pull to frustrate Washington. Even without American arms, Nasser had developed a powerful new weapon in Radio Cairo, from which he could broadcast challenges both to the British at Suez and the French in Algeria. *Voice of the Arabs* had first announced its campaign on August 20, 1953, with Nasser's ringing declaration: "We must follow the policy of a total war—the people's war. The enemy is now fighting us with money, hostile propaganda and the agitation of minds. *This is the cold war between us and imperialism.*" [33]

British and American diplomats pondered how to respond to Nasser's challenge and emerged with something they called Project Alpha. Put the onus on Nasser, said its authors. If he wanted aid, he should accept his role as the key to peace in the Middle East and abandon thoughts of a new Egyptian dynasty: "We shall therefore need to offer inducements to Egypt." But there could be no yielding to his views on the Baghdad Pact, not even as an inducement "to move towards a Palestine settlement." Military aid for Egypt could be considered only after a resolution of the Arab-Israeli conflict. On the toughest question, the Palestinian refugee problem, the proposed solution was out of Lewis Carroll's *Alice's Adventures in Wonderland*. Israel was expected to agree to accept 75,000 refugees over several years, while the rest—nearly a million—would have to be absorbed into other Arab countries. The United States and Great Britain would put up much of the money for resettlement of the 75,000 in the form of long-term loans, but 30 percent of the estimated $300 million would have to come from Israel and "world Jewry."

There was actually little new in the Alpha Project except the promise of economic aid for the high dam at Aswan. During the secretary's 1953 visit, Naguib had pressed for American aid to build a new dam on the Nile. The project was crucial, he argued then, so as to bring new lands under cultivation to feed Egypt's rapidly growing population. Over the long term, Egypt would need $100 million to start the Aswan Dam and related projects. He had also appealed for "immediate" economic aid in the form of grants to obtain American wheat, because cotton sales to dollar areas had lagged, creating an immediate exchange crisis.[34] It was suggested that Alpha might be a way to secure Egyptian participation in international water projects on the major rivers that flowed from Syria and Jordan into Israel. Israel would have to be warned that its refusal to cooperate could prevent the United States from offering a long-sought security guarantee, "and that she would have to bear the onus for failure of our efforts to progress toward peace."[35]

There was precious little reason to believe that Project Alpha would succeed in persuading Israel to take such steps. In the fall of 1953, when the Eisenhower administration enjoyed almost complete public support after a Korean truce, Dulles found himself fending off a storm of criticism from Jewish groups when he suspended economic aid to Israel in an effort to force it to halt efforts to divert water from the Jordan River. In a confrontation with Dulles, the leader of one group, congressman Jacob Javits, warned that he planned to release a statement decrying the decision as unfair and harmful to Israel's economic development. Dulles retorted that his statement was full of inaccuracies, and suggested that "the group might spend some time working with representatives of the Israeli Government to try to change their policy of presenting the world with faits accomplis. Cooperation seemed to be a one-way street as far as Israel is concerned." A final peace settlement with Israel, he insisted, depended very much on increased American influence in the Arab world, with its strategic position in the Cold War and the "petroleum reserves upon which our military planning depends." On this occasion, the threat worked: Israel agreed to cooperate with the United Nations on an international plan for the Jordan River. But nothing was really resolved.[36]

Ambassador Byroade always doubted that Alpha had much of a chance. Still, he conceded, "some good may yet come out of [the] situation which has been locally one of deterioration." If Washington played its cards right, maybe the Northern Tier alliance would persuade the Egyptian leader both of what he had to do to achieve American military aid, and that he could never expect military aid for any group of countries under his leadership unless there was a solution to the Arab-Israeli situation. Nasser saw he was in danger of being isolated between Israel and the Northern Tier. There was no doubt about that. But a worse outcome was far more likely: "These feelings of frustration could . . . lead him to seek neutrality and general non-cooperation with the West." Indeed, there were ominous signs. Nasser was now insisting on a land connection with other Arab countries through the Negev desert—more than just a corridor, as imagined in various schemes of Project Alpha, but "the whole of [the] Negev south of Beersheba." The Israelis were not likely to go along with that concession, given their own plans for the Negev. And therein was the central problem. There were very few "apparent advantages for Arabs in Alpha proposals themselves."[37]

The Neutralist Road to Power

Byroade's pessimistic prediction about Nasser's next move came true sooner rather than later. In April 1955 in Bandung, Indonesia, representatives of more than twenty-five nations with a total population of over 650 million people met at the conference of Asian and African nations and asserted that "colonialism in all its manifestations is an evil which should speedily be brought to an end." As a leader of the new neutral nations bloc that emerged from the conference, it appeared that Nasser had found an excellent opportunity to bring pressure on Washington. Byroade and Kim Roosevelt had attempted to dissuade him from attending a conference where they said he would be up against the cleverest Communist of all, Chinese foreign minister Chou En-lai. American policy makers had belittled the conference beforehand and Secretary Dulles declared with patronizing contempt that neutralism was "an immoral and short-sighted conception."[38]

It galled American policy makers that the Chinese claimed to represent a "neutral" nation in the Cold War, but they had not anticipated that something much worse would happen at Bandung when Nasser broached the question of Soviet arms for Egypt. Nasser had met Chou at Rangoon on the way to the meeting, and posed his question of questions. Did the foreign minister think the Russians might be prepared to sell arms to Egypt? Chou said they might: "Do you want me to explore?"[39]

Nasser came home a hero and a major player. He now had good reason to believe the Soviet Union would entertain a bid for arms, and provide him with a way around American hurdles. Egypt's cotton exports had fallen by 26 percent in little over a year, the result, in part, of American agricultural subsidies that permitted U.S. farmers to dump cotton on the world market. China and Russia offered an alternative outlet for the cotton, and a barter deal for arms that would not require cash payments in scarce dollars or pounds. Journalist Kennett Love wrote that Nasser's return from Bandung marked the time when his three-year endeavor to base Egyptian policy on friendship with the United States "began to fade into history's limbo of lost opportunities. . . . It became Egypt's door out of the parochialism of the Arab world into the new horizons of awakening Africa and Asia."[40]

From a longer-term perspective, Egypt's escape from neocolonialism was much more problematic than Love suggested. But Bandung shook the branches at least. A self-styled neutralist bloc emerged from the conference with its own "Big Three," Yugoslavia's Marshal Tito, India's Pandit Nehru, and Gamal Abdel Nasser. Nehru had played a big role in impressing on Nasser the latent power of both the neutralist position and leverage with the great powers. American and British officials were aware that Egyptian and Soviet diplomats had begun talking about cotton for arms deals but thought Nasser was simply trying to use a Bandung-inspired bluff to make himself stand out above Nuri al-Said as the founder of a great Arab empire.

On August 26, 1955, Dulles outlined the essentials of the Alpha Plan in a speech to the Council of Foreign Relations, asserting that the central issue was the "pall of fear that hangs over the Arab and Israel people alike." He proposed an international loan to aid in resettlement of the refugees, and expressed willingness to "join in formal treaty engagements to prevent or thwart any effort by either side to alter by force the boundaries between Israel and her Arab neighbors." But what were those boundaries to be? The Alpha Plan envisioned two small triangles ceded to Egypt and Jordan that met at their points in the Negev. A road from Egypt to Jordan under Arab sovereignty would pass over an Israeli road from Beersheba to Eilat. As historian Steven Freiberger points out, "Dulles wanted the Arabs to compare what the Soviet Union and the United States had to offer. Moscow could provide weapons for war, but only Washington could offer the possibility of redressing Arab griev-ances."[41] No one gave a direct answer to Dulles's speech. But Am-bassador Byroade was informed by one of Nasser's aides on September 21, 1955 that an arms deal with a Soviet bloc country was now an accomplished fact.

Grabbing on to Acheson's familiar credo—negotiation from strength—and throwing it back at the Eisenhower administration was a remarkable show of bravado. But that was only the beginning. On September 27, 1955, Nasser formally announced the arms deal at the opening of an exhibition of military pictures. When the de-tails came out, the agreement with Czechoslovakia startled ob-servers around the world. It totaled more than $200 million, and included 200 MiG-15 fighter planes, 50 Ilyushin bombers, 60 half tracks equipped with 122 mm cannons, and 275 T-34 tanks. The Russian agreement to sell weapons meant, first of all, that the United States could no longer control the distribution of arms in the area to keep the lid on an arms race. The French, for example, were quick to transfer advanced Mystere IV fighters from NATO to Israel. While American policy makers were not happy with this de-velopment, they did nothing to block the transfer on grounds that, as Dulles put it at a news conference in October, it was difficult to be "critical of countries which, feeling themselves endangered, seek arms which they sincerely believe they need for their defense."[42]

Where would Russian arms go next? Was it now possible that the Russians could make similar deals with Saudi Arabia, thereby threatening the American position at Dhahran air base, the origi-nal entry point for the U.S. military into the Middle East negoti-ated by Roosevelt and Truman? British foreign minister Harold MacMillan suggested countering the Russian move with more aid to the Baghdad Pact. We could encourage Jordan and Lebanon to join the pact, he added, almost as if that were a new idea that just popped into his head. Macmillan's chief aide, Evelyn Shuckburgh, suggested drily that maybe it was time for a quid pro quo: the West to give up trying to form defense pacts everywhere, and the Soviets to abandon the arms deal? Moscow might ask whether we are interested in a neutral Middle East.[43]

Everyone present knew the answer to that question. Dulles said he abhorred "neutralism." But this was because his efforts at pact making were only secondarily directed at creating a military front against Russia, and aimed above all at controlling the international behavior of otherwise quarrelsome states and building up internal strength to resist "subversion." "Our efforts are directed at an Arab-Israel settlement," he repeated for the umpteenth time. The Russian move had to be considered in that light, as something entirely separate from the Northern Tier. Still, he said, the last thing he wanted was to push the Baghdad Pact like a stick into Nasser's eye. It was a tough situation all around: "If Nasser rejects the [Russian] offer, he may well be overthrown and we could get something worse." He worried as well that Russian arms in Egypt would be looked on in the United States as "a major defeat." What alternatives were there? He had not been able to bring pressure on either side in the Arab-Israeli dispute prior to the arms deal, so how could he do so now? "If Egypt lines up with the USSR, I doubt that U.S. public opinion would permit us to use coercive restraints in the event of an Israel attack."[44]

Fears of an Israeli attack on Egypt were reason enough to up the ante, however, by making a greater effort to persuade the Israelis to be more yielding, on the one hand, and trying to convince Nasser, on the other, to make the Russian arms deal a one-time operation. Perhaps, Dulles mused, the arms deal was not a completely negative development. Israel would also feel new pressure, and therefore "might give up a bigger slice of the Negev."[45]

Showdown at the Aswan Dam

Reports that the Russians were now ready to consider extending aid to build the Aswan Dam added to the pressure to find a way to redirect the Egyptian revolution into safe channels. Nasser, indeed, encouraged Ambassador Byroade to think of the arms deal as just a detail, a bump in the road. During one conversation he pointed out the window to the Nile and said, "Mr. Ambassador, we're worrying about all these details while all that water is flowing into the Mediterranean. That's more important." Besides the obvious problems of fending off congressional criticism that loans for the Aswan Dam rewarded Nasser for playing the Russian card, there were other objections to going ahead with the project. It would be the largest "public works" project ever undertaken, under secretary of state Herbert Hoover, Jr., told the Egyptian ambassador—larger than all the public works built in the United States since 1900.[46]

On the bright side, there were a few indications that the Egyptians were ready to seek a settlement with Israel on several issues. If that happened, the Aswan project would proceed more smoothly in Congress. On November 17, 1955, the Egyptian foreign minister met with Ambassador Byroade and his British counterpart and informed them that his government was ready to move toward a settlement with Israel at the earliest practicable date. Egypt believed there was a "51 percent chance" of success. If Egyptian-Israeli issues could be resolved, Cairo would then take the lead with other Arab countries, even in the face of severe opposition. Hence he was now willing to put forward, in general terms, Egypt's position on all outstanding questions. And to start things off, Mahmoud Fawzi agreed that repatriation of refugees in large numbers was not possible, and would, in fact, be "quite restricted." For most, resettlement and compensation was the only answer. In such a settlement, Egypt would also agree to end the economic blockade and allow freedom of transit on the canal. As for Egyptian territorial demands, all Cairo wanted at this stage was agreement in principle that there would be "continuity of Arab sovereign territory," and not merely a corridor. Hearing the proposal, the Americans could conclude that the only hitch at this stage appeared to be Egypt's unwillingness to meet face-to-face with Israeli leaders to work out any of the outstanding issues.[47]

The hitch became a major obstacle, nevertheless, when Eisenhower sent his special envoy, Robert Anderson, to talk with Nasser and Ben-Gurion. Meanwhile, the World Bank's Eugene Black, the negotiator handling the bulk of the details for an international loan to start work on the Aswan Dam, found the going rough in reaching agreement with Cairo on terms of the contract. As the negotiations dragged on, Dulles intervened with Black to prevent any "take it or leave it" ultimatum. Vitally important considerations were at stake for the entire Western world, cabled Undersecretary Hoover to Black, and these took precedence over normal business considerations.[48]

Dulles still faced a big problem with Congress, however, and had no idea, really, how he was going to get around objections from diverse pressure groups that included not just pro-Israeli legislators who objected to funding anything that would strengthen Nasser, but also advocates of cotton growing states fearing Egyptian competition in world markets. His task became almost impossible, finally, when Nasser extended diplomatic recognition to the People's Republic of China, bringing into the picture another highly emotional factor working against Dulles's fading hopes to promote his favored solution to the Middle East imbroglio. China was particularly difficult for Dulles because he had repeatedly insisted that the final word had not been spoken on the triumph of the Communist revolution and the legitimacy of the People's Republic of China. He found himself in an awkward spot by now advocating aid to a nation that had defied his ban on direct dealings with Beijing.

Robert Anderson's meetings with Nasser left the Egyptian leader with a sense that the Americans had no serious understanding of what they asked of him in the way of a face-to-face meeting with an Israeli leader. Anderson was in Cairo for three days, Nasser complained to Kermit Roosevelt, and in that time he expected Nasser to agree to arrange a meeting with Ben-Gurion. It was certainly true that Eisenhower and Dulles had impressed on Anderson the need to move quickly before the 1956 election campaign made it impossible to avoid a partisan shouting match that, while it would not lead to a Democratic victory, would cause more problems in carrying out any Middle East initiative. But he could not be seen to be seeking peace with Israel in that way, Nasser told Roosevelt, for that would "give Nuri Said a weapon with which to destroy him."

Roosevelt replied that Nasser's reluctance to move forward totally ignored U.S. problems: "Specifically it does not recognize the dilemma we will all be in should Israel launch a preventive war."[49]

Dulles was well aware of both Nasser's fixation on Iraq as a major threat to his position and of the continuing British effort to regain something of their lost position with the Arabs by encouraging Jordan to join the Baghdad Pact. Indeed, London went so far as to present Jordan with a gift of ten jet fighters and an offer of $11 million for the Arab Legion, commanded by Sir John Glubb (Glubb Pasha). Glubb Pasha was the stuff of modern legend, on view in newsreel clips that romantically portrayed British command of the Middle Eastern situation, teeming with ramrod-straight cavalry and proud horses on parade. He had come to the new kingdom when Jordan was created after World War I and represented in his person the old Kipling servant of the British monarchy deputized to a lesser ruler in need of such protection from local enemies. But King Hussein complained that Sir John sought control over Jordan's relations with the outside world. If Glubb and his masters had their way, Hussein charged, there would be no Arab commanders in the Legion until at least 1985. The ensuing uproar inside Jordan over the British "gift" was the final straw. King Hussein dismissed the longtime commander, removing yet another symbol of British prestige and power. Infuriated by this turn of events, Eden blamed Nasser's meddling, considering it proof that the Egyptian leader would not be satisfied until he ruled supreme throughout the entire area. And this episode proved to be the beginning of the Suez crisis that followed. Eden, it should be said, was under terrific pressure from both Conservatives and Labour for the continuing retreat from the Middle East. The prime minister hoped to tag Nasser as the Soviet Union's Mussolini, a willing servant of the Kremlin whose ambitions fit into the scheme of Russian plans for dominance across the area. The arms deal and the possibility that the Soviets would finance the Aswan Dam made such accusations at least "headline plausible," even if Nasser had cracked down hard on Communists at home.

British maneuvering with Jordan, however, did not please

Washington. For one thing, Eden's ploy—despite its anti-Nasser objective—alarmed the Israelis, a complication that Dulles did not want as he attempted to recalibrate the Alpha Project in the face of Nasser's refusal to meet with an Israeli leader. What emerged was called the Omega Plan, a much more coercive program characterized by punishment rather than reward. Musing privately on preliminary sketches for the plan, Eisenhower applauded the objective: to isolate Nasser from potential allies such as Saudi Arabia. Of course, playing up to Saudi Arabia entailed other problems, but it was essential to bring Nasser to understand that he could not achieve his objective of being "the most popular man in all the Arab world," and that he would have to settle for a lesser place in the order of things. "I am certain of one thing," mused Eisenhower in private. "If Egypt finds herself thus isolated from the rest of the Arab world, and with no ally in sight except Soviet Russia, she would very quickly get sick of that prospect and would join us in the search for a just and decent peace in that region." [50]

The Omega Plan for bringing Nasser around to Ike's way of seeing things was explained in a memorandum Dulles prepared for the White House. The plan included cutting off various aid programs (either existing or planned), expanding Iraqi radio capabilities to counter Radio Cairo's *Voice of the Arabs*, encouraging the British to keep a strong foot in Jordan, increased support to the Baghdad Pact (still without formal membership), as well as support for pro-Western elements in Lebanon in ways designed to influence public opinion, and other initiatives that remain classified even today. Two points stood out above all others. One was to delay the conclusion of the previously imperative negotiations on the Aswan Dam loan, and the other was to improve the American position in Saudi Arabia: "We must find ways, in connection with the negotiation of a new air base agreement which should be promptly concluded, of assuring King Saud that some of his military needs will immediately be met and others provided for subsequently." [51]

"We would want for the time being to avoid any open break," Dulles added, "which would throw Nasser irrevocably into a Soviet satellite status and we would want to leave Nasser a bridge back to good relations with the West if he so desires." Perhaps he worried more than Eisenhower did about what the Egyptians might do in the future, but his "bridge back" was a pretty creaky structure. American policy had now gone all the way from welcoming the Egyptian revolution to hoping for an opportunity to put Nasser in his place—or even out of his place. It was certainly true that the administration had domestic problems with any policy that appeared to be strengthening anti-Israel forces in the Middle East, as well as problems with Egypt's quest to lead "anti-imperialist" movements on the African continent through Radio Cairo and possible aid to insurgents—but Washington's diplomacy qualified only at the level of "tough love."[52]

While Israel continued to put pressure on the State Department for arms sales, warning that Egypt was preparing for war, Dulles cast a wary eye on the progress of Soviet-Egyptian negotiations on a loan for the Aswan Dam. He was more than pleased that a visit to Cairo by a high-ranking Moscow emissary had led nowhere. "The Egyptians were now back," he advised Eisenhower on July 13, 1956, "saying they would take our proposal on the original terms and withdraw their own counter proposals." There were still questions about congressional approval, he said, but "also our views on the merits of the matter had somewhat altered." He concluded by saying that would "consult" with the president next week.[53]

Dulles received advice from his assistants that Nasser was in an exposed position as a result of the apparent breakdown in Cairo negotiations with Russian foreign minister Dmitri Shepilov. He was scheduled to go to Moscow, wrote George Allen, and "unless he obtains a commitment from the West before his trip . . . his bargaining position will be severely deflated and he may end up with no dam at all." Allen followed this note with a recommendation that when the Egyptian ambassador called, the American offer should be withdrawn—regardless of whether Nasser proposed to accept the original conditions imposed by the World Bank—and he should be told that future aid for other projects would depend on "whether Egypt ceases to engage in acts inimical to interests of the West."[54]

As he observed the developing mood in Washington, Henry Byroade sought to warn his superiors what they risked by such a dramatic action. "Neutralism exists over a large portion of this part of the world," he wrote. Washington's policy was based on the idea that the Arab nations must support American policy on all Cold War issues, an unrealistic demand. If the United States continued to view them "as either in enemy camp or as 'fellow travelers' I fear that before too long we will begin to appear in [the] eyes [of] these people as being the unreasonable member of East-West struggle."[55]

Dulles met with Eisenhower on the morning of July 19, 1956, and told him the offer should be withdrawn, adding novel reasons for the decision, such as avoiding being blamed for the "austerity" that would follow when the Egyptians had to start paying for the project. Besides, the Soviets would have a hard time explaining to their own people and to the satellite nations why they were undertaking such a project to benefit Egyptians when living standards remained low at home. The president said he concurred with "the Secretary's view," but which of Dulles's views he did not say.[56]

Later that day Dr. Ahmed Hussein called on Dulles to receive the bad news that, in fact, Nasser had predicted he would hear before he left Egypt. Dulles wasted no words. He got right to the point without the usual exchange of pleasantries, listing the reasons why the United States had decided not to undertake the project. He began in the style of this-hurts-me-more-than-it-does-you patronizing mode of disappointed parents, asserting that the decision was based on a concern for long term Egyptian-American relations because the costs would "superimpose" a heavy burden on the Egyptian economy. The immediate impact of an announcement that the United States was undertaking the project might be good, but it would not likely last long. He had also to consider, Dulles went on, the impact on the American people, who were, frankly, not happy about Egyptian actions over the past several months. He hoped that in the future, "tranquility" would return to Egyptian-American relations so that the kind of cooperation Americans desired could be resumed.

Hussein attempted to respond to the issues, including the accusation about the Russian arms aid and the recognition of Communist China, adding as well that rumors that Egypt had tried to interfere with negotiations over the extension of the lease at Dhahran were not true. Dulles sincerely hoped that was the case, but it was better to put the project "on the shelf" to await a better atmosphere for big projects. Hussein, with a reputation for being pro-American, decided there was nothing more to be gained by arguing specific points with Dulles. He wished now, he said, to speak personally. He sincerely hated to see the Russians take advantage of the situation, but he knew they were making a "very generous" offer, one that would be more advantageous on technical and financial points than what the Americans had offered. He had argued vigorously with Nasser not to accept those terms before he had had his chance to change minds in Washington, but the Egyptian leader was under strong pressure to accept the offer before he left for Moscow.

Dulles then recited the argument he had used with Eisenhower as the second reason why the United States should back away from the Aswan Dam. The Soviets would find it hard to undertake such a project in light of the low living standards of their people. Whereas the United States could easily handle the costs "because of the tremendous magnitude of its national production," the Russians would be forced to scrape up the money from an already-pressed economy. It sounded no less curious in this second go-round than it did when Dulles first used the argument that morning in the White House. In his opinion, moreover, the only way the Russians could justify such expenditure was if they expected great political advantages—so many, in fact, that it would endanger Egyptian independence. Looking for still more arguments, he implied that the United States never bargained over such matters: "We could not undertake to try to match the Russians in any offers which might be made to Egypt or to other countries." He ended with yet another weird assertion that even a diplomatic greenhorn would know to be untrue: "We did not wish to give the impression that the decision . . . was in any way unfriendly or represented a retaliation for actions of the Egyptian Government. He still saw a bright future in Egyptian-American relations."[57]

There were many things revealed here in Dulles's arguments that few then or now have commented on. One thing especially stands out: given the secretary's comments about the Soviet economy and standards of living, why was it so difficult for Americans to devise a foreign policy that relied on something else besides "defense pacts"? His stress on the ability of the American economy to meet the Soviet challenge in the third world without real strain, moreover, sounded a very different note than the public alarms about the worldwide threat of "International Communism." The issue was a complicated one, but somewhere near to the heart of it was a stubborn reality: the United States had little interest in manifestations of self-determination that would challenge the vision of the American Century. That had been clear in the Iranian oil crisis, and it was equally clear in dealings with the Egyptian revolution.

Egypt Takes the Suez Canal

Further, no one doubted that the way the rebuff had been planned and delivered signaled a turning point in U.S.-Egyptian relations. The administration was expected to try a "get tough" line now with Nasser, wrote diplomatic correspondent Dana Adams Schmidt in the *New York Times*, perhaps even joining the Baghdad Pact: "It will probably be some time before Mr. Eisenhower sends another pistol to an Egyptian leader." The Dulles bombshell landed on Cairo just as Nasser was returning from a "Big Three" conference of neutrals held at Brioni in the Adriatic. On July 24 Nasser delivered a scathing attack on Washington, with the Russian ambassador sitting close by with a big smile on his face. The United States, he asserted, had given out false and misleading statements, making it seem that the "Egyptian economy is unsound and throwing shadows of doubt on the Egyptian economy." This was contrary to the principles of international relations: "I look at Americans and say: May you choke to death on your fury!" Interviewed after the speech, the Russian ambassador, Yevgeni Kiselev, confirmed that "we are ready to finance the Aswan High Dam if Egypt asks for it." Two days later Nasser gave his full answer to Dulles in another public speech. After declaring the arms deal necessary to "defend ourselves so that we would not become refugees like the Palestinians," he turned to the dam. As the crowd clapped and roared he talked about how the canal was built, and how "Egypt became the property of the canal. . . . It is no shame for one to be poor and to borrow in order to build up one's country; what is a shame is to suck the blood of a people and usurp their rights." He finished the speech with a six-paragraph decree nationalizing the canal company, and as he spoke Egyptian forces moved into the company's offices and took charge. "Today, O citizens," Nasser shouted over the tumult, "with the annual income of the Suez Canal amounting to . . . $100 million a year, $500 million in five years, we shall not look for the $70 million of American aid. . . . Now, while I am talking to you, brothers of yours, sons of Egypt, are rising up to direct the canal company and undertake its operation. Now, at this moment, they are taking over the canal company—the Egyptian canal company! not the foreign canal company!"[58]

Nasser had dropped the other shoe: the arms deal and now the canal. His action had made it clear that Israel's long-standing desire to break through the economic boycott that kept its ships out of the canal and its determination to secure control over the Straits of Tiran would go for naught except by military action. But Israel would not dare attack Egypt, it was obvious, without assurances from the British and French that they could count on support disguised as neutral intervention to separate the combatants.[59]

The ultimate objective of such a war would not be to reacquire the canal company, but to get rid of Nasser, a goal the United States now shared—but not in such a reckless manner. While Dulles and Eisenhower were accused of sending ambiguous messages to their close Cold War allies, they made it clear time and again that the United States never intended to shoot its way through the Suez Canal, or to support anyone else in such a venture. Whatever American intelligence knew about Anglo-French plans, Dulles followed a policy throughout the summer of 1956 of devising various schemes—none of which had any chance of success—as delaying tactics. All of his proposals for international supervision of tolls and canal employees assumed continued Egyptian "ownership" of the canal, even if in limited fashion as to day-to-day operations. "It might even be necessary to minimize the role of Britain and France," he advised the president, "assuming dependable alternatives could be found." One of the problems, however, was that Asian countries were too apt to be swayed by political slogans, he said, "such as 'colonialism,' 'imperialism,' 'Asia for the Asians,' etc." Put another way, Dulles feared that the political and military consequences of a direct assault on Egypt's right to nationalize the canal company would spread like a plague across Africa, Asia, and back to Latin America—where he had had trouble enough ousting a "radical" regime in Guatemala. There were risks aplenty in managing the world without doing such great damage to the already-sagging reputation of the United States as a revolutionary inspiration for newly emerging nations.[60]

Yet he knew the British were planning war—foreign minister Selwyn Lloyd told him so during one of the seemingly interminable conferences on the canal's future that summer. The plans were such, Lloyd said, that "there would be a button pushed early in September and after that everything would happen automatically and be irrevocable." According to Lloyd, Dulles was the only one who could stop it. "During this conversation Mr. Lloyd showed obvious emotional strain," the secretary recorded in a memorandum. Perhaps Dulles, knowing Washington did not approve the use of force, thought the British and French would at the last minute pull back and not push the button. Or perhaps he thought, let them try and we will step in to halt it and unhitch our albatross from around our neck. Was it even possible to glimpse a new dawn along the Suez, with a grateful Egypt renouncing its apostasy in treating with Russia?[61]

It is unlikely he really wished for the latter to happen. However much he chafed at British and French maneuvering and wished for a clean slate, he did not like being in the middle. The Soviets were playing their own waiting game, Dulles told congressional leaders. It was an evil game aimed at taking advantage of Israeli-Arab animosity to move into a position of great influence. Most Arab leaders feared Nasser's ambitions, but they feared more his great popularity with the peoples of their own countries. Our problem, he concluded to general agreement, was how to guide the new nations from colonialism to independence in an orderly way: "We must have evolution, not revolution."[62]

One of the legislators asked about the Israeli role in the crisis. They were keeping quiet, Dulles said, on the calculation that whatever happened would benefit them in one way or another. He was disturbed that they had rejected all of UN secretary general Dag Hammarskjöld's suggestions for strengthening the armistice, and the secretary general felt there was nothing more he could do with them. In any event, the next moves were up to the British and French. He did not imagine, however, that the next move would be to encourage Israel to attack Egypt, thereby allowing the British and French to intervene to "protect" the canal.

There were discussions at the United Nations about a proper remedy for Nasser's brazen challenge to the oil-needy Western European nations, and an interesting opinion from Harold Macmillan that foretold later American maneuvers before the 2003 invasion of Iraq. The British foreign secretary, who, if anything, was more insistent on using military force than Anthony Eden, told the American ambassador in Paris that he hoped the Russians would veto any resolution, because that would fragment domestic opposition that otherwise "would have been shocked by the use of force without a prior appeal to the U.N."[63]

Dulles also met with Macmillan and stressed that economic and political means for bringing Nasser to bay would be more effective. He was particularly careful to stress his hope that nothing would be done before the American election in November. Macmillan seemed to provide assurances that it would not be overly costly to hold matters in "abeyance," but he did not offer a guarantee that no military action would be taken. On the eve of the war, in late October, Dulles confessed to Eisenhower that he was "really baffled" about the actual purposes of the British and French: "Perhaps they did not know themselves." He had the impression, Dulles said, that they believed American policy was just for the election period, and that after that was over "we might back them in a policy involving the use of force."[64]

Dulles believed he had a promise that there would be no military action before the election, but afterward was a different matter. The war actually began before the election, infuriating Eisenhower, who told all his advisers that the United States would "redeem our word about supporting any victim of aggression." The war plan had been that Israel's invasion and drive to the Suez would trigger an ultimatum from the British and French that the two sides must stop their fighting and retreat so many miles from the canal area. It was assumed, apparently, that in the aftermath Egyptians would then dispose of Nasser themselves, allowing a "reasonable" leader to emerge with whom it would be possible to do business on a "normal" basis. The Israeli invasion was thus a ruse for the main objective of an Anglo-French strike—to get rid of Nasser. The few second-level officials who knew of these plans were appalled at what Eden's protégé, Anthony Nutting, called "this sordid conspiracy."[65]

On the night of October 29, 1956, the Israelis began their attack, as agreed, heading toward the Suez Canal. And, as also arranged, the British and French issued their ultimatum to both sides demanding that the military forces disengage. The ultimatum was a ruse to justify air attacks on Egyptian airfields and a paratroop landing at Port Said. From that point onward, nothing went right. The strategy came completely undone at the end of a week's fighting when Washington threatened to end support for the pound sterling and forced the leader of the "alliance," British prime minister Anthony Eden, to end the adventure. The invasion failed in every respect, especially in its primary object of removing Nasser from the scene. Instead, the Egyptian leader retaliated by sinking huge concrete blocks and ships in the canal, shutting down all tanker traffic. Known ever after as the "lion's last roar," it was a sad ending for Eden's role before and during World War II as a vigorous opponent to appeasement of Nazi Germany.

At least two aides, chair of the Joint Chiefs Admiral Radford and CIA director Allen Dulles had suggested waiting a bit before intervening to see how things would go as British bombers appeared over Cairo. Maybe getting rid of Nasser would be quick and easy? The president wanted none of that. It was too risky: "If we do not now fulfill our word Russia is likely to enter the situation in the Middle East." A British diplomat present at one of these conversations wondered if the United States would not first go to the United Nations before stepping into the affair, perhaps hoping to give a little time for a fait accompli? That was his idea, said Ike, but not to cause a delay: "We plan to get there first thing in the morning—when the doors open—before the USSR gets there."[66]

Eisenhower Stops the Show

It had finally come down to what Washington had hoped all along to avoid, a choice between taking sides with old allies, or striking out on a different path. "When you get into [a] case like this," Eisenhower told an aide, "you just gotta go your own way. . . . What you gonna do—fight the whole Moslem world?" Over the next few days the Suez crisis grew into a perfect storm of bad news. Soviet premier Nikita Khrushchev threatened to launch ICBMs at the British and French, even as Moscow sent tanks into Budapest to suppress the Hungarian freedom fighters, who, it was claimed, had responded to encouraging broadcasts from Radio Free Europe by taking up arms against the Communist regime. It was doubly infuriating, therefore, that the Soviets could pose as defenders of the Egyptian revolution while smashing down buildings in Hungary to get at the Freedom Fighters and crush the uprising. And to make matters still worse, Hungary exposed Dulles's "liberation" policy as little more than a rhetorical flourish on old themes. The secret was out—liberation really meant disengaging from the old colonial powers, not driving the Soviets back beyond the Polish frontier.

Eisenhower believed there was a good chance that the Soviets did fear losing Eastern Europe and would flail out in the Middle East in a spasm of desperation: "The British and French took the worst possible case they could to fight on—and proceeded to get all of us in a hole." In an effort to cheer him up, apparently, some aides told him there were CIA reports that Nasser was fretting that he might have to go. Eisenhower's sarcastic reply silenced them: "Tell Nasser we'll put him on St. Helena and give him a million dollars." But he was deeply worried, never-theless, about the outcome: "There has to be some way out of this impasse."[67]

Both Moscow and Washington sponsored UN resolutions demanding a cease-fire and immediate withdrawal, but the British and French stood fast, neither landing additional forces nor leaving. Matters had reached a point, noted one State Department aide, where either Nasser or Eden falls. It was to be Eden. Chancellor of the Exchequer Harold Macmillan saw the handwriting on the walls of Number 11 Downing Street, and became the first to turn in his hawk's talons for a dove's softer wings. "I'm inclined to think that those who began this operation," Eisenhower told his aides, "should be left to work out their own oil problems—to boil in their own oil, so to speak."[68]

Angry as he was, Eisenhower hated cutting off his "right hand," as he called the British even at the height of the crisis. But there was some good news from the Middle East: ambassador Raymond Hare in Cairo reported that the American stand had turned things around in terms of Arab attitudes toward Washington. Suddenly the United States appeared to the Arabs as a champion of the right. This stiffened Eisenhower's stand against doing anything about the British financial predicament, as the pound grew weaker by the day, almost by the hour. Treasury secretary George Humphrey told "Rab" Butler, a candidate to succeed the ailing Eden, whose personal health had declined alongside British financial health, that his country was in defiance of the United Nations by not withdrawing its forces, and that American help would not come until a general settlement had been reached.[69]

Far from achieving its objective of toppling Nasser, Suez made him stronger. The Egyptian leader loved to ruminate about how the crisis had brought the United States into the Middle East as a defender of the new regime while finishing off the Baghdad Pact as a serious rival. "It might even be said," recalled Nasser's confidant, Mohamed Heikal, "that Eden was responsible for Nuri Said's death, for no Arab leader could be Britain's friend and Nasser's enemy after Suez. Suez cost Britain the Arab world." Eden left office ill, his career destroyed. "It was," quipped Nasser, "the Curse of the Pharoahs."[70]

The Search for a New Doctrine

Eisenhower might have improved the American image in the Middle East—dramatically so—but images are insubstantial things lasting only for brief moments until the rent comes due. It is worth noting at this point that no future president would take the chances Ike did in attempting to preempt wars in the Middle East—Quite the opposite. Dulles had been thinking meanwhile what the next step in the Middle East should be. Nasser's "victory" at Suez had elevated him to a high point on the Nile, but the elimination of the British presence or threat also encouraged the hope that the United States could now once again seek to concentrate Arab thoughts on "International Communism." More and more it appeared that the best option left for achieving a turnaround was Saudi Arabia, or, as some thought of it, ARAMCO Land. The Saudi royal family had profited highly from its original decision to grant the oil concession, but the economics of the Suez crisis (when Middle Eastern oil could not move through the canal) had made the king anxious about the future, and especially concerned with Nasser's spreading influence. Old quarrels with Iraq and Jordan had to be forgotten and closer relations with the Americans encouraged. Dulles knew of these desires and thought about how he might turn things around with a new "charter" for the Middle East.[71]

Even so, the Saudis would have to understand that they would have to play ball with other American plans. On January 5, 1957, even before his inauguration for a second term, Eisenhower sent to Congress a message asking for authority to act to combat the challenge of "International Communism" in the Middle East. "International Communism, of course, seeks to mask its purposes of domination by expressions of good will and by superficially attractive offers of political, economic and military aid," he said. "But any free nation, which is the subject of Soviet enticement, ought, in elementary wisdom, to look behind the mask."

A new responsibility fell to the United States, he went on, accepting the idea that Suez had changed the lines in the Middle Eastern drama, to assist any nation or group of nations in resisting a takeover by "International Communism." He wanted approval beforehand, therefore, in the form of a congressional resolution to use military force if it ever became needed to rescue any of these countries from such a dire fate: "It would . . . authorize such assistance and cooperation to include the employment of the armed forces of the United States to secure and protect the territorial integrity and political independence of such nations, requesting such aid, against overt armed aggression from any nation controlled by International Communism."

As the situation developed with Congress, however, Secretary Dulles was hard-pressed to explain the meaning of the term "International Communism." After a decade, the same question that went unanswered at the time of the Truman Doctrine—whence came the threat?—arose again, and once again it could only be finessed by calling on Congress not to leave the president exposed and shivering in the Cold War. "International Communism" had been chosen as a cover to slip over Eisenhower's real aim of preventing the spread of Nasserism. The argument had to be made to Congress, therefore, that the Russian arms sales had the potential to convert Egypt into one of those countries controlled by "International Communism." Where in 1953 Dulles had promised to make Egypt's army a real force in the Middle East—if the revolution took the right turns—now it was being held up as a danger to other Arab countries! The great fear, policy makers said, was that Russian arms meant greater influence, from the logistics to the increased number of military advisers. Nasser's personal ambitions, it was thought, would inevitably make him susceptible to Soviet guidance and, it was also argued, turn the Egyptian army into a Russian auxiliary. At least that was the way the case was presented to Congress. There was another way to explain the situation, however. Dulles would never put it in these words, but the contest in his mind was really about which force would succeed colonialism: "International Communism" or "International Capitalism." Congressional hearings on the proposed resolution revealed the difficulty of stretching the rationale to a breaking point. Senator Henry "Scoop" Jackson raised the question of whether the situation was really such an emergency as Dulles implied, since he had already testified that there seemed no likelihood of a Soviet military attack in the near future:

SENATOR JACKSON: How about the military threat?

SECRETARY DULLES: The Soviet military threat?

SENATOR JACKSON: International communism, that is the way you are using it. You don't use "Soviet" in the resolution?

SECRETARY DULLES: I say countries controlled by international communism.

SENATOR JACKSON: Yes. Well, they are synonymous, but for the purpose—

SECRETARY DULLES: No, it is much broader. For instance, China we consider controlled by international communism.

SENATOR JACKSON: You feel that Red China is now independent of the Soviet Union or not subject to their domination at the present time?

SECRETARY DULLES: We believe that both Russia and mainland China are subject to the control of international communism.

SENATOR JACKSON: Who controls international communism?

SECRETARY DULLES: Well—

SENATOR JACKSON: Well, is it a joint operation between Russia and China? Are they operating jointly, do you think, as copartners now?

SECRETARY DULLES: International communism, Senator, is a phrase which I assume has a meaning from the standpoint of the Congress because it uses it very frequently, and the phrase "countries controlled by international communism" is a phrase which we did not invent. We picked it out of the present Mutual Security Act as a phrase which Congress—

SENATOR JACKSON: We want to know what it means in connection with this legislation.

SECRETARY DULLES: It means the same thing here, Senator, exactly as it meant and means in the Mutual Security Act.

SENATOR JACKSON: What did it mean in the Mutual Security Act?

SECRETARY DULLES: Congress passed the act and I assume knows what it meant.

SENATOR JACKSON: You folks in the executive branch administer it. What does it mean?

SECRETARY DULLES: Well, international communism is a conspiracy composed of a certain number of people, all of whose names I do not know, and many of whom I suppose are secret. They have gotten control of one government after another. They first got control of Russia after the First World War. They have gone on getting control of one country after another until finally they were stopped. But they have not gone out of existence. International communism is still a group which is seeking to control the world, in my opinion.[72]

Testimony in Executive Session before the Senate Foreign Relations Committee on the Eisenhower Doctrine further demonstrated that it had more to do with concern about the spread of Nasserism than it did with that secret conspiracy—all of whose names Dulles did not know—of "International Communism." When Admiral William C. Radford, chair of the Joint Chiefs of Staff, came under heavy questioning about whether the doctrine would lead to an arms race in the Middle East, he repeatedly stressed that there was no intention to send much heavy equipment into the area. Instead, the aim was to influence the military behavior of the countries from within and to build up pride so as to resist the temptations of seeking aid from Russia as Egypt had done. He did not expect a Russian attack. The only possibility was an attack through Iran, but he thought Moscow knew anything like that would mean world war. If that were so, Senator Richard Russell asked, would the military aid under the doctrine build up a military force "of real value to the free world"?

Radford was honest and straightforward, a trait often missing in such briefings then and later: "Well, first the consideration is to generate forces in friendly countries that can maintain internal security." Pride was a big part of it. "They love to have the heavy equipment that they can parade down the main street on independence days and things like that, and show the people that they have what they feel is real armed strength."[73] In assessing the Middle East situation, Radford went on, the key thing to keep in mind was the tremendous influence of the Egyptians, a result, in large part, of the universities in Cairo, "sort of the center of Moslem religious activities." But that was not all, according to the admiral. Egyptian schoolteachers and bookkeepers carry on the education and day-to-day business affairs throughout the area: "Since Nasser came into power, to some extent before, but since he came into power, he has organized these Egyptian representatives all through the Middle East, and he is in a position to stir up trouble politically in various countries."[74]

The keys to turning the situation around, Radford and Dulles agreed in their testimony, was to counter Egyptian influence with a program to tamp down the rivalries between Egypt and Iraq—who threatened to outbid each other in terms of anti-Israel rhetoric—and to create a new force in the Middle East: Saudi Arabia. Saudi Arabia was the country of choice for several reasons, but mostly because, as Dulles put it, the king "is in a sense the titular head of their religion; their Mecca, their holy places, are in his territory, and he has a very great potential influence in the area. And we have got, in our opinion, to be able to build him up and build around him."[75]

Waiting for Saud

In a sense, it was back to square one—back even to the time Roosevelt played host on board an American warship in the Suez Canal as he waited for a royal visitor to arrive. FDR wanted an air base and a settlement of a future problem. Thus it was that on a cold day, January 30, 1957, Eisenhower now stood waiting for King Saud to land in the president's personal plane, the *Columbine*, which had been put at the king's disposal in New York. A call from the Saudi ambassador to the State Department had informed Secretary Dulles that the king "would cancel his visit to U.S. if he [was] not repeat not met at airport by the president." This was the first time Eisenhower had done anything like that, and it marked the next step in the relationship Roosevelt had initiated in 1945—but this time with the much higher price tag of $100 million.[76]

King Saud spent a week in Washington, another sign of great favoritism over Nasser's Egypt. The final communiqué began with a firm statement of Saudi Arabia's "vital importance" to the Middle East, and how the interests of world peace required that it be strengthened "for the maintenance of its own stability and the safeguarding and progressive development of its institutions." If more evidence were required about the purposes of the Eisenhower Doctrine, this communiqué would seem to have settled the matter. The bulletin also committed the Saudis to settle "justly" problems of the Middle East area by peaceful means, an oblique reference to the Arab-Israeli imbroglio, and the sort of commitment long desired from Egypt. Saud also agreed that he would work to improve relations between the United States and other Arab countries. In exchange, the United States would provide money to enhance the capabilities of the Dhahran air base and provide assistance for strengthening the Saudi military.[77]

Dulles confirmed to British ambassador Harold Caccia the details of the military aid program, including plans for the air base and the agreement to sell $100 million in arms over a five-year period. The ambassador expressed concern at the magnitude of the program, but the secretary appeared unconcerned: "I said that we doubted it would have any serious impact on the area." Another sort of criticism came from Rep. George McGovern of South Dakota: "Do we build strength against communism by contributing American tax dollars to perpetuate this kind of feudal despotism?"[78]

The answer to McGovern's question, of course, was that the Eisenhower Doctrine was about containing—and eliminating—Nasserism as a force in the Middle East. "If we could build [Saud] up as the individual to capture the imagination of the Arab world," the president wrote his secretary of state on the eve of the king's visit, "Nasser would not last long." The real problem was that there was no other likely candidate for this assignment. Iraq's Nuri al-Said was too polarizing and had disqualified himself by falling in with British plans for the Baghdad Pact; Lebanon's Camille Chamoun was the Christian president of a small, divided country; and Jordan's King Hussein could not by any stretch of the imagination be seen as an international figure, being barely able to keep the lid on his own country.[79]

While the final communiqué contained some ambiguous phrases, and did not specifically mention the threat of "International Communism," it could still be read as an endorsement of American policy objectives, including an affirmation that all questions should be settled justly without war. That was enough to allow Eisenhower to take a strong line with Israel over its continuing occupation of Egyptian territory. He did so in a public address to the nation on February 20, 1957. Although the UN Emergency Force was in position on the armistice lines and at the Gulf of Aqaba, he said, the Israelis were still refusing to withdraw: "This raises a basic question of principle. Should a nation which attacks and occupies foreign territory in the face of United Nations disapproval be allowed to impose conditions on its own withdrawal?"

Eisenhower held a powerful hand for the moment, having been reelected with a huge margin, and having obtained from Egypt concessions on future international traffic in the Suez Canal and the Gulf of Aqaba. It was hard, even for many pro-Israel senators and representatives, to see why that should not be enough. Ike's promise that the Egyptians would be held accountable satisfied, at least for the time being, nervous Israelis and their American supporters. The emerging American relationship with Saudi Arabia might cause concern in some quarters, but there, again, it looked as if the United States had succeeded at last in finding a counterforce to Nasser, one whose conservatism contrasted with the supposed incendiary objectives of the Egyptian leadership.

Meanwhile, the administration had succeeded in another objective, making peace with its closest ally, Great Britain. Harold Macmillan, the sometime Suez hawk who had split with the ailing Anthony Eden, had become prime minister, a development much encouraged by Eisenhower. He was welcomed in Washington as one who understood the shift in the Anglo-American balance of power in the Middle East, and who could be counted on to play his part with loyalty and enthusiasm. At a dinner meeting in Bermuda's Mid Ocean Club in late March, the new prime minister raised what he called the $64 question, a reference to the once-popular quiz show: What was the United States going to do about this completely unreliable man, Nasser? Did Washington intend to proceed with a series of inducements to win his favor and in that way solve long-term problems relating to the Canal and Israel? Ike replied somewhat ambiguously that one could not at the same time seek his cooperation and combat him. Macmillan persisted. He assumed, he said, that did not mean we were wedded to him and would not be unhappy if indigenous forces in Egypt brought about his downfall. Dulles intervened to say that the United States was not required to support him internally, "as against internal forces and indeed we would welcome certain types of change in Egypt." But that was different from an international campaign. Macmillan nodded that he was satisfied with this answer to the $64 question.[80]

A few months later Macmillan and Eisenhower authorized a top secret effort to topple a left-leaning Syrian government that had reached several economic agreements with the Soviet Union. The CIA-MI6 plan to stage fake border incidents as an excuse for an invasion by Syria's neighbors and to depose the government by "internal" action failed, in large part because the man the administration had been hoping to build up as the spiritual leader of the Arabs—

and successful rival to Nasser—refused to play along at any stage. Even while he had been in Washington, King Saud warned Dulles that he was exaggerating Communist control in Damascus; and when the Syrians made their overtures to Russia, Saud blamed the United States. Like Egypt, the king wrote, the Syrians had turned to Russia because they could not get arms from the United States, "while at the same time economic and military assistance to Israel is plentiful. . . . If those requests had been heeded, the situation would not have reached the present point."[81]

"The retreat from the initial embrace of the Eisenhower Doctrine looked to be turning into a rout," writes Robert Vitalis, as the king found himself the target of Arab nationalists like Nasser's confidant, Mohamed Heikal, who mocked him as nothing but a stooge for the Americans. Secretary Dulles admitted to Senator Mike Mansfield that Arab countries were turning away from any military action against Syria: "The Secretary said that public opinion in the Arab world was such that the Arab leaders felt they had no other choice." He lamented that Soviet propaganda had great influence with the "mobs in the Arab world," a result of U.S. association with Israel. He had been reading over position papers from a decade earlier, just before the emergence of the state of Israel: "It was amazing to what extent and with what accuracy these papers had predicted the troubles which would follow the emergence of a State of Israel."[82]

The troubles had only begun for American policy. In early 1958 Syria and Egypt merged into the United Arab Republic (UAR), a union that only lasted three years but looked for a time to be the predecessor of a general movement for unity under Nasser's leadership. This development brought about another twist in American policy. Having failed to make King Saud the man of the hour, the administration turned back to Nasser, however tentatively, with offers to resume wheat sales and other small steps in the direction of rapprochement. The Eisenhower Doctrine was now considered somewhat embarrassing, as the supposed beneficiaries were not only not queuing up like children in front of the ice cream wagon, they were fleeing the scene. The only stalwart appeared to be Lebanon's

Camille Chamoun, who ironically proved to be the reason for its unhappy ending. Chamoun proved the old Lippmann thesis about the weaknesses of the U.S. Cold War "containment" policy. Pundit Walter Lippmann had contested George Frost Kennan's prescriptions for dealing with the Soviet Union in a series of articles in 1947 that pointed out, among other things, that containment would inevitably put Washington into the hands of weak allies who would twist things around to suit their particular needs.[83]

Chamoun called on his American allies to secure for him a continuation of his presidency by fair means or foul. He planned to force an amendment to the constitution that would allow him to remain in power. Ambassador Robert McClintlock urged the administration to support him lest his succumbing to internal pressures demoralize pro-Western elements all through the Middle East. Like the Truman Doctrine, the "domino" thesis had a stranglehold on American policy makers and led them into the shadow of the valley of death over and over again. "We must see that he wins and wins handsomely," said McClintock. When Chamoun made his move, a rebel movement grew that Americans feared was being funded and supported by Nasser. It was true that Radio Cairo spared no epithet to denounce Chamoun, but it was harder to say that Egypt was behind the rebellion. Dulles told Afghan prime minister Sardar Mohammed Daud that Nasser was a highly volatile personality: "At times he seemed calm and reasonable; at other times he was highly emotional, and whipped up Pan-Arabism, much as Hitler had whipped up Pan-Germanism, as a means of promoting an extension of his power." When Nasser, in fact, proved to be the calm personality on the scene with a compromise proposal for Lebanon, the American government turned him down. "This would add to Nasser's prestige," Dulles said, "and seriously discourage Iraq and other pro-Western elements in the area."[84]

Obsession with Nasser as a symbol of resistance to American control, as well as an intransigent obstacle to an Arab-Israeli settlement, dominated thinking about the Middle East and filtered out alternatives to jumping into Lebanon feetfirst. So, despite being unable to find that "International Communism" had taken over

Lebanon, the United States landed nearly ten thousand troops in Lebanon on July 15, 1958. The most miraculous thing about the intervention was that the American soldiers did not fire a shot. Nonetheless, the Arab world's reaction to the intervention essentially spelled the end of the Eisenhower Doctrine. It died for lack of a plausible Communist threat to counter, or perhaps because the administration could find no suitable personality to champion an anti-Nasser crusade. On January 19, 1959, Dulles had a conversation with Israeli ambassador Abba Eban. The subject turned to Iraq and a revolution in that country that had brought down Nuri al-Said. Eban hoped that the United States would not throw support to Nasser in an effort to counter supposed Communist inroads in Iraq. "I said if one has to make a choice," Dulles sighed, "between the Communists and Nasser, I suppose Nasser is a lesser evil."[85]

The policy Dean Acheson had first declared with regard to the Egyptian revolution, and adopted by John Foster Dulles, had been to channel its nationalist fervor into pro-Western outlets. But the realities of the Middle Eastern situation could not be forced into an anti-Communist popular front. The effort proved to be Mission: Impossible, with serious consequences for the future. In the ten years since 1947, the Truman Doctrine had expanded, and the British had been replaced in the Middle East. Washington had its clear field—although it proved to be more of a minefield than a safe landing spot. The question was not whether Nasser was a danger to the Middle East—in the sense of Moscow's Mussolini, as Anthony Eden charged—but whether Washington had succeeded in making it impossible—first in Iran, then in Egypt, and finally in Iraq—for change to come about without invoking the Cold War to sustain a counterrevolutionary ethos that created new crises by sowing the area with dragon's teeth.

6

BE CAREFUL WHAT YOU WISH FOR

My thoughts have often turned to the Middle East, an area which has contributed so much to the religious and cultural heritage of the world today, and whose potential for further rich contributions to civilization is great. As an American I am proud that the concepts of our founding patriots, of Abraham Lincoln, Woodrow Wilson and Franklin Roosevelt, have played so great a part in the emergence of vigorous, independent Arab states, respected as sovereign equals in the international community.

—President John F. Kennedy,
letter to Arab leaders, May 11, 1961

There will never be unanimity as to what our broad interests are in the internal affairs of other nations. Nor will there be unanimity on the question of why it is necessary to intervene. . . . For our nation to remain economically strong, we must have access to strategic materials and technologies. When nations attempt to limit our access to these resources, we must have a capacity to circumvent their efforts.

—Richard Bissell, *Reflections of a Cold Warrior*, 1996

We believe we must resist firmly all efforts to force us to undertake intervention of any type in the internal affairs of Iraq unless and until it is clear that the domestic communists stand to gain control of Iraq in the absence of such intervention.

—State Department memorandum, December 18, 1961

What to do about Egypt's Nasser after the Suez crisis occupied much of the debate in the administration leading up to the promulgation of the Eisenhower Doctrine, but it was very far from being the only concern for policy makers. Indeed, when the Egyptian leader cracked down on domestic Communists, putting hundreds in jail, the fears caused by the arms deal with the Soviet bloc eased up a little. In itself, of course, Nasser's action in cracking down on Communists was hardly enough to win him a good conduct medal from Congress or the administration; for there was still the question of his unwillingness to make peace with Israel, and, despite Dulles's complaints, the anti-American broadcasts emanating from Radio Cairo to the Arab world and Africa continued. Thus the riddle of how to deal with Nasser continued to trouble Washington watchers on the Nile.

Besides those concerns, moreover, there was the question of where his ambition to lead a pan-Arab renaissance would wind up taking Egypt. Certainly there were fears the movement could endanger American military bases and the equally treasured assured access to the oil fields of the Middle East. Then came a series of unwelcome surprises. In February 1958 Egypt and Syria joined in forming the United Arab Republic with its capital in Cairo. The idea apparently originated in Damascus in part out of concern to block a leftist surge in that country. But it was not altogether a welcome development even to Nasser, who was somewhat unsure about such a prospect. No sooner had the world digested this news than in July a bloody revolution in Iraq brought to power Abdul Karim Kassem, who almost immediately began taking steps that put him outside the lines Americans had been drawing around the "Free World" since the establishment of the Truman Doctrine.

The July revolution in Iraq toppled the monarchy and its pro-Western prime minister, Nuri al-Said, who had been one of the original signers of the Baghdad Pact three years earlier. His British supporters had urged the pact on him as a way of gaining security against external threats, but it made him an easy target for Radio Cairo's accusation that he was nothing more than a "lackey of Western imperialism." Nasser and Nuri al-Said were old rivals and enemies, and at first Kassem's triumph was cheered as a victory over the charismatic Egyptian derided by his enemies in the Arab world as a would-be new pharaoh.

One immediate result of the Iraqi revolution was the first test of the Eisenhower Doctrine in Lebanon, when American troops rushed in to save one of Washington's friends. Lebanon's president, Camille Chamoun, was maneuvering to stay in power against a popular uprising and had called the American ambassador to warn him that the Iraqi revolution constituted an expansion of both Soviet and Egyptian power; as usual in these appeals, he claimed that the fate of his country hung in the balance. He demanded American troops rescue him and his government. Eisenhower and Dulles were alarmed, and set about to pull Chamoun's chestnuts out of the supposed deadly crossfire. Congressional leaders were called to the White House in a repetition of the scene in 1947 when Dean Acheson stepped in to elevate Secretary Marshall's calm briefing about the situation in Greece and Turkey to world-changing proportions. Secretary Dulles duly warned the legislators that sending a military force to Lebanon might start something that could not easily be finished, and thus increase "the anti-Western feeling of the Arab masses." But not to go in would make it appear that the United States was weak. "The first consequence of not going in," he said, "would certainly be that the non-Nasser governments in the Middle East and adjoining areas would be quickly overthrown." And if that were not enough, "the impact of our not going in, from Morocco to Indochina, would be very harmful to us. Turkey, Iran and Pakistan would feel, if we do not act, that our action is because we are afraid of the Soviet Union. They will therefore lose confidence and tend toward neutralism."[1]

His careful choice of words here should not go unnoticed. What he wished to impress on the legislators, ostensibly at least, was the Soviet threat—the rationale, after all, for the Eisenhower Doctrine—but what he really stressed was the matter of preventing conservative Arab leaders from losing confidence in the ability of the United States to keep them in power, and attempting to save themselves by kowtowing to the masses by moving out of the Western orbit and onto the treacherous (in all ways) path of neutralism. American troops landed in Lebanon, but, remarkably enough, no shots were fired either by them or against them. Undertaken as a move to preempt a Communist takeover, historian H.W. Brands notes that it was really a matter of symbolism: "to demonstrate to conservative regimes in the Middle East that the United States cared for their survival and to demonstrate to Nasser that Washington wouldn't retreat in the face of his anti-Western agitation." In the event, however, Chamoun was quickly persuaded to yield to new leaders approved not only by his American "rescuers" but also by Nasser.[2]

Empire on the Installment Plan

Such were the complexities of life early in the Pax Americana—especially in the Middle East. These conundrums were much on the minds of legislators when Dulles testified before the Senate on the need for the Eisenhower Doctrine. In that setting the secretary was even more explicit about his primary concerns. North Carolina's Sam Ervin pointed out that the United States had not joined the Baghdad Pact, even though it consisted of nations who had declared their willingness "to stand by the free world at any possible Armageddon with Russia." It had refused to join, he said, out of concern that we might "anger or irritate some other countries in the Middle East which have not been willing to stand up beside the free world." How did that square with the administration's insistence that the Senate support the doctrine as a way to block Moscow from advancing into the area?

Dulles replied that the administration had announced in no uncertain terms its support for the Baghdad Pact—but it was true that "we do not want to become involved in Arab politics, which the Baghdad Pact is also involved in." Ervin jumped in like a Carolina hound scenting the fox: "Absolutely. And that is what you will get us embroiled in under this resolution." No, not at all, protested Dulles: "It just keeps us out of being embroiled in it." But the senator was way out in front of the administration witnesses:

SENATOR ERVIN: You were asked a number of times what expenditures you proposed to make of the $200 million in the event—or in the release from restrictions, and you suggested only one, and that was this: You suggested it might partly be used, in part, to bolster the security forces of each individual nation of the Middle East, so that their government might not be overturned by internal forces; did you not? Did you not state that, make that suggestion?

SECRETARY DULLES: I said one of the purposes would be to sustain the internal security forces of these countries; yes, sir.

SENATOR ERVIN: So that their governments could be stabilized against internal forces; did you not use those terms?

SECRETARY DULLES: I think so; yes.

SENATOR ERVIN: So that would put us having Uncle Sam sticking his nose in all of the nations of the Middle East in order to maintain the status quo; would it not? And if that would not mess us up in Arab politics, what would it do?

SECRETARY DULLES: I think that to maintain a government which is strong enough not to be overthrown by subversion is not to become involved in Arab politics.

Ervin was not buying into that obfuscation: "Well, it certainly is taking the side of that government against the side of the people of that country which do not want that government; is it not?" Backed into a corner, the secretary played the Truman Doctrine card: "I do not believe that the kind of internal security forces we are trying to build up here would be used against the general will of the people unless it is stirred up and organized by international communism. That is the great danger, and if that is the purpose of it, then we want to have the forces to resist them."[3]

A decade earlier, secretary of state Dean Acheson had displayed considerable uneasiness when trying to answer a similar question. At the time that the North Atlantic Treaty was under debate, Acheson was confronted by another traditional conservative, Wisconsin Republican Senator Alexander Wiley, who asked him to look at the proposed treaty and to consider the meaning of "attack" on one of its members. It was possible, was it not, Wiley asked, that after one of the countries became a member that it could then "become Communist through the application of, let us call it, ideas. That would not be covered [under the rubric 'attack']?"

SECRETARY ACHESON: A purely ideological offensive would not be covered. If you would have a combination of the use of force with an internal fifth column, of course it would.

SENATOR WILEY: Now we are getting down to where I was going to lead you. An internal fifth column would be force if it were connected with the so-called mother country, Russia.

SECRETARY ACHESON: Well, what I was trying to point out is that what you are likely to get is both the use of external force and the use of internal revolution, as you have in Greece. . . . That would clearly be an armed attack. *Whether you would reach the same conclusion if the thing were entirely generated from inside, with external political stimulation, is another question.*[4]

Acheson slipped through a narrow crack here by squeezing together two *"use's,"* implying they were one and the same as directed from Moscow: "external force" and "internal revolution." American policy makers were helped enormously by the Soviets in securing congressional approval for both the Truman Doctrine/NATO and the Eisenhower Doctrine, first by exploding their atomic bomb in 1949, and then by launching Sputnik in 1957. Both came as profound shocks. In the case of the Eisenhower Doctrine, moreover, the Russian arms deal with Egypt had the effect of both reducing Sam Ervin's concern about meddling in internal Arab politics of countries supposedly threatened by subversion, and, most interesting of all, easing the task of sending arms to Israel to match the arms Cairo received. Prior to the arms deal the United States had been constantly on the spot—actually two spots—trying to field complaints from Israel's supporters and at the same time fending off

Egyptian complaints that American promises were always about tomorrow.

In the Executive Session hearings on the Eisenhower Doctrine, Senator Wiley, who had become a Truman Doctrine cheerleader— "My America is stepping out into a new field, reaching out and, yes, without mincing words, assuming the function of the British Empire, which she so gallantly handled in the century that is past"— proved to be prescient about American attitudes toward the United Nations in future decades: "So it seems to me that . . . we are going to play ball with the United Nations as long as it is necessary; but if they do not do the job, we are not going to permit the ball to be taken from us."[5]

Indeed, but the trick was to keep the ball moving so fast that the naked eye could not focus on the loose seams.

A New Player

Kassem's takeover in Iraq provided the first real test after Lebanon of the Ervin thesis about the likely results of the Eisenhower Doctrine, for almost as soon as he came to power he began changing the "internal" situation in much more dangerous ways so far as Washington was concerned. He left the Baghdad Pact with scarcely a nod in the direction of his Western benefactors, then undertook to challenge the Iraq Petroleum Company (IPC), an enterprise with major British, American, and Dutch components, and threatened Kuwait's existence as an independent sheikdom. Nine months after he overturned the monarchy and killed strongman Nuri al-Said, said *Time* magazine, "the land that some say was the Garden of Eden is a place of terror, plot and counterplot."[6]

Kassem had welcomed support from the Iraqi Communist Party. "Above all," said *Time*, "Iraq today is a land where cautious men do not openly criticize the Communist Party." It dominated the mobs, the magazine claimed, the press, and parts of the government: "Such is the nightmarish atmosphere that in at least one Iraqi city (Basra) the populace is firmly convinced that Communist-led unions have prepared a list of local employers, merchants and professional men to be liquidated as soon as opportunity offers." According to his son, Sergei, Soviet premier Nikita Khrushchev was delighted with Kassem's quick decision to disassociate himself from the Baghdad Pact: "According to the standards of the time, that meant Iraq became automatically 'ours,' 'like us.'" Khrushchev issued a blustery public statement that the Soviet Union would support the anticolonial revolution not simply with words, "but by armed force if necessary."[7]

Khrushchev had blustered earlier during the Suez crisis that he had ICBMs ready to defend Egypt if the invaders dared to keep up their attacks, but, of course, the real force that got the British, French, and Israelis to back off was American financial pressure on the pound sterling and warnings to Israel about economic aid. Nevertheless, Stalin's successor believed he had called the tune in both instances, and he was emboldened to seek new ways to agitate nationalist sentiments in the Middle East and elsewhere in what was then called the third world. At the time of the 1958 revolution, Nasser and Khrushchev were meeting in a Russian city after the Egyptian had been visiting in what was then Yugoslavia. "I liked him very much," Khrushchev wrote in his memoirs about Kassem.[8]

But they were both to be disappointed. Nasser wished to return to Egypt immediately because he believed that with Nuri gone, Iraq might well become the third state in the UAR. "This was a completely understandable desire," recalled Khrushchev, "but as it turned out, neither Nasser's hopes nor our own information about Kassem were borne out. Kassem turned out to be highly unstable politically." Nasser's efforts to engender Pan-Arabism in Iraq soon met with a rebuff, and the divisions it caused were only one source of an ongoing religious, ethnic, and class conflict that Kassem could never bring under control.

While he was in power, Kassem attempted to encourage Iraqi nationalism through the creation of a three-man council that would include an Arab Sunni, an Arab Shia, and a Kurd in an effort to overcome ethnic divisions. He closed British military bases, purged the government of Western advisers and contractors, and promised the Kurds in the north greater autonomy: "If you tour any part of this country, you will see how extensive misery, poverty, and deprivation are in the life of the people. The wealth of this country was robbed and wasted in the interest of imperialism and the foreigner."[9]

Kassem's rhetoric might not be any worse than Nasser's tirades when he nationalized the Suez Canal, but he soon mounted real threats to important American interests, the IPC and Kuwait. Successor to an oil company dating back to the final days of the Ottoman Empire, the IPC came into being in 1929. Composed of major oil companies from Europe and the United States, IPC promised Iraq a 20 percent share in properties it developed, a promise it never fulfilled. As a result, IPC's relations with the host country became fraught with discord over the years, especially as Iraq's leaders considered how the oil companies manipulated production quotas with Kuwait. These interlinked questions dominated Iraqi politics before, during, and after Kassem's reign, until they culminated in Gulf Wars I and II. Kassem's challenge to IPC, in turn, led the company to favor Kuwait and other Middle Eastern oil producers over Iraq. Baghdad's chief complaint was that IPC enjoyed a vast concession over much of the country since the time of its formation but had developed only a tiny fraction of the territory, protecting lands with oil potential it wished to reserve for future use. The oil companies also decided which fields to pump in which countries. Immediately after the July 1958 revolution, Kassem had assured London and Washington that he did not intend to nationalize the oil fields. But he was aware that even post-Mossadeq Iran as well as Saudi Arabia were able to force negotiations on new concessions for land not covered in the original concessions, an option not possible for Iraq given the size of IPC's concession.[10]

Kassem opened negotiations with the IPC with a big chip on his shoulder. He was determined to force the company to relinquish 60 percent of its concession area so as to permit new oil exploration arrangements. He insisted as well that IPC double its output of Iraqi oil and construct refineries so that more of the profits from sales would remain in the country. IPC responded with a vague promise to increase output, "depending on market conditions." It would make no other commitment—on any issue. Strengthened by a glut in crude supplies, IPC chose to sit tight, just like AIOC had done, and with the same purpose of retaining full control over every aspect of the industry. "One is forced to conclude that company behavior," wrote a keen observer, "indicated a decision to make an example of Iraq and that there was a strong political flavor to this decision."[11]

That would hardly be surprising given the still-recent episode in Iran, when the CIA and British intelligence effectively called a halt to a government bent on nationalization. The success of that enterprise further emboldened IPC to resist Kassem's demands. The Iraqi leader was not yet convinced, however, that he would be defeated, despite the companies' many advantages, and despite the divisions opening up beneath him, especially between pro-and anti-Nasser factions. Trying to see through the sandstorms of Middle Eastern politics, American policy makers quietly supported Nasser's efforts to unseat Kassem with his pan-Arab, anti-Communist campaigns. That was a far from comfortable posture, for, even if handled with the utmost delicacy, they still could not see what the Egyptian leader's activities might produce. Too-open support for Nasser might give his Communist enemies in Iraq and other Arab countries the opportunity to call him an "imperialist stooge," read a State Department paper on the Iraq situation, but it would be equally dangerous to run the risk of discouraging him from expanding his campaign: "At the same time it should be borne in mind that Nasser's current conflict with the Communists, while opening up new opportunities for the West, has not altered his basic pan-Arab goals which include the elimination of the remaining positions of Western, and particularly British, influence in the area."[12]

The fruitless negotiations between Baghdad and the IPC continued until 1961, when Kassem issued law 80, under which the constituent companies were permitted an area of exploitation little bigger than their current fields. Law 80 stripped them of 99.5 percent of the original concession. In retaliation for the Iraqi action, the IPC held down production in that country, while increasing it in Kuwait, Iran, and Saudi Arabia.[13] In December 1960 Kassem injected an extraneous argument into his fight with the IPC, accusing the French company involved in the consortium with various crimes against Muslims in Algeria, where Paris struggled to hold on to its colony, and of secretly selling oil to Israel. These were designed to ward off France's IPC cohorts from taking action against him as he sought to break down the company's united front against Iraqi demands. He also announced, after a December 1960 meeting in Baghdad at which the Organization of Petroleum Exporting Companies was founded, that his government was considering nationalizing the French company, Société Française des Pétroles—in effect separating it out so he could acquire a larger share of overall IPC royalties, from 50 percent to 61.6 percent.

The immediate stimulus to the founding of OPEC, however, was a 1960 law the U.S. Congress passed that placed lower quotas on Venezuelan and Persian Gulf oil imports in favor of the Canadian and Mexican oil industries. Eisenhower explained that the new law reflected national security needs for assured land access to energy supplies in times of war. But it had the immediate effect of lowering the price of oil from Venezuela and the Gulf.[14] Venezuela actually took the lead in forming the organization, which included not only nations in the Middle East but also other countries in Latin America. OPEC did not really flex its muscles until the 1973 Yom Kippur War, however, when the Arab countries boycotted Western countries and used that conflict as a reason to raise crude oil prices. It was the first time since the original Western explorations of "new worlds" around the globe that the shoe was on the other foot in relations between raw-materials economies and consuming nations—and it pinched!

Coup Time

Saddam Hussein emerged as a CIA hireling in various plots to remove Kassem from 1959 to 1963, an era of "special ops" that commenced with the restoration of the shah of Iran in 1953 and later included the overthrow of Diem in Vietnam. He was a key player in the coup that began in Baghdad on Feburary 8, 1963, ostensibly the idea of army officers who put Kassem on trial and ordered him shot on television. His body disappeared and was not found until 1974, apparently in an effort to defeat any attempt to make him a martyr. In the bloody aftermath and the house-to-house hunt for "Communists," more than eight thousand Iraqis were killed, a campaign managed by the Ba'ath Party, which Hussein found a useful vehicle to speed his rise to power.

"We really had the T's crossed on what was happening," said James Critchfield, the lead actor in the Iraq drama that played out in February 1963 with Kassem's downfall. "We regarded it as a great victory." Critchfield had been recalled from the German front in the Cold War by CIA director Allen Dulles shortly before Christmas 1959 to head up Middle East operations: "I found this an exciting assignment. Europe had become extremely stable after the Warsaw Pact. I very enthusiastically went to the Middle East." Dulles made no bones about what he was to do: prevent the Soviet Union from taking advantages of vulnerabilities resulting from World War II to increase its influence in this strategic area.[15]

These vulnerabilities included the steady British retreat east of Suez, of course, and the Arab reaction to the creation of the state of Israel. But, as Critchfield also acknowledged, neither the Soviets nor the United States really understood the deeply ingrained desire for independence following the years of colonial experience. The ultimately successful effort to get rid of Kassem began in the spring of 1959, when his negotiating demands on the IPC were accompanied by both increased influence of the Communist Party and a series of gestures toward the Soviet Union. It took a long time— nearly four years, continuing from the Eisenhower administration to the New Frontier years of John F. Kennedy. As events unfolded after Kassem's demise, moreover, Washington found itself on a tiger's back with no safe way to get off over the next twenty-five years. Nothing changed during that time except that the stakes got bigger, and so did the risks. Allen Dulles told the Senate Foreign Relations Committee in 1959 he had concluded that "Iraq today is the most dangerous spot on earth."[16]

At a National Security Council meeting on April 2, 1959, the CIA director explained why that was so—why Iraq was such a dangerous place. President Eisenhower had mused about the continuing Nasser problem, wondering how it might be possible to support Nasser's domestic anti-communism without promoting Cairo's dominance among Arab countries. But he was even more troubled by the worsening situation in Iraq. "It seemed to the President," recorded the note taker, "that if we were really going to undertake to save Iraq, we should have to begin to do so now." Allen Dulles pointed out that the situation "was very complicated." Not all U.S. friends had the same view of the situation as American policy makers, he said. Eisenhower kept coming back to Nasser as a possible ally and instrument for getting rid of Kassem: "He still did not understand why Nasser could not make common cause with Qasim [Kassem] against Communism." It just wouldn't work out, explained Dulles, because there was far too much bitterness between them to hope for such a solution.[17]

Under secretary of state Douglas Dillon interjected that if it became known that the United States was "plotting with the UAR against Iraq," the result would simply be to drive Baghdad "further and more rapidly into Communism." The discussion resumed two weeks later at the next National Security Council meeting. DCI Director Dulles reported that he was "extremely pessimistic" about the Iraqi situation, although the British and Turkish governments now seemed to agree with Washington about the nature of the threat. He added another piece to the emerging picture of presumed Soviet gains, the "so-called repatriation of a number of Kurds from the Soviet Union. . . . There were undoubtedly a number of Soviet agents included among them."[18]

These remarks led to a very long discussion of what to do about Iraq. Dulles had framed the question perfectly in terms of the Truman Doctrine rationale for opposing subversion supported by an outside power. Throughout the Cold War, from Latin America to Southeast Asia, this rationale fit closely with American notions about the "agent" theory of revolution, specifically that since the United States was a trustworthy anti-imperialist nation dedicated to self-determination, those revolutions that mixed nationalism with Marxism were fomented by agents, and therefore could not be considered genuine expressions of self-determination.

As the discussion went on, vice president Richard Nixon commented, "It seemed unlikely that we could find any middle ground between Communistic control of Iraq and control by Nasser." He had difficulty, he said, in seeing how any of the alternatives they had discussed did not have serious liabilities in terms of American relations with the Arab countries. But in the end, "we simply could not tolerate a Communist take-over in Iraq and . . . we were therefore engaged in building a case to prevent this from happening or for overthrowing a Communist regime in case one became established in Iraq."

General Nathan Twining, chair of the Joint Chiefs, picked up on Nixon's point and took it to a logical conclusion: "We could easily take over Iraq by military force if the appropriate preparations were made in advance." But if we went that route, he said, it would be necessary to prepare public opinion. Treasury secretary Robert B. Anderson, the cabinet's strongman after John Foster Dulles resigned and died shortly thereafter, warned against repeating the error of talking while the Communists took over half of Indochina. He believed that the domino thesis was far more applicable in the Middle East than in Southeast Asia. How long could we wait to take action? The people of the United States would understand— after all there had been no fuss when American forces landed in Lebanon the previous summer. The administration should set up a group whose sole duty should be to develop plans to prevent a Communist takeover: "We do not want another Dienbienphu."[19]

Here was the first comparison of Vietnam and Iraq, one that would help to propel the United States into both Gulf Wars. But the real importance of this discussion and what followed was the logic (given their assumptions) of pursuing a unilateral course of action to get rid of the problem, in this case Kassem, although it applied with equal force in later situations. Actually, such a group as Anderson recommended had already been assigned to that task, chaired by assistant secretary of state William Rountree. He opened its first full meeting on April 27, 1959, with a statement that there was "a certain amount of confusion regarding our objectives concerning a post-Kassem regime in Iraq." The meetings of this special group continued over the next few months, and ranged across the possibilities of encouraging Nasser to intervene—an action sure to be vehemently opposed by Israel as well as other American friends in the area—to organizing something of an exile government made up of refugees from the prerevolution era, to warning Kassem that we would intervene regardless of whether he wanted Washington's aid in defeating the Communists. The discussions also revealed an unsurprising division between Iraqi "doves" in the State Department and "hawks" from Defense and the CIA.

In October 1959 the group reviewed all the alternatives and heard from one member that the most likely path was assassination accomplished by a military coup: "The army could possibly seize control with less chance of chaos in this contingency."[20] There was an eerie similarity in all these discussions to those in the White House in 1991 after Saddam Hussein invaded Kuwait, even down to the complaint voiced by participants that they were getting nowhere by looking and listening (or, in that case, waiting for economic sanctions to force a withdrawal). The two biggest questions in both instances were how to sell the war to the public, and how to handle the threat of civil war and chaos. These were major concerns, although policy makers in the run-up to Gulf War II in 2003 professed to believe that American troops would be greeted as liberators after Saddam Hussein's reign of terror.

There was a process set in motion while the special committee debated that eventually led to an army coup and Kassem's removal, but it took nearly four years to come to fruition. It took Critchfield and his associates that long to implement Eisenhower's original mandate to save Iraq for the West. After a failed assassination attempt in 1959, one of the conspirators escaped to Cairo where, under the watchful eyes of his CIA contacts, Saddam Hussein bided his time. In a later interview Critchfield suggested only that he and his colleagues in the Middle East were well informed about the changing situation in Baghdad, and especially the Ba'ath Party, which they had regarded as a good alternative to Kassem: "Our analysis of the Ba'ath was that it was comparatively moderate at that time, and that the United States could easily adjust to and support its policies." In this same interview, however, he admitted that he had not identified the radical movement inside Ba'ath that would come to the fore after the 1963 coup.[21]

Those radical elements eventually brought to power the young conspirator, Saddam Hussein, who had escaped to Cairo, and who returned in 1963 to play a role in the massacre of thousands of Ba'ath enemies. "Quite clearly after Saddam Hussein took power, America slowly developed, not a hostility," said Critchfield, "but enormous reservations about the ability of the Ba'ath to constructively bring Iraq along. But during those years, the oil companies continued to deal with Iraq, and there were a lot of American business interests."[22]

Although he was tipped off by a variety of sympathetic leaders, such as Yugoslavia's Marshal Tito, Kassem had convinced himself he could deal with any conspiracy. Inside Iraq the CIA contact man with dissident members of the armed forces was William Lakeland, nominally an assistant military attaché. Even before the success of the coup, the embassy contacted the rebels and promised them early diplomatic recognition. Ali Saleh Sa'adi, the minister of the interior in the first post-Kassem government, quipped, "We came to power on a CIA train." The point man in this operation was Saddam Hussein.[23]

The best news of all was that the new government was neither pro-Nasser nor pro-Communist. "It is almost certainly a net gain for our side," National Security Council aide Robert Komer wrote president John F. Kennedy. Lakeland offered U.S. arms to the new government in exchange for Russian weapons Kassem had acquired, including MiG-21 fighter jets that the Defense Department wished to have to study their features.[24]

In the first postcoup memorandum on dealing with the new government, the State Department stressed that it was important not to be seen as "overshadowing": "Any indication of interference in Iraqi internal affairs must be avoided. We must also be careful to avoid creating the impression that we sired the regime or are now trying to father it." Without smothering the regime with love, the United States should look into various aid programs, including police training, and "if the new regime has immediate budgetary problems, we would support an Iraqi request to IPC for a loan. . . . We shall of course encourage American businessmen to seek opportunities in Iraq and we shall as appropriate encourage the Iraqis to do business with them."[25]

Prominent businessmen did arrive in Baghdad in large numbers, including representatives of oil companies previously excluded, and Robert B. Anderson, who negotiated a sulfur concession for the Pan American Sulfur Company. Said Aburish comments wryly that "the CIA-Iraqi connection was yielding economic benefits." But it was short-lived. The first sign of trouble was when Baghdad asked Washington to recall William Lakeland. In the short term, secretary of state Dean Rusk wrote to the president, the new regime looked a lot better than Kassem, "and it sets up a new power pole in the Arab world in fact competing with Nasser." Rusk added, however, that "in the longer term we see problems: (a) Iraqi bias against monarchies (Saudi Arabia and Jordan), (b) Iraqi hostility toward Israel, and (c) Iraqi pan-Arabism including a demand for Arab control over Arab resources (oil)."[26]

Nasser Again

If it was supposed that the United States had found a way of containing Nasser, or at least finding a balance of power, disappointment arrived early, even in the short term. President John Kennedy had opened a correspondence with Nasser in an effort to demonstrate that the Democrats were determined not to be one-sided in the Arab-Israeli dispute. One of his chief advisers on the Middle East, Robert Komer, went so far in a conversation with Israeli representatives as to say that the real problem began with the Soviet bloc arms deal. That was a common enough statement, but Komer then added that this "military threat to Israel" was brought on in large measure by American and British mistakes in dealing with Nasser.

"We ourselves had contributed to this situation by our policy in the mid-fifties vis-à-vis Nasser. It was in reacting to US/UK policy that he turned to Moscow, and we didn't want to make this mistake again."[27]

Komer and others were not always so blunt about supposed past errors, but they hoped to reinvigorate the lapsed dialogue with Cairo—or at least not lose touch with Nasser. A few days before a meeting with Israeli foreign minister Golda Meir in late December 1962, Kennedy addressed the Egyptian leader in very cordial terms about policies toward Yemen—where Nasser supported a new republican government, and Saudi Arabia supported the old regime—and a variety of other questions. Kennedy said he was pleased to learn that Egypt was interested in restoring tranquility in Algeria and helping its economy. "As you know," he wrote, "I have long taken a special interest in Algeria and I share your judgment that the success of the Algerian Government in its efforts to bring stability to this key country is very much in the interest of both our nations." He intended to provide "several tens of millions of dollars in hard relief aid to Algeria," Kennedy went on, and he hoped Nasser would encourage that country to pursue such policies as would "enhance our ability to be of such help."[28]

There was much between the lines here, for while Nasser certainly knew that Kennedy's "special interest in Algeria" went back to the 1950s, when the senator had criticized French efforts to suppress the nationalist uprising, he could also take note that JFK seemed now to be repudiating the French for their role in the Suez crisis. Paris had justified its joining in the Anglo-French-Israeli invasion not simply because of the canal nationalization, but also because of Nasser's support for Algerian rebels. And there was more in this message: "We stand with you on the position of principle that the UAR has taken at the Colombo Conference in opposition to the acquisition of territory by armed force. I believe that a similarity of outlook on this and many other issues has created a community of interests which argues well for the success of our cooperative endeavors."[29]

That sentence could be read as both an implied warning to Israel

not to start a new war and some indication of support for the return
of Palestinian refugees. However one looks at this message, Kennedy protected himself by sending it to his ambassador in Cairo to
be conveyed "orally," not as a formal signed letter. Three days later
the president met with Golda Meir at his vacation "White House"
in Palm Beach, Florida. The Cuban missile crisis and its diplomatic
aftermath were much on his mind, but now he was worried about a
renewed military conflict between Egypt and Israel. Kennedy's guest
began the conversation with a long rendition of Egypt's supposed
preparations for such a war, including recent information that
Cairo was "making preparations for radiological warfare." By that
she apparently meant, some form of dirty nuclear bomb to contami-
nate vast areas of Israeli territory. With the recent Cuban showdown still reverberating in American ears, it no doubt seemed to
her a good time to bring up a possible new threat. "It seems" she
said, "that if the refugees can't come back, the Egyptians think that
at least the land should not be available to Israelis." Her country
had information, she said, that Nasser had established a secret
budget for developing these weapons of at least $220 million per
year.[30]

As for the refugees themselves, she asked, what was behind the
Arab demands that they be allowed to return? Arabs living in Israel
already constituted 11 percent of the population. Given the Arab
pronouncements in the United Nations "for hours and hours" that
Israel has no right to exist, the real motive becomes clear: "This is
the situation. Israel knows about Arab plans to bring Arabs back to
Israel and then to make an Algeria out of Israel." The returning
Arabs would stir up trouble, and the Israeli government would do
what any government would do to protect itself, and then the Arab
countries would rush in to help these "refugees." Meir's description
fit, of course, the Truman Doctrine's original description of the way
subversion worked, and she was at pains to point out Israel's alle-
giance to the "Free World."

After this long presentation, the foreign minister said she understood that the president's position "causes all sorts of people to put
their problems on his shoulder. Israel does this too. The United

States has taken on the responsibility for the free world. Israel is part of the free world." Kennedy picked up on her final point. She was right, he said. U.S. interest in maintaining the balance of power worldwide had led it into "disputes which are not part of what we see as the central struggle, i.e., the struggle of free peoples against the Communist Bloc." He moved on quickly, however, to add that the U.S. relationship with Israel was comparable only to its relationship with Great Britain. But if that were so, he doubled back again, it was also true that Israel's security would not be enhanced if the United States abandoned its efforts with the Arab Middle East and "maintained our ties only with Israel."[31]

From that point, Kennedy discussed various ways that Israel could help the United States help Israel, such as by not taking unilateral actions on questions like the diversion of water from the Jordan River, and especially by cooperating with Washington's efforts to monitor Israel's atomic energy project. Meir was conciliatory but noncommittal, and this issue would continue to disturb policy makers up until Kennedy's death. Lyndon Johnson was less persistent in efforts to discover Israel's atomic secrets; as the Vietnam War expanded, he became more concerned about not challenging a valued ally, from whom he hoped to get support in rallying American Jews behind the defense of South Vietnam's government.

Kennedy had deliberated long and hard before agreeing to supply Israel with Hawk antiaircraft missiles, fearing it would become a slippery slope to an accelerated Middle East arms race. He finally concluded that providing the missiles Israel wanted might offer him some leverage in arguing with Israeli leaders over the dangers of nuclear weapons, as well as in pointing out the willingness of the Soviet Union to match whatever Israel accomplished in that regard with aid to Arab countries. There was always the preelection calculus to consider. With the 1962 congressional races pending, JFK had finally agreed to the sale, crossing his fingers that he could persuade Israelis of his determination to defend their country, thereby eliminating a supposed need for Israel to develop nuclear weapons.[32]

Kennedy's hopes were quickly dashed. Pressure only intensified after the Hawk missile debate until, as the State Department had long feared, the United States became the major supplier of Israeli weaponry. Israel always had one key trump card to play in negotiations over its arms requests: the unwillingness of the United States, under either Kennedy or Johnson, to countenance a bilateral security treaty with Israel. The possibility that such a "trip wire" in the Middle East would alienate the Arab countries—and the consequent fear that the United States could become involved in a nuclear war over boundary lines not settled by the original Arab-Israeli War or the Suez crisis—was simply too much of a risk even for the pro-Israel contingent in Congress to overcome. Foreign Minister Meir had played a related card in her December 1962 conversation with Kennedy, suggesting that the next conversation over refugees should be in Jerusalem, with Israeli and Arab diplomats negotiating directly. It was obvious that neither Nasser nor anyone else would accept such a bid, thereby allowing Meir to leave behind her visit with JFK a warning: if Egypt would not deal directly, it was because it was planning to carry out Arab threats to Israel's existence.

Sand Traps

The Kennedy Administration made several complicated moves to try to placate Nasser over the Hawk sales, including an aid program that would supply Egypt with free wheat, a deal worth several million dollars. Nevertheless, when the sales were announced, the Egyptian press erupted in fury. Every weapon given to Israel, thundered a paper with close attachments to Nasser, "has been used to shed Arab blood." Outside Nasser's circle, the reaction was more muted in other Arab countries, including Iraq and, especially, Saudi Arabia.[33]

Saudi Arabia was much more concerned about Nasser's actions in the developing civil war in Yemen, located at the bottom of the Arab peninsula. When a medieval-style ruler was overthrown at the end of 1961, a full-scale war erupted between supporters of the old regime, backed by Riyadh, and leftist "republicans" aided by Egypt and the Soviet Union. The war would rage on for six years, from 1963 to 1969, and would become Nasser's Vietnam, tying down seventy thousand of his troops and, his critics would say, weakening him fatally at the time of the 1967 Six-Day War. When the struggle in what would become known as North Yemen began, the British faced an insurgency against its protectorate, Aden, led by the Front for the Liberation of South Yemen and the National Front. These movements succeeded in securing a British withdrawal and the unification of the two territories as the People's Democratic Republic of Yemen.

Egypt's intervention in the Yemen situation confirmed in the minds of U.S. policy makers that Nasser's role was never going to be a constructive one. Whatever the missed opportunities in the 1950s, he was now considered beyond redemption. But waiting him out was a nerve-wracking experience, akin, some would say, to Mark Twain's quip about walking five miles while holding a wildcat by the tail. Nasser's aid in setting up the Palestine Liberation Organization was yet another "example" of irresponsibility, it was argued. Even the title—PLO—invoked Nikita Khrushchev's 1961 speech that Kennedy had seized on to rev up his support for counterinsurgency operations in Southeast Asia. On January 6, 1961, the Soviet premier had asserted, in a speech that haunted Kennedy's nightmares, "liberation wars and popular uprisings will continue to exist as long as imperialism exists. . . . Such wars are not only admissible but inevitable. . . . We recognize such wars. We help and will help the people striving for their independence." Having alerted his administration to the idea that here was the major challenge of the times, Kennedy did his turn at scaring hell out of the country in a speech to Congress on March 28, 1961: "The free world's security can be endangered not only by a nuclear attack, but also by being nibbled away at the periphery . . . by forces of subversion, infiltration, intimidation, indirect or non-overt aggression, internal revolution, diplomatic blackmail, guerrilla warfare or a series of limited wars."

Kennedy's speech not only updated the Truman Doctrine's contentions about the need to resist outside support for subversive forces, but added new rationales—intimidation, nonovert aggression, even diplomatic blackmail—to the list, thereby completing the transformation of the doctrine into fully imagined counterinsurgency theory. Kennedy's announced goal was to keep ahead of the Russians at every step on the escalation ladder from the Peace Corps, to the Green Berets, all the way to MIRVs.

Eventually the Yemen situation would resolve itself, and both Nasser's forces and British troops would leave the area. Once the latter were gone from the old Aden protectorate, the British retreat East of Suez was very nearly complete. At the end of November 1967, the last two thousand remaining British soldiers were airlifted by helicopters to ships waiting offshore. The following day, the People's Republic of Southern Yemen (later renamed the People's Democratic Republic of Yemen) officially declared its independence. A civil war continued between republicans and royalists but the great alarms that had been raised about a Soviet move to take Britain's place faded for the time being. The sky had not fallen. King Faisal of Saudi Arabia did make a plea for American aid to the royalists, but the U.S. ambassador cut short the discussion: "I told him this was not in the cards."[34]

American reluctance to increase its role in Yemen was partly the result of the deepening crisis in Southeast Asia, where president Lyndon Johnson saw many of his hopes and plans for the Great Society sink beneath the rice paddies or get blown apart by Rolling Thunder. Vietnam also had an impact on Johnson's Middle Eastern policies in a variety of ways, especially, one could argue, on Washington's attitude toward the Six-Day War in 1967, when the president's popularity was already on the wane. LBJ did not encourage the Israelis to launch their attacks, but he thought he had no good alternative to offer to prevent war when the Egyptians closed the Straits of Tiran, the narrow passageway that provided Israel an access to the Red Sea and beyond.

On a mission to probe American intentions if Israel attacked Egypt—and thus to avoid another debacle like Suez—Israeli chief of intelligence General Meir Amit provided a briefing for defense secretary Robert McNamara on June 1, 1967, that once again sounded like Dean Acheson's famous declamation to congressional leaders in February 1947 when the British had signaled they could no longer hold the fort in Greece and Turkey. Acheson, it will be remembered, had drawn a truly scary picture that day of the Russians moving all the way to North Africa and beyond, a rolling Red tide of subversion and conquest. McNamara now asked Amit if he thought the Russians knew in advance of the blockade on the Straits of Tiran? He was interested, obviously, in discovering whether this had, in fact, been a coordinated plan between Cairo and Moscow. Probably not, said Amit, but they were not reluctant to take advantage of it. Then he held forth on the true meaning of the blockade. The blockade of Tiran, he began, was merely window dressing. A "grand design" was now evident, which he termed the "Domino Effect," a loaded phrase sure to bring attention to his next words.

Egypt, with Russian backing, "hopes to roll up the whole of the Middle East all the way to the borders of Russia, to include Iran, under Arab domination." While this would affect Israel right away, "the long range effect would be deeply inimical to U.S. interests." General Amit would not go so far as to say that the "design" was behind Cairo's "original move" in blockading the straits, but it had offered Russia an opportunity to implement long-term plans, "whatever the origins of the present confrontation." The only option for Americans was to support Israel with weapons and economic support.

Johnson's Dilemma

It was a fascinating performance by Amit, one that presumed several things about the relationship between Russia and Egypt in a manner certain to stimulate Cold War fears, yet at the same time suggested there did not have to be a Russian-American confrontation if the United States stepped in to aid Israel in eliminating the threat from Nasser. He invoked the "Domino Effect" and, by implication, wars of national liberation everywhere as a given of Soviet imperial behavior. After the meeting, however, Amit wondered if he had been convincing. McNamara had not really responded to his suggestions for all-out aid to Israel, and he asked one of his hosts who drove him away from the meeting if he should try to see President Johnson? No, responded Admiral Rufus Taylor quickly, he could be sure McNamara would convey Amit's position to the White House: "I urged him to get a night's sleep and go back to Israel as soon as possible because he would be needed more there than here."[35]

American leaders had understood the Israeli position on all these issues for a long time, and were leery of giving an absolute guarantee to their emissaries about borders. They did not agree, moreover, that Washington was damned in the eyes of Arab leaders no matter what course it chose. Most of all they did not want to be in a position where a border dispute could drag the United States into military action against an Arab country. Where they agreed with Israel was in seeing Nasser as an obstacle—if not quite in the way the Israelis did, or claimed they did, as a threat to the nation's very existence.

Kennedy's efforts to kindle warmer relations between Cairo and Washington failed despite the aid he had offered for wheat purchases in the United States, in part because the Hawk missile sales, but also because the Egyptian intervention in the Yemeni wars made Nasser appear to be a frontman in the struggle for an increased Soviet presence in the Arab world. But Soviet connections aside, it was more worrisome that he constantly revealed himself as an opportunistic leader with continuing aspirations to bring about Arab unity by focusing on Israel and the Palestinian refugees. When Lyndon Johnson succeeded Kennedy, he tried anew to start up a dialogue with Nasser, even as his aides stressed that Egypt's prospects would not really change unless its leadership gave up on playing to the Arab man in the marketplace and refocused on economic development.

Walt Rostow, then chair of the State Department's Policy Planning Council, forwarded a memorandum to Johnson on April 14, 1964, authored by the council's Middle East expert, William R. Polk, that, Rostow asserted, answered the key questions about how the United States could go about getting what it wanted from Nasser. It was the best statement of the problem he had seen, commented Rostow in a covering note, laying out why it was necessary "to maintain the delicate stick and carrot balance with Cairo." Egypt's prospects, and therefore its usefulness to the United States, began Polk, depended on economic growth, for with its population increasing at the rate of 3 percent a year, doubling every twenty-five years, demands for a better life, if not met, will force its leaders to turn to more radical politics internally and closer relations with the Soviet bloc.[36]

Why did this matter to the United States? It mattered because Egypt was a leader of the Arab states and a major force in the Afro-Asian and nonaligned groups, and "occasionally opposes our interests." Polk then listed what was at stake: "These include investments in oil, which earn roughly $1 billion yearly, Wheelus Field [an air base in nearby Libya] in which U.S. pilots assigned to NATO are exercised [sic.], the Suez Canal, the use of Arab airspace and landing facilities . . . and security of Israel." On all these, Egypt was in a position to help or oppose the United States. Or simply to keep silent: "In general, our interests are served by Egyptian inactivity."[37]

Egyptian inactivity was a far different role for Cairo than Dulles had envisioned for Nasser in the American scheme of things. "Since we cannot, apparently, destroy Nasser or replace him with a viable and more moderate government and since we do not want him to rely completely upon the USSR or to be replaced by a more radical government," the only alternative was to assist Egyptian development. "The U.S. contribution, mostly PL 480 wheat, just about equals the difference between the population growth (3 percent) and the rise in GNP (5–6 percent)." Maintaining this delicate balance, as Rostow called it, would have to be implemented as well in terms of other actions. And Polk repeated for emphasis, "If we cannot destroy Nasser, what we should do is to moderate his positions so that they remain below the threshold of real danger to our interests." How? There were various ways to accomplish this objective: direct threats of force, actions in the United Nations Security Council, supplying defensive arms to Israel, and cooperation with friendly intelligence services such as those in Jordan.

How far had these measures succeeded? There had been just enough economic growth to stave off a genuine crisis, and there had not been a renewed outbreak of hostilities. This was hardly comforting news to the White House, especially as Polk reported that the situation was volatile and that Nasser would never trust the United States about Israel, which he feared as the United States feared the USSR: "He talks of renewed war but lacks the capacity to fight it. Our best guess is that he does not want war." The final word? "Nasser will never become our creature." The United States would have to put up with a lot but make sure that Nasser knew where the lines were drawn, and that it has the strength and will to protect our interests. The key to maintaining the situation in rough equilibrium, however, was not to permit a Middle East arms race to reach a point where the Egyptians, concerned about an Israeli atomic bomb, might call on the Soviets, leading to a Cuban-style showdown, "where we would not have all the cards as we did in the Cuba crisis."

Polk's blunt memorandum, especially the "if we cannot destroy Nasser" as its starting point, sounded ironically fitting after the American role in the removal of the obstinate Vietnamese leader Ngo Dinh Diem a few months earlier. When Polk wrote his memo Vietnam had not yet become the deadly swamp where Johnson's cherished ambitions for the Great Society vanished into the mists; but very soon this war impinged on American policy in the Middle East, increasing Johnson's concerns about support for his policy among Jewish groups at home, thereby increasing Israel's leverage with the White House. Almost all the recommendations in the Polk memo were acted on over the next several years, as Washington sought to keep Nasser hemmed in so that he could not endanger U.S. interests.

Johnson encouraged Nasser to correspond with him, declaring in one letter in early 1964 that while the "next few years will be a strain on both of us," the two nations had so much to gain through maintaining good relations that "we must both strive to maintain and expand them rather than letting our two nations drift apart." But later that year, on Thanksgiving Day, African students in Cairo burned down the American library next to the embassy, followed a few days later by the accidental shooting down of an airplane owned by a friend of LBJ's. As it happened, the wheat deal was up for renewal at that moment, and when the Egyptian minister of supply asked ambassador Lucius Battle about plans for a new pact, he was told it was a bad time to press Johnson about a supply of wheat. Somehow the message Battle wished to convey got garbled into a threat not to supply any more wheat. "By God," Battle was quoted when the encounter was repeated to Nasser, "I cannot discuss this at all because we do not like your behavior." [38]

Nasser had been on his way to Port Said to deliver a speech on the anniversary of Egypt's "victory" in the 1956 war, and he used the incident as a takeoff point in a bombastic speech attacking Johnson personally. "The American Ambassador says that our behavior is not acceptable. Well, let us tell them that those who do not accept our behavior can go and drink"—he paused and asked the audience, "From where?" The shout came back "From the sea!" "What I want to say to President Johnson is that I am not prepared to sell Egyptian independence for thirty million pounds or forty million pounds or fifty million pounds. We are not ready to discuss our behavior with anybody. We will cut the tongues of anybody who talks badly about us. This is clear and this is frank." [39]

Nasser soon regretted those words, and there was an admission/ apology forthcoming from Cairo that it had all been a misunderstanding. The wheat deal was renegotiated, but on a short-term basis. Johnson kept at it, nevertheless, inviting Anwar al-Sadat, the president of the Egyptian National Assembly, to visit the United States in early 1966 after Nasser said he could not come because of the tense state of relations and the likelihood he would be subject to protests. "It will do more harm than good," he told the president. "I will be picketed and the Zionist groups will demonstrate against me and it will only make matters worse." [40]

Johnson gave Sadat the full treatment, receiving him in the Oval Office by pointing to the walls covered with signed photographs of heads of state and saying, "I like you. I admire your country . . . I like President Nasser. . . . Now look, I have a space here waiting for a picture of President Nasser. Why doesn't he send me one? Why do we make enemies of each other? We should be friends."[41]

Having pictures on the wall of "third world" leaders in the Vietnam years (and after) conveyed a double meaning: friendship and coonskins. Sadat brought with him a letter from Nasser expressing satisfaction at the recently improved relations between the two countries, which offered LBJ the opportunity to point out that in recent years the United States had given Egypt more than $1 billion in aid, but that it had been tough sledding all the way because of Cairo's frequent denunciations of American policy. He had to operate in a goldfish bowl, Johnson went on, given the press and public interest. Yet whatever problems were still unresolved, he hoped that they could be "discussed quietly among ourselves and not announced to the public over loudspeakers." Then he turned to substance, wondering if it would not be possible for Saudi Arabia and Egypt to get together to work on a settlement for Yemen? Finally, there was a subject he knew from his aides was a very big issue in Arab-Israeli antagonism: the prospect of an Israeli atomic bomb. "We were watching the situation closely," Johnson said. The United States was not as "alarmist" on the subject as Egyptians, but, certainly, would be against such a development, "because of our firm policy against the proliferation of nuclear weapons."[42]

Kennedy had indeed pressed the Israelis hard about the purpose of the nuclear reactor at Dimona in the Negev desert. He had stressed the importance of international inspections over and over again, particularly in the summer of 1963. The Israelis evaded the president's questions as best they could, and made sure the inspectors, when they came, were kept away from areas that indicated work on weapons. Their mantra was that Israel would not be the first to introduce such weapons into the area, but it would never be the last. There was an ambiguity here about the meaning of "introduce." It could mean first to build a bomb or first to use a bomb; or it could mean if someone else built one ready to use, preemption was a proper answer. However that might be, Kennedy's death signaled a

change, with Lyndon Johnson not eager to push matters to a confrontation: "[Prime Minister] Eshkol decided to permit regular
American visits to the reactor and then set about making sure that
Israel's guests never found anything. For his part, Lyndon Johnson
proved more willing to be convinced by the sham inspections because he had less stomach than Kennedy for an all-out slugfest over
Dimona."[43]

How closely Sadat had been informed about Johnson's reluctance to monitor Israel's atomic progress is hard to say, but the Egyptians constantly raised the issue in conversations with American
policy makers. They also linked Israel's military preparations to
plans for territorial expansion, as Sadat did during his visit in a talk
with secretary of state Dean Rusk. Israel's small size plus its policy of
encouraging immigration, he said, made expansion "inevitable."
Hence the need for his country to be armed to the teeth. Sadat's
portrayal of the situation was almost a mirror image of Meir's outline to Kennedy of Egypt's military aspirations. Rusk then asked in
Yoda-like manner if it was fear of Israeli expansion, or the existence
of Israel that governed Egyptian attitudes? Both, said Sadat. If it
were the former, Rusk replied, "something might be done, if latter
not so sure."[44]

Rusk did not mean to convey in the slightest any intention of
questioning Israel's right to exist, only to bring Sadat back to serious
thinking about Egypt's role. The Americans believed that Nasser
was out of touch on several questions. He faced a dilemma in trying
to be the leader of an Arab resurgence without committing himself to a solution of the Palestinian refugee question, which would
inevitably raise the question of Israel's existence as a Jewish state.
The refugee numbers had now reached over one million, and talk
of their absorption into Israel or someplace else in the Middle East
made no one happy or willing to act. Nasser had created the Palestinian Liberation Organization, it was argued, as a way of maintaining control of the situation, but with Syria prodding him, as well as
other Arab countries joining in a chorus of criticism that he did not
do more, the stage was set for another major conflict.

The Six-Day War

The Syrians had permitted PLO raiders to strike out of the Golan Heights, and matters came to a head in April 1967 when an armed Israeli tractor cultivating land in a disputed area was fired on. In the ensuing "battles," which included mortar attacks, tank fire, and an aerial dogfight, several Syrian MiG-21s were destroyed. Events began moving at a rapid pace in the aftermath. Nasser was told by Moscow that Israel was massing troops on the Syrian border, indicating that it was a challenge he could not ignore. The reports were not true, but so many forces had been set in motion that momentum was the deciding factor. Nasser took two steps near the end of May that helped to push the Middle East into war by sending his forces into the Sinai and closing the Gulf of Aqaba to Israeli shipping. Richard Helms, CIA director, told the White House, however, that Nasser's move into the Sinai did not signal an intention to launch a military attack on Israel. The Egyptians were embarrassed, read Helms's notes for the meeting, because they had not helped the Syrians in April, so they "made a big show of marching into Sinai, partly to show good faith, partly in hopes of deterring the Israelis" from more retaliatory attacks.[45]

American intelligence did not believe Egypt wanted a war in the near future, nor that it was any match for Israel militarily. But Nasser had opened the way for his antagonists to take advantage of the situation. Israel promptly sent its most skillful negotiator to Washington, foreign minister Abba Eban, essentially to learn if the United States had any real plan for international action to force open the narrow waterway at the bottom of the Gulf of Aqaba. If there was not a plan, that would create a rationale for unilateral Israeli military action. Eban was also concerned to learn if there was any prospect of repeating what happened in the 1956 Suez crisis, when the United States forced Israel to give up its gains from the invasion of Egypt. President Johnson made a statement in one of the sessions with Eban that is sometimes interpreted as giving the Israelis an amber light. "With emphasis and solemnity," read notes of this meeting, "the President repeated twice, Israel will not be alone unless it decides to go it alone." [46]

One could interpret that to mean that while the United States would not join in a military attack, it would stand aside while Israel did the job it needed to do. Yet just before that statement, "Johnson had said, "Israel must not make itself responsible for initiating hostilities." That could, of course, be a coded signal that Israel must come up with some sort of "excuse" for starting a war, not unlike the events leading to Suez in 1956. But given what American intelligence believed about Egyptian capabilities, Johnson's careful formulation was more likely a delaying tactic. No matter what Eban pictured as Cairo's ability to wage an offensive war, neither Johnson nor Defense Secretary McNamara thought an Egyptian attack was likely, or if it did come, it would end quickly in defeat. But Eban countered LBJ's strategy with a proposal he knew the president constitutionally could not accept: an Israeli-American security pact modeled on the NATO alliance guarantees. LBJ said only, as if that were a substitute, "You will whip hell out of them." [47]

To Eban's next proposal, that American and Israeli intelligence services join together to render an accurate assessment of the Egyptian threat, the president was decidedly cool: "We do not want to establish any joint staff which would become known all over the Middle East and the world." McNamara, he said, should see if there was some way to accomplish such a purpose without a formal organization. On that point, the Pentagon head commented drily that his people did not feel they were getting the proper information from the Israelis, so perhaps such an exchange would indeed be useful. McNamara's suggestion for an equal exchange was much less appealing to Eban.

After leaving Johnson, Eban talked with Arthur Goldberg, the U.S. ambassador to the United Nations, who told him that the most important thing about his mission was whether he had convinced Johnson of Egypt's culpability and Israel's innocence: "If it was established in the American mind that Egypt's action was illicit, then Israel could hardly lose. Either she would gain international support against the blockade or if she acted alone, she would

have the United States committed to the doctrine of Israel's recti-
tude and Cairo's guilt."[48]

Eban had accomplished that mission: he felt comfortable, if not
absolutely certain the United States would not behave as it had
after Suez. How much was owed to Eban's skillful diplomacy, however, can be argued. Johnson was concerned about support for his
war in Vietnam. He was inclined, therefore, to be wary about involving the United States in another war, but given Nasser's bom-
bast and threats—both public and private—to destroy Israel, he
could take the high road and get credit with those in the Jewish
community who were doubtful about the war in Southeast Asia.
The skillful diplomacy was actually his, for he fended off Eban's direct overtures while conveying the impression that Israel did not
have to worry about another Suez debacle. LBJ had said Israel would
not be alone unless it initiated hostilities, but he had not said that it
would be stopped from doing so.

That was the only green light LBJ gave, having reluctantly concluded that he could not prevent the Israelis from taking matters
into their own hands. His repeated statement that Israel would only
be alone if it went in alone then becomes simply an acknowledgment of what American policy had been over the years: an effort to
play a role in the final settlement of accounts, which could only be
done if the United States indeed refused to give Tel Aviv a NATO-
type security guarantee that would offend the Arab countries in the
worst possible way.

LBJ could also look back and say that he and Kennedy had given
Nasser every "break," even if, as one expert had put it, that it was
only because they could not destroy him; but now the Egyptian
strongman had brought this on himself by his ambition to unify the
Arab world under his leadership. On the eve of the Israeli attack,
Walt Rostow wrote Johnson a memo that summed up where matters stood and how the United States could achieve its main objectives. It was premised on the argument that whatever they said
about Israel and the Palestinian refugees, moderate elements, and
that meant, he said, "virtually all Arabs who fear the rise of Nasser,
. . . would prefer to have him cut down by the Israelis rather than by

external forces." In other words, exactly what Johnson had accepted as his role, not as cheerleader for the Israelis, let alone military ally. Beyond the immediate crisis, Rostow argued, the "radical nationalism represented by Nasser" was waning. "Arab socialism and other such doctrines have not proved successful":

> Just beneath the surface is the potentiality for a new phase in the Middle East of moderation; a focusing on economic development; regional collaboration; and an acceptance of Israel as part of the Middle East if a solution to the refugee problem can be found. But all this depends upon Nasser's being cut down to size.
>
> The problem before us is whether this crisis can be surmounted in ways which lead on to that historical transition and which avoid: the destruction of Israel, on the one hand, or the crystallization of a bloc unified only by a hostility to Israel, which would require us to maintain Israel as a kind of Hong Kong enclave in the region.[49]

All this was vintage Rostow, and similar to arguments he had been making about the Vietnam War as a necessary application of force to pave the way for the emergence of a true revolution focusing on economic development and regional collaboration. In that case, it all depended on Ho Chi Minh being "cut down to size."[50]

With the Six-Day War, Israel made a big leap from a petitioner to a very different position as military ally of the United States. From 1948 to 1967, the White House had attempted to maintain a delicate balance between domestic politics and foreign policy requirements. It had tried, especially in the Dulles years, to bring about a settlement of the Arab-Israeli conflict by convincing the leaders of the Egyptian Revolution that their future success was best placed in American hands. All those efforts had failed, and not just because Nasser refused to deal with Israel. But his stance on Israel, while it made it difficult for those who really sought to back an Arab "nationalist" in the struggle with "International Communism," finally resulted in Johnson's ability to rationalize American options at the time of the Six-Day War in a way that also established common grounds within the U.S. government.

At the outset of the Russo-Japanese War in February 1904, when the Japanese fleet attacked Russian ships at Port Arthur, President Theodore Roosevelt actually rejoiced, claiming that Japan was "playing our game" in a private letter to his son. Later, of course, TR played the role of mediator and peacemaker between the two countries, and won the Nobel Prize for his efforts. His object in supporting Japan, and then presiding over the peace talks, was to maintain a balance that would allow American interests to expand in Asia without threat of a conflict with either power. LBJ's attitude toward Israel was based on the same premise, exactly as Walt Rostow had pointed it out to him: that an Israeli triumph of arms could produce support for a moderate Arab leadership to step to the fore in place of Nasser's unbridled nationalism and ambitious agenda.

In both cases, however, unleashing a war did not serve long-term purposes nearly as well as the presidents hoped it would. From this point of view, the question of what kind of light Johnson gave to Abba Eban is less important, for he probably could not have stopped the Israelis from going to war in any event—and certainly not without running risks that appeared at the time greater than the course he pursued of first trying to convince Eban that his government could not go to war expecting overt support from the United States, then letting him understand by what he did not say that Washington would not repeat Eisenhower's intervention to save Nasser from his fate.

Ultimately, however, Japan turned against the United States at Pearl Harbor, while in the aftermath of the Six-Day War, the United States would find that Israel's position as a military power to be reckoned with by the Arabs did not resolve the issue in the way Rostow predicted. When the war began, Johnson ordered Rostow to assemble a group of "wise men" to advise him on American policy. Among those summoned was Dean Acheson, who, by common acknowledgment, was the titular head of the knights of the Cold War roundtable. Rostow recorded Acheson's musings on the central dilemma that would face policy makers after the quick victory and the occupation of new territories by the Israelis, which would create an even greater number of refugees and a lasting obstacle to the idea of a "modernization" way out of the American predicament. "There was an interesting moment, as I remember it. Mr. Acheson looked back on the whole history of Israeli independence and, in effect, said it was a mistake to ever create the State of Israel."[51]

The war began on June 5, 1967, with a series of Israeli air raids on Egyptian air bases that within the span of a few hours had all but eliminated Cairo's air force. At the same time, Israeli infantry moved into the Sinai, and a ferocious tank battle ensued over the next two days. It was a brutal war in the desert with the aim of destroying Egypt's capacity for war and killing as many of the enemy as possible. Although there had been pledges by Israeli leaders that the war was not about territory, with the successful capture of Jerusalem and the Golan Heights such vows were almost immediately all but forgotten. Johnson, moreover, did not insist on an early truce, but delayed applying pressure for a cease-fire until Israel had achieved its territorial objectives on all Arab fronts: Egypt, Syria and Jordan.

The Legacy

Although Nasser had been cut down to size, other problems grew in the wake of the Six-Day War. Even as Israeli military forces routed the Egyptian air forces and shattered its defenses—in the process demonstrating the inferiority of Russian-supplied weapons, much to the delight of American observers—Johnson received a CIA briefing on anti-American demonstrations all over the world that also included a warning that the Arab countries would stop selling oil "to any country which takes part in or supports Israel in the fighting. Baghdad radio said this morning that the pumping of Iraqi oil has been stopped 'because of US and UK attitudes.'"[52]

This time it proved a false alarm. The threat did not become a reality until the Yom Kippur War in 1973. But by then the Egyptians had a new leader, Anwar Sadat, who, after launching that war, did a turnabout and became an American ally. Nasserism as a challenge to American hegemony had been vanquished. President Richard Nixon took advantage of that breakthrough, and, citing the Vietnam War as an example of the wrong way to run an empire, turned to regional stabilizers—especially the shah of Iran. From the time of the Truman Doctrine, the shah had complained about being shortchanged in comparison to other client states in the region. Nixon promoted him to regional stabilizer-in-chief and ordered that he be provided with the latest weapons in the American inventory. After a 1972 meeting with the shah, he instructed that F-14 and F-15 aircraft, laser-guided bombs, and uniformed technicians be made available to the "Government of Iran as quickly as possible."[53]

The shah's appetite for the latest American jet fighters eventually proved his undoing, as the Ayatollahs and their supporters crumpled up his regime like used tinfoil in the 1979 revolution. The search for someone who could replace the shah—who, truth be told, had never lived up to American hopes—eventually turned to Saddam Hussein. Some months after the Six-Day War, a new coup in Baghdad provided the second step in the rise of Saddam Hussein. From the beginning there were rumors that this coup, like the one in 1963, had been midwifed by the Central Intelligence Agency. In March 2003, as the United States initiated Gulf War II to remove Saddam, a former National Security Council aide, Roger Morris, wrote in the *New York Times* that he had contacts with CIA officers, including Archibald Roosevelt, a grandson of president Theodore Roosevelt, who boasted "about their close relations with the Iraqi Baathists."[54]

Morris's story was picked up by Reuters, with a reporter adding a comment that such a version of how Saddam came to power was "a far cry from current American rhetoric about Iraq—a country that top U.S. officials say has been liberated from decades of tyranny and given the chance for a bright democratic future." Agency sources immediately denied the Morris story. The idea that Saddam ever received CIA payments was "utterly ridiculous." With the failed search for weapons of mass destruction, the time for such boasting, as had been the case when the coup managers toppled Mossadeq in 1953, had long since passed. Morris stuck to his guns and made an oblique reference to 1953 in remarks to another reporter, David Morgan: "We climb into bed with these people without really knowing anything about their politics." Except, he might have added, that they seemed to offer an alternative to uncooperative leaders whose ambitions challenged American goals. "We tire of these people," Morris went on, "and we find reasons to shed them."[55]

Morgan remained skeptical, but while his efforts to find out the truth turned up many denials from government officials, others told him that the United States had to face up to the unintended consequences of its policies. "There are always some unintended consequences," a former aide to Henry Kissinger, Helmut Sonnenfeldt, told him. He added this dramatic statement: "There were unintended consequences in World War I that brought the rise of Hitler."

Like Hitler did for some conservatives at the outset of his rise to power, Saddam appeared manageable to his CIA handlers. James Chritchfield, who ran agency affairs in the Middle East at the time, told *Frontline* interviewers that Washington eventually developed reservations about Saddam's regime and the Ba'ath Party, however. After the Six-Day War, he said, Soviet influence began to decline in the Middle East. So what was there to worry about? "We thought that Saddam Hussein might be brought along in that sense—showing increased interest in working with the United States, its instruments, and its government, because of the infatuation for modern technology. This was Saddam being totally pragmatic."[56]

What spoiled the plan, of course, was the 1979 Iranian revolution, which stoked Hussein's ambitions to seize the mantle of the Arab awakening, while at the same time it tempted the Reagan administration to use him as a firewall against the spread of the new menace centered in Tehran. Reagan's efforts were no more successful in the end than had been the earlier attempt to co-opt Nasser and the Egyptian revolution. As Chritchfield noted of Saddam, he stopped being "pragmatic": "When he was interested in making a bigger and better missile or a bomb, he wasn't interested in it to increase American influence in the region. He was interested purely in increasing his own influence." That quest, concluded the former CIA agent, had been seriously underrated, and was still "a very prevalent characteristic of the Middle East."

From the moment the Truman Doctrine was presented to Congress in 1947, there were warnings aplenty voiced by legislators about the consequences of sending arms to prop up regimes in the Middle East. Pentagon spokesmen insisted that they had the situation under control, that through MAAGs and other close supervision, the weapons supplies would never constitute a problem. Every time Congress wound up supporting the president's requests in the name of fighting "International Communism," when in reality it feared the domestic and international consequences of repudiating the president.

The rising American empire in the Middle East was never a smoothly operating set of policies. It was hampered most by the intractable problem of the ongoing Arab-Israeli crisis. Roosevelt could see that at the beginning, even in his talks with the Three Kings. Truman simply forged ahead along a path of least resistance domestically. Dulles and Eisenhower tried to steer American policy along a narrow line, and hoped to seize on the Suez crisis to restore Washington's reputation in the Arab nations. But while they succeeded in a move that completed the transition begun when the British alerted American policy makers they could no longer hold the line in Greece and Turkey; like Acheson and Truman, they could not bring Nasser along the way they had hoped when Dulles suggested he would make the Egyptian army into a real force, provided he cooperated with Washington in organizing a Middle Eastern front against "International Communism." LBJ stopped trying.

Twenty years after the Truman Doctrine, the Six-Day War came in the midst of the Vietnam debacle and led American policy makers to rely more on surrogates. In a way, Israel was one. Its victory in that war did produce a change with Anwar Sadat. But the denouement, first, of the open embrace of the shah and then of the more ambiguous endorsement of Saddam Hussein in the aftermath of the Iranian revolution exposed weaknesses in the founding assumptions of the Truman Doctrine that cracked apart on September 11, 2001.

EPILOGUE

George W. Bush announced a war on terror after September 11, 2001. He made it clear that his policies were not to be a continuation of the Truman Doctrine, which, he implied, had relied upon supporting the status quo over more than five decades, and finally produced the radical forces surrounding Osama bin Laden. His critique of past American policies certainly had a point, but his confidence in the "shock and awe" method of transforming the Middle East and using Iraq as a beacon light for an area awaiting such transformation just as fatefully led to more "unintended consequences."

After seven years and a war in Iraq whose costs would mount into the trillions of dollars, the real perpetrator of the 9/11 attacks had not been caught, and American forces still had not brought peace to Afghanistan. A new president, Barack Obama, immediately ordered a review of American strategy that led to a new focus on Afghanistan and border areas with Pakistan. Noting that both Presidents Bush had promised that Iraq would not be another Vietnam, Obama promised that Afghanistan would not be another Iraq. Even as he did so, the White House announced that American forces in Afghanistan would be augmented by 17,000 new troops, while further reinforcements would depend on the final outcome of the strategy review.

For some observers, that left the door ajar a bit too much on the edge of the Hindu Kush, especially, it was pointed out, when the goals of the military strategy remained unclear. Before he was replaced in early 2009, General David McKiernan, the American commander in Afghanistan, had asked for thirty thousand troops, while others, such as General David Petraeus, commander of Central Command in the Pentagon, and retired Colonel Jon Nagl, a respected counterinsurgency adviser, talked about building an

Afghan army of more than one hundred thousand. But no one had any real estimate of how long it would take or, in the case of the proposed Afghan army, how a country as poor as Afghanistan could afford such a huge military establishment.

One goes down to the end of the road, warned Senator Walter George during secret hearings on the Truman Doctrine. Was this where it ended, on mountain trails searching out all the local Taliban and Al-Qaeda fighters who had spread across into Pakistan? "After seven years of war," wrote a veteran observer of the Iraq campaign, "Afghanistan presents a unique set of problems: a rural-based insurgency, an enemy sanctuary in neighboring Pakistan, the chronic weakness of the Afghan government, a thriving narcotics trade, poorly developed infrastructure, and forbidding terrain."[1]

Besides these obstacles, the Afghan situation presented other problems to any foreign army—not least in the danger of alienating the population by raids on suspected hiding places that killed or injured "civilians" (who were, in any case, hard to distinguish from the supposed enemy) or by drone aircraft dropping bombs on targets selected thousands of miles away by "pilots" seated at computer consoles. Upon Obama's election, Afghan president Hamid Karzai repeated the warning he had given his predecessor: "We cannot win the fight against terrorism with airstrikes. This is my first demand of the new president of the United States—to put an end to civilian casualties."[2]

In this regard, the authors of the Truman Doctrine had been concerned that American policy not produce a backlash: "We now take full cognizance of the tremendous value of this area as a highway by sea, land and air between the East and West; of its serious consequences which would result if the rising nationalism of the peoples of the Middle East should harden into a mould of hostility to the West."[3]

General McKiernan, however, preferred to focus on the issue as he saw it. Afghanistan was vital to American national security— the original rationale of the Truman Doctrine. He had heard, he told a military newspaper, about all the warnings, that Afghanistan had been called the "graveyard of empires" because of what had happened to the British and Russians over two centuries when they tried to control the country. In this situation, he said, U.S. efforts have the support of both the international community and the Afghan people: "It is in our vital national security interests to succeed here." Comparing the American presence in Afghanistan with past failures, he warned, was an unhealthy occupation.[4]

In the years of the Pax Britannica, Lord Curzon, viceroy of India, spoke like McKiernan of vital interests: "Turkestan, Afghanistan, Transcaspia, Persia . . . they are the pieces of a chessboard upon which is being played out a game for the domination of the world."

For America, the game began with a rendezvous with three kings.

NOTES

1. Introduction to a Doctrine

1. U.S. Senate, Committee on Foreign Relations, Historical Series, *Legislative Origins of the Truman Doctrine: Hearings Held in Executive Session*, 80th Cong., 1st sess., 1947 (Washington, DC: GPO, 1973), pp. 21–22.

2. Thanks to Marc Favreau here, for his suggestions about formulating the argument of the book in the clearest possible way.

3. Harry S. Truman, *Memoirs: Years of Trial and Hope* (Garden City, NY: Doubleday, 1956), pp. 102–5.

4. Ibid.

5. C.P. Trussell, "Congress Is Solemn," *New York Times*, March 13, 1947.

6. Ibid.

7. Peggy Noonan, "The President Within: George W. Bush Is Downright Trumanesque," *Wall Street Journal*, November 16, 2001, www.opinionjournal.com/columnists/pnoonan/?id=95001471.

8. The account here is taken from one of the first tellings of the story by Joseph Marion Jones, a State Department aide at the time, in *The Fifteen Weeks: An Inside Account of the Genesis of the Marshall Plan* (New York: Viking Press, 1955), pp. 139–42.

9. Cited in Lloyd C. Gardner, *Economic Aspects of New Deal Diplomacy* (Madison: University of Wisconsin Press, 1964), p. 283.

10. Dean G. Acheson to George C. Marshall, March 15, 1947, U.S. Department of State, *Foreign Relations of the United States, 1947*, vol. 5, *The Near East and Africa* (Washington, DC: GPO, 1971), pp. 120–21 (hereafter cited as *FRUS, 1947*, vol. 5).

11. A recent evaluation from a post–Cold War perspective is Geoffrey Roberts, *Stalin's Wars: From World War II to Cold War, 1939–1953* (New Haven, CT: Yale University Press, 2006), pp. 310–14.

12. U.S. Senate, *Legislative Origins of the Truman Doctrine*, p. 198 (emphasis added).

13. Curtis E. LeMay with MacKinlay Kantor, *Mission with LeMay: My Story* (New York: Doubleday, 1965), pp. 204–6.

14. "Memorandum by the Joint Chiefs of Staff," March 13, 1947, *FRUS, 1947*, vol. 5, pp. 110–14.

15. "Memorandum of Conversation," February 24, 1947, ibid., 43–44.

16. "Minutes of the First Meeting of the Special Committee," February 24, 1947, ibid., 45–47.

17. Melvyn P. Leffler, *A Preponderance of Power: National Security, the Truman Administration, and the Cold War* (Stanford: Stanford University Press, 1992), p. 144.

18. U.S. Senate, Committee on Foreign Relations, *Executive Sessions of the Senate Foreign Relations Committee*, 85th Cong., 1st. sess., 1957 (Washington, DC: GPO, 1979), pp. 140–43.

2. The United States Moves into the Middle East

1. For accounts of Roosevelt's "surprise," see the official "Memorandum of Conversation," 9:00 P.M., February 10, 1945"; and an undated, untitled memorandum by Harry Hopkins, both in the Harry L. Hopkins Papers, box 337, Franklin D. Roosevelt Library, Hyde Park, NY (hereafter cited as Hopkins Papers).

2. "American Economic Policy in the Middle East," Report by the Coordinating Committee of the Department of State, May 2, 1945, U.S. Department of State, *Foreign Relations of the United States, 1945*, vol. 8, *The Near East and Africa* (Washington, DC: GPO, 1969), pp. 34–39 (hereafter cited as *FRUS, 1945*, vol. 8).

3. Ibid.

4. See Lloyd C. Gardner, *Economic Aspects of New Deal Diplomacy* (Madison: University of Wisconsin Press, 1964), p. 220.

5. Press secretary Steve Early to Jonathan Daniels, no. 104, undated [February 1945], Franklin D. Roosevelt Papers, Map Room Collection, box 22, Franklin D. Roosevelt Library, Hyde Park, NY (hereafter cited as Roosevelt Papers).

6. Gardner, *Economic Aspects of New Deal Diplomacy*, p. 273.

7. Early to Daniels, no. 108, undated [February 1945], Roosevelt Papers, Map Room Collection, box 22.

8. Ibid.; and see Thomas W. Lippman, *Inside the Mirage: America's Fragile Partnership with Saudi Arabia* (Boulder, CO: Westview Press, 2004), p. 125.

9. Thomas W. Lippman, *Arabian Knight: Colonel Bill Eddy USMC and the Rise of American Power in the Middle East* (Portola St. Vista, CA: Selwa Press 2008), pp. 135–36.

10. James Moose to Cordell Hull, September 25, 1943, and Hull to Franklin Roosevelt, March 30, 1943, both in Roosevelt Papers, Official File 3500.

11. Roosevelt to Ibn Saud, January 9, 1939, Official File 3500, Roosevelt Papers; and "Suggested Procedure Regarding the Palestine Question," undated memorandum [1945], Hopkins Papers, box 170.

12. Roosevelt to Abdul Aziz Ibn Saud, July 7, 1943, Roosevelt Papers, President's Secretary's File (PSF) Arabia.

13. Roosevelt, "Memorandum for the Secretary of State," August 15, 1943, ibid.

14. "King Ibn Saud," undated memorandum, Hopkins Papers, box 170; and Edward Stettinius to Roosevelt, January 9, 1945, Roosevelt Papers, PSF Arabia.

15. "Memorandum of Conversation Between the King of Saudi Arabia and President Roosevelt," February 14, 1945, *FRUS, 1945*, vol. 8, pp. 2–3.

16. Gordon Merriam, chief, Division of Near Eastern Affairs, Department of State, memorandum to Jonathan Daniels, March 17, 1945; and Daniels's note on the memorandum, with clipping from the *New York Herald Tribune*, March 17, 1945, both in Roosevelt Papers.

17. Summary of correspondence with Prince Abdul Ilah, March 10, April 2, April 10, and April 12, 1945, Roosevelt Papers, Official File 3500.

18. William Eddy to Secretary of State, March 3, 1945, *FRUS, 1945*, vol. 8, p. 7.

19. Ibid., 9.

20. Gerald Posner, *Secrets of the Kingdom: The Inside Story of the Saudi-U.S. Connection* (New York: Random House, 2005), p. 23.

21. David S. Painter, *Oil and the American Century: The Political Economy of U.S. Foreign Oil Policy, 1941–1954* (Baltimore: Johns Hopkins University Press, 1986), p. 33; and State Department memorandum, April 21, 1941, Roosevelt Papers.

22. Painter, *Oil and the American Century*, p. 33.

23. Ibid., 37.

24. Daniel Yergin, *The Prize: The Epic Quest for Oil, Money, and Power* (New York: The Free Press, 2003), p. 401.

25. Patrick Hurley to Roosevelt, June 9, 1943, Roosevelt Papers, PSF Saudi Arabia.

26. Painter, *Oil and the American Century*, pp. 42–44.

27. James Landis to Hopkins, August 29, 1944, Hopkins Papers, box 332.

28. Lippmann, *Inside the Mirage*, pp. 33–35.

29. Landis to Hopkins, September 4, 1944, Hopkins Papers, box 332.

30. "Cairo Questionnaire," *Time*, October 18, 1943, p. 20.

31. Reinhold Niebuhr, *The Irony of American History* (1952; repr., Chicago: University of Chicago Press, 2008), p. 36.

32. Stettinius to Roosevelt, January 8, 1945, *FRUS, 1945*, vol. 8, p. 847.

33. Acheson to Eddy, September 11, 1945, ibid., p. 952.

34. Eddy to Secretary of State, July 15, 1945, ibid., pp. 929–30.

35. Eddy to Secretary of State, September 13, 1945, ibid., pp. 955–57.

36. Acheson, "Memorandum of a Conversation," May 28, 1945, ibid., pp. 902–3.

37. Acheson, "Memorandum to the Secretary of State," October 9, 1945; and Gordon Merriam, "Draft Memorandum to President Truman," undated [1945], both in ibid., pp. 43–48.

38. Truman to Ibn Saud, September 12, 1945, ibid., pp. 953–54.

39. Eddy to Secretary of State, July 15, 1945, ibid., pp. 929–30.

40. Loy Henderson, "Memorandum of Conversation," July 31, 1945, ibid., pp. 1000–1005.

41. Thomas Donnelly, "Rebasing, Revisited," American Enterprise Institute, December 6, 2004, www.aei.org/publications/pubID.21657/pub_detail.asp.

42. For a discussion of these questions, see Mark Lytle, The Origins of the Iranian-American Alliance, 1941–1953 (New York: Holmes & Meier, 1987), pp. 16–34. Much of the information in the next few paragraphs is taken from this source.

43. Roosevelt to the Shah, September 2, 1941, Roosevelt Papers, PSF Iran.

44. Adolf A. Berle, diary entry, October 5, 1943, Papers of Adolf A. Berle, box 215, Franklin D. Roosevelt Library, Hyde Park, NY (hereafter cited as Berle Papers).

45. Pat Hurley to Roosevelt, November 7, 1943, Hopkins Papers, box 332.

46. "Memorandum of a Conversation," October 10, 1941; and "Memorandum by the Chief of Near Eastern Affairs," November 5, 1941, both in U.S. Department of State, Foreign Relations of the United States, 1941, vol. 3, The British Commonwealth, the Near East and Africa (Washington, DC: GPO, 1959), pp. 374–76, 373.

47. Gardner, Economic Aspects of New Deal Diplomacy, p. 228.

48. Painter, Oil and the American Century, pp. 77–78.

49. Ibid., 78.

50. See Lytle, Origins of the Iranian-American Alliance, pp. 55–57.

51. Ibid.; and see FRUS, 1945, vol. 8, pp. 523–26.

52. Elliott Roosevelt, As He Saw It: The Story of the World Conferences of F.D.R. (New York: Duell, Sloan and Pearce, 1946), p. 197.

53. See James Goode, The United States and Iran, 1946–51: The Diplomacy of Neglect (New York: St. Martin's Press, 1989); and Mostafa Elm, Oil, Power, and Principle: Iran's Oil Nationalization and its Aftermath (Syracuse, NY: Syracuse University Press, 1992), pp. 300–301.

54. Millspaugh to Harry Hopkins, January 11, 1944, Hopkins Papers, box 332.

55. Arthur C. Millspaugh, Americans in Persia (Washington, DC: Brookings Institution, 1946), pp. 47–48.

56. Roosevelt to Hull, January 12, 1944, Roosevelt Papers, PSF Iran.

57. Donald Connolly to Hopkins, January 11, 1944, Hopkins Papers, box 332.

58. Connolly to Hopkins, August 7, 1944, ibid.

59. Lytle, Origins of the Iranian-American Alliance, p. 38.

60. Gardner, Economic Aspects of New Deal Diplomacy, p. 230.

61. Robert Patterson to Secretary of State, Novemberr 23, 1945, FRUS, 1945, vol. 8, pp. 452–53.

62. Conference of Chiefs of Mission in the Near East with President Truman, November 10, 1945, ibid., p. 18; and memorandum of conversation, July 6, 1945, U.S. Department of State, Foreign Relations of the United States: The Conference of Berlin (The Potsdam Conference), 1945 (Washington, DC: GPO, 1960), vol. 1, pp. 997–98.

63. Thucydides, *History of the Peloponnesian War*, trans. Rex Warner (New York: Penguin Books, 1972), p. 464.

64. U.S. Congress, House of Representatives, Committee on Foreign Affairs, *Hearings: Assistance to Greece and Turkey*, 80th Cong., 1st sess. (Washington, DC: GPO, 1947), p. 43.

3. The Truman Doctrine Protectorate

1. Harry S. Truman, *Memoirs: Year of Decisions* (Garden City, NY: Doubleday, 1955), p. 455 (emphasis added).

2. "Special Message to the Congress on Greece and Turkey: The Truman Doctrine," March 12, 1947, *Public Papers of the Presidents: Harry S. Truman, 1947* (Washington, DC: GPO, 1963), pp. 176–80.

3. Alexander Kirk to Cordell Hull, April 25, 1944, quoted in William Roger Louis, *The British Empire in the Middle East, 1945–1951* (Oxford: Clarendon Press, 1984), p. 183 (emphasis added).

4. The Potsdam debate is reproduced in Lloyd C. Gardner, *Architects of Illusion: Men and Ideas in American Foreign Policy, 1941–1949* (Chicago: Quadrangle Books, 1970), pp. 80–81; the Murphy quotation is from p. 82.

5. James Clement Dunn, "Memorandum for the Secretary," August 16, 1945, John Foster Dulles Papers, Seeley G. Mudd Manuscript Library, Princeton University, Princeton, NJ (hereafter cited as Dulles Papers).

6. "Record of the Fourth Meeting of the Council of Foreign Ministers," September 14, 1945, U.S. Department of State, *Foreign Relations of the United States, 1945*, vol. 2, *General: Political and Economic Matters* (Washington, DC: GPO, 1967), pp. 167–75.

7. Charles E. Bohlen, "Memorandum of Conversation," September 14, 1945, ibid., pp. 163–66; and "Conversation Between Secretary of State and Molotov," September 23, 1945, FO 371/47883, Foreign Office Records, Public Record Office, Kew, London, UK (hereafter cited as Public Record Office).

8. See Gregg Herken, *The Winning Weapon: The Atomic Bomb in the Cold War, 1945–1950* (New York: Knopf, 1980), p. 50; and James V. Forrestal, diary entry, October 16, 1945, Papers of James V. Forrestal, Seeley G. Mudd Manuscript Library, Princeton University, Princeton, NJ (hereafter cited as Forrestal Papers).

9. G.L. McDermott, "The Straits," November 16, 1945, FO 371/48699, Public Record Office; and Arnold Offner, *Another Such Victory: President Truman and the Cold War, 1945–1953* (Stanford, CA: Stanford University Press, 2002), p. 112.

10. James F. Byrnes, *All in One Lifetime* (New York: Harper, 1958), pp. 333–34, recounts the Moscow exchanges over Iran. The argument that Russia feared sabotage directed from Iran was discounted then and later, but Lytle, *Origins of the Iranian-American Alliance*, pp. 150–52, suggests there may have been serious reason for concern.

11. Truman, *Memoirs: Year of Decisions*, pp. 604–6.

12. On Stalin's aims in the 1946 Iranian "crisis," see Fernande Scheid Raine, "The Iranian Crisis of 1946 and the Origins of the Cold War," in *Origins of the Cold War: An International History*, ed. Melvyn P. Leffler and David S. Painter (1994; repr., New York: Routledge, 2005), pp. 93–110; and *New York Times*, September 13, 1947.

13. *New York Times*, October 22 and 23, 1947.

14. On the White Paper, see Tom Segev, *One Palestine, Complete: Jews and Arabs Under the British Mandate*, trans. Haim Watzman (New York: Henry Holt, 2001), pp. 438–43.

15. Ibid., 442.

16. Sidney Gruson, "Britain Maps Strategy with Palestine as Key," *New York Times*, August 4, 1946.

17. Michael Cohen, *Truman and Israel* (Berkeley: University of California Press, 1990), pp. 67–70.

18. Press conference, August 16, 1945. This reference and others to Truman's press conferences have been taken from the Truman Library Web site, www.trumanlibrary.org, "Public Papers" page, unless otherwise noted.

19. Press conference, October 18, 1945.

20. Louis, *British Empire in the Middle East*, pp. 428–29.

21. The complicated 1945 deliberations and correspondence can be followed in *FRUS, 1945*, vol. 8, pp. 679–844, especially Roosevelt's letter to Ibn Saud, April 5, 1945, p. 698.

22. "Memorandum of Conversation," October 22, 1945, ibid., pp. 779–83.

23. "Memorandum by the Minister to Saudi Arabia," October 26, 1945, ibid., pp. 790–91.

24. "Memorandum by the Director of the Office of Near Eastern and African Affairs," November 13, 1945, ibid., pp. 11–18.

25. John Keay, *Sowing the Wind: The Seeds of Conflict in the Middle East* (New York: W.W. Norton, 2003), p. 340.

26. Text of Stalin's "reply" in the *New York Times*, March 14, 1946.

27. Memorandum by Felix Belair Jr., April 29, 1946, Papers of Arthur Krock, box 1, Seeley G. Mudd Manuscript Library, Princeton University, Princeton, NJ (hereafter cited as Krock Papers).

28. Forrestal, diary entry, August 15, 1946, Forrestal Papers.

29. Ibid., August 21, 1946.

30. C.L. Sulzberger, "War Speculation Held Unjustified," *New York Times*, August 21, 1946; and James Reston, "U.S., Russia, Join Issue on Dardanelles' Fate," *New York Times*, October 6, 1946.

31. Reston, "U.S., Russia, Join Issue on Dardanelles' Fate."

32. *New York Times*, November 9, 1946; and minute by J. Donnelly, September 5, 1945, FO 371/44557, Public Record Office.

33. Attlee to Bevin, January 3, 1947, FO 800/502 (SU/47/2); and Offner, *Another Such Victory*, pp. 169–73.

34. Offner, *Another Such Victory*, p. 199.

35. James Reston, "Truman Asks Aid to Greece; British Unable to Bear Cost," *New York Times*, February 28, 1947, pp. 1, 10.

36. "Excerpts from Telephone Conversation Between Honorable James Forrestal . . . and Mr. James Reston of the New York Times," March 13, 1947, Papers of Joseph Marion Jones, Harry S. Truman Library, Independence, MO.

37. Arthur Krock, "Some Questions Arising Over the 'Truman Doctrine,'" *New York Times*, March 20, 1947.

38. Reproduced in the *New York Times*, March 30, 1947.

39. Notes on "Rough Draft of the President's Message to Congress in Regard to Greece," March 9, 1947, Papers of George M. Elsey, Harry S. Truman Library, Independence, MO (hereafter cited as Elsey Papers), available on the Truman Library Web site, www.trumanlibrary.org (emphasis added); and James Reston, "The Big Question: What Will Our World Role Be," *New York Times*, March 15, 1947. For a general discussion of the speech drafts, see Gardner, *Architects of Illusion*, pp. 219–21.

40. Gardner, *Architects of Illusion*, pp. 211–12.

41. "Churchill Hails U.S. Policy as Stabilizing Middle East," *New York Times*, April 12, 1947.

42. *New York Times*, March 25, 1947.

43. U.S. Senate, *Legislative Origins of the Truman Doctrine*, p. 22 (emphasis added).

44. Ibid., 198 (emphasis added).

45. Ibid., 160 (emphasis added).

46. "X" (Kennan), "The Sources of Soviet Conduct," *Foreign Affairs Quarterly* 25 (July 1947): pp. 566–82.

47. Ilan Pappé, *The Making of the Arab-Israeli Conflict, 1947–1951* (New York: I.B. Tauris, 2001), pp. 24–25.

48. Segev, *One Palestine Complete*, pp. 158–59; and Simha Flappan, *The Birth of Israel: Myth and Realities* (New York: Pantheon, 1987), pp. 38–39.

49. Draft memorandum by Dean Rusk, May 4, 1948, U.S. Department of State, *Foreign Relations of the United States, 1948*, vol. 5, *The Near East, South Asia, and Africa* (Washington, DC: GPO, 1976), pp. 894–95.

50. Memorandum of conversation, May 12, 1948, ibid., pp. 972–76.

51. Truman, *Memoirs: Years of Trial and Hope*, pp. 168–69.

52. Read by Clifford at the White House meeting, May 12, 1948, *FRUS, 1948*, vol. 5, pp. 977–78.

53. Ritchie Ovendale, *The Origins of the Arab-Israeli Wars* (London: Longman, 1984), pp. 123–24, 130.

54. R.H. Hillenkoetter to Truman, *FRUS, 1948*, vol. 5, p. 1200.

55. Louis, *British Empire in the Middle East*, p. 545.

56. Secretary of State to Acting Secretary of State, May 12, 1950, U.S. Department of State, *Foreign Relations of the United States, 1950*, vol. 5, *The Near East, South Asia, and Africa* (Washington, DC: GPO, 1978), p. 161 (hereafter cited as *FRUS, 1950*, vol. 5).

57. "Conversation with the Egyptian Ambassador," April 13, 1950, Papers of Dean Acheson, box 66, Harry S. Truman Library, Independence, MO (hereafter cited as Acheson Papers).

58. J.R. Childs to Secretary of State, April 3, 1950, "Visit to Saudi Arabia of Assistant Secretary the Honorable George C. McGhee," Papers of George C. McGhee, box 2, Harry S. Truman Library, Independence, MO.

59. The speech can be read and downloaded at the Truman Library Web site, www.trumanlibrary.org.

60. The speech can be read and downloaded at the Truman Library Web site, www.trumanlibrary.org.

61. Kennan, untitled memorandum, January 22, 1952, Records of the State Department Policy Planning Staff, box 48, National Archives, College Park, MD.

62. Stephen Kinzer, *Overthrow: America's Century of Regime Change from Hawaii to Iraq* (New York: Times Books, 2006), p. 124.

4. The Iran Oil Crisis

1. Acheson, "Interview between the President and the Shah of Iran," November 18, 1949, Acheson Papers, box 65.

2. Acheson, "Iranian Desire for Greater Security Assurances from the United States," November 18, 1949, ibid.

3. Harriman quoted in Stephen Kinzer, *All the Shah's Men: An American Coup and the Roots of Middle East Terror* (New York: Wiley, 2003), p. 109.

4. "The Present Crisis in Iran," undated [April 1950], *FRUS, 1950*, vol. 5, pp. 509–18.

5. Memorandum of conversation, "Call of the Iranian Ambassador on the Secretary," April 27, 1950, Acheson Papers, box 66.

6. George McGhee, *Envoy to the Middle World: Adventures in Diplomacy* (New York: Harper & Row, 1983), p. 74.

7. Memorandum of conversation, January 24, 1950, *FRUS, 1950*, vol. 5, pp. 13–15.

8. McGhee, *Envoy to the Middle World*, p. 76; and Kinzer, *All the Shah's Men*, p. 72.

9. McGhee, *Envoy to the Middle World*, p. 323.

10. Steve Marsh, *Anglo-American Relations and Cold War Oil* (New York: Palgrave Macmillan, 2003), pp. 45, 51, 54.

11. George Elsey, "President Truman's Conversations with George M. Elsey," notes of June 26, 1950, Elsey Papers.

12. McGhee, *Envoy to the Middle World*, pp. 326–27.

13. Ibid., pp. 327–28.

14. Elm, *Oil, Power, and Principle*, p. 85.

15. Kinzer, *All the Shah's Men*, p. 54.

16. "The Stake in Iran," *New York Times*, March 23, 1951; and "Iran's Crisis Deepens, But Premier Stays On," *New York Times*, September 23, 1951.

17. Louis, *British Empire in the Middle East*, p. 687.

18. Dean Acheson, *Present at the Creation: My Years in the State Department* (New York: W.W. Norton, 1969), p. 503; and memorandum of conversation, April 27, 1951, Acheson Papers, box 68.

19. Berle to Robert Hooker, May 11, 1951, Berle Papers, box 217.

20. "United States Position on Iranian Oil Situation," May 18, 1951, Papers of Harry S. Truman, President's Secretary's File (PSF), box 157, Harry S. Truman Library, Independence, MO (hereafter cited as Truman Papers).

21. Kinzer, *All the Shah's Men*, pp. 108–9.

22. Ibid.

23. Memorandum of conversation, "Iranian Oil Problem," October 10, 1951, Acheson Papers, box 61. The U.S. State Department's *Foreign Relations of the United States, 1952–1954*, vol. 10, *Iran (1951–1954)* (Washington, DC: GPO, 1989), published to answer critics of the series, leaves out this document (hereafter cited as *FRUS, 1952–1954*, vol. 10).

24. Krock, "Private Memorandum on a Visit to the President," May 24, 1951, Krock Papers, box 1.

25. Mohammed Mossadeq to Truman, June 11, 1951, encl. in Acheson to Truman, June 13, 1951, Truman Papers, PSF, box 157. Once again, this document is not printed in *FRUS, 1952–1954*, vol. 10, where only a note of the response is made on p. 62.

26. William Korns to Gordon Gray, September 21, 1951, Truman Papers, Psychological Strategy Board Files, box 7.

27. Ibid.

28. "Memorandum by the Acting Secretary of State," September 21, 1951, *FRUS, 1952–1954*, vol. 10, pp. 163–64.

29. U.S. Senate, Committee on Foreign Relations, *Executive Sessions of the Senate Foreign Relations Committee (Historical Series)*, vol. 3, pt. 2, 82nd Cong., 1st sess., 1951 (Washington, DC: GPO, 1976), pp. 457–59.

30. Elm, *Oil, Power, and Principle*, p. 176.

31. Ibid.

32. Memorandum of conversation, October 23, 1951, *FRUS, 1952–1954*, vol. 10, pp. 241–44.

33. Acheson, *Present at the Creation*, p. 504.

34. Memorandum of conversation, October 24, 1951, Acheson Papers, box 69.

35. Ibid.; and Elm, *Oil, Power, and Principle*, pp. 185–86.

36. Acheson to the Department of State, November 10, 1951, *FRUS, 1952–1954*, vol. 10, pp. 278–81; Acheson quotation from p. 279.

37. Mossadeq to Truman, November 10, 1951, Truman Papers, Official File 134-B, box 591.

38. Michael Clark, "Truman Receives Mossadegh Today," *New York Times*, October 23, 1951, p. 7.

39. Albion Ross, "Mossadegh Hailed by Crowds in Cairo," *New York Times*, November 21, 1951.

40. Special to the New York Times, "Iran's and Egypt's Premiers Avow Close Ties," *New York Times*, November 23, 1951.

41. Steering Group on Preparation for Talks Between the President and the Prime Minister, "Negotiating Paper: Middle East Command," January 4, 1952, Truman Papers, PSF.

42. Steering Group on Preparation for Talks Between the President and the Prime Minister, "Negotiating Paper: General Middle East Paper," December 31, 1951, ibid.

43. Ibid.

44. Steering Group on Preparation for Talks Between President and the Prime Minister, "Iran," January 5, 1952, ibid.

45. Dean Acheson, "Memorandum of Dinner Meeting," January 8, 1952, U.S. Department of State, *Foreign Relations of the United States, 1952–1954*, vol. 6, *Western Europe and Canada* (Washington, DC: GPO, 1986), pp. 730–39.

46. Ibid.

47. Acheson, "Memorandum of a Dinner Meeting," January 6, 1952, ibid., pp. 742–46.

48. Records of the "Princeton Seminar," December 13, 1953, Truman Library.

49. Painter, *Oil and the American Century*, p. 184.

50. Lytle, *Origins of the Iranian-American Alliance*, pp. 202–3.

51. Memorandum of conversation with the president, "Iran," July 31, 1952, Acheson Papers, box 71; and Churchill to Truman, August 16, 1952, Truman Papers, PSF. It is interesting that Acheson's references to Qavam have been excised out of the version of this conversation in *FRUS, 1952–1954*, vol. 10, p. 428.

52. Churchill to Truman, August 16, 1952; and Truman to Churchill, August 18, 1952, both in Truman Papers, PSF. Versions of the letters appear in *FRUS, 1952–1954*, vol. 10, pp. 445–47.

53. Elm, *Oil, Power, and Principle*, pp. 252–54.

54. Acheson to Truman, October 1, 1952, encl. Churchill to Truman, September 29, 1952, Truman Papers, PSF. See also *FRUS, 1952–1954*, vol. 10, pp. 479–80.

55. "Memorandum of Meeting at the White House Between President Truman and General Eisenhower," November 18, 1952, Truman Papers, PSF.

56. J.C. Kitchen, "Memorandum of Meeting with Oil Company Representatives," December 4, 1952, Acheson Papers, box 72.

57. "Memorandum of Discussion," March 4, 1953, *FRUS, 1952–1954*, vol. 10, pp. 692–700; quotation from p. 699.

58. C.M. Woodhouse, *Something Ventured* (London: Granada, 1982), pp. 110–11.

59. Ibid., p. 118.

60. James Risen, "How a Plot Convulsed Iran in '53 (and in '79)," *New York Times*, April 16, 2000.

61. Robert C. Doty, "Mossadegh's Foes Predict His Fall," *New York Times*, March 28, 1953.

62. Associated Press, "Mossadegh Forces Oust Rashani," *New York Times*, July 2, 1953, p. 1.

63. Eisenhower to Mossadeq, June 30, 1953, Papers of Dwight D. Eisenhower, Ann Whitman File, box 29, Dwight D. Eisenhower Library, Abilene, KS (hereafter cited as Eisenhower Papers).

64. Gordon Mattison to Department of State, July 13, 1953, *FRUS, 1952–1954*, vol. 10, pp. 734–5; and Kermit Roosevelt, *Countercoup: The Struggle for the Control of Iran* (New York: McGraw-Hill, 1979), p. 18.

65. Roosevelt, *Countercoup*, p. 116.

66. *New York Times*, July 22, 1953, p. 1.

67. Kinzer, *All the Shah's Men*, pp. 167–69; and Kennett Love, "Shah Flees Iran After Move to Dismiss Mossadegh Fails," *New York Times*, August 17, 1953.

68. Kinzer, *All the Shah's Men*, pp. 188–91.

69. Kennett Love, "Shah Back in Iran, Widely Acclaimed; Prestige at Peak," *New York Times*, August 23, 1953, p. 1.

70. Quoted in Elm, *Oil, Power, and Principle*, p. 309.

71. Ibid., pp. 312–13.

72. Ibid., pp. 316–17.

73. Memorandum of discussion, May 27, 1954, *FRUS, 1952–1954*, vol. 10, pp. 1008–12.

74. Special to the New York Times, "Schwarzkopf Declines Comment," *New York Times*, August 20, 1953, p. 3; and James Risen, "Secrets of History: The CIA and Iran," *New York Times*, April 16, 2000, p. 1.

75. "Memorandum for the President," undated [August 26 (?), 1953], Eisenhower Papers, Whitman File, box 32.

76. "USIS Country Plan," June 20, 1956, ibid., White House Office NSC Staff, box 44.

77. "NSC Discussion with Mr. Herbert Hoover, Jr.," May 25, 1954, ibid., box 42.

78. "Memorandum of Conversation: Iranian Oil Negotiations," June 1, 1954, ibid., box 43.

79. "Discussion Paper re Iran," August 22, 1956; and "Draft Paper re Iran," August 22, 1956, both in ibid., OCB Central Files, box 44.

80. NSC Planning Board, "United States Policy Toward Iran," December 21, 1953, ibid., Office of the Special Assistant for National Security Affairs, NSC Policy Papers, box 8 (emphasis added).

81. Operations Coordinating Board, "Analysis of Internal Security Situation," December 14, 1955, ibid., NSC Staff Papers, box 43.

82. Dulles to Eisenhower, December 7, 1956, ibid., White House Central File, box 875.

83. MAAG Tehran to USCINCEUR, December 19, 1959, ibid., Office of the Staff Secretary, International Series, box 8.

84. Ibid.

85. Eisenhower to the Shah of Iran, March 12, 1960, ibid., Whitman File, International Series, box 32.

86. Phillip J. Halla to McGeorge Bundy, February 8, 1961, ibid., White House Office, NSC Staff Records, box 4.

87. William Burr, quoted in "U.S.-Iran Nuclear Negotiations in 1970s Featured Shah's Nationalism and U.S. Weapons Worries," Electronic Briefing Book, no. 268, National Security Archive, January 13, 2009, www.gwu.edu/~nsarchiv/.

88. Kissinger to American embassy in Tehran, received August 11, 1974, Papers of Gerald R. Ford, Confidential File, Middle East, box 13, Gerald R. Ford Library, Ann Arbor, MI (hereafter cited as Ford Papers).

89. Borzou Daragahi, "U.S. Policies Led to Iran Revolt, Study Says," Los Angeles Times, October 17, 2008.

90. Kissinger to Ford, undated [December 20 (?), 1975], Ford Papers.

91. See Roosevelt, Countercoup; and Steven R. Weisman, "U.S. Program Is Directed at Altering Iran's Politics," New York Times, April 15, 2006.

5. Damming the Egyptian Revolution

1. Kennett Love, Suez: The Twice-Fought War (New York: McGraw-Hill, 1969), pp. 170–71.

2. Ibid., 173.

3. Ibid., 177.

4. Mohamed H. Heikal, Cutting the Lion's Tail: Suez Through Egyptian Eyes (New York: Arbor House, 1987), pp. 17–18; and Mohamed Heikal, The Cairo Documents: The

Inside Story of Nasser and His Relationship with World Leaders, Rebels, and Statesmen (New York: Doubleday, 1973), p. 16.

5. Charge in the United Kingdom to Secretary of State, January 7, 1949, p. 187; and Truman to Mark Ethridge, April 29, 1949, p. 957, both in U.S. Department of State, *Foreign Relations of the United States, 1949*, vol. 6, *The Near East, South Asia, and Africa* (Washington, DC: GPO, 1977) (hereafter *FRUS, 1949*, vol. 6).

6. Caffery to Secretary of State, January 25, 1950, *FRUS, 1950*, vol. 5, p. 702.

7. "Memorandum of Conversation," January 31, 1950, ibid., pp. 712–15.

8. Eliahu Elath to Acheson, February 13, 1950, pp. 736–41; and McGhee to Acheson, March 25, 1950, pp. 816–17, both in ibid.

9. Ibid., p. 135n6.

10. Miles Copeland, *The Game of Nations: The Amorality of Power Politics* (New York: Simon & Schuster, 1969), p. 58.

11. Memorandum of conversation, "Visit of Prime Minister of Israel," May 8, 1951, Acheson Papers, box 68.

12. Copeland, *Game of Nations*, p. 59; and "Visit of Prime Minister of Israel," May 8, 1951, Acheson Papers.

13. Donald Neff, *Warriors at Suez: Eisenhower Takes America into the Middle East* (New York: Simon & Schuster, 1981), pp. 68–69; and Love, *Suez*, pp. 180–81.

14. Barry Rubin, "America and the Egyptian Revolution, 1950–1957," *Political Science Quarterly* 97, no. 1 (Spring 1982): pp. 73–90; and memorandum of telephone conversation, January 27, 1952, *Foreign Relations, 1952–1954*, vol. 9, *The Near and Middle East* (Washington, DC: GPO, 1986), pt. 2, pp. 1756–57 (hereafter cited as *FRUS, 1952–1954*, vol. 9).

15. Rubin, "America and the Egyptian Revolution."

16. "Caffery to Secretary of State," September 18, 1952, *FRUS, 1952–1954*, vol. 9, pt. 2, pp. 1861–62.

17. "Secretary of State to Caffery," September 30, 1952, ibid., pp. 1863–65.

18. Heikal, *Cutting the Lion's Tail*, pp. 34–35.

19. Love, *Suez*, p. 265; and Dulles to Eisenhower, June 13, 1953, Dulles Papers, White House Memos, box 1.

20. "Memorandum of Conversation," May 11, 1953, *FRUS, 1952–1954*, vol. 9, pt. 1, pp. 8–18.

21. "Memorandum of Conversation," May 12, 1953, ibid., pp. 19–25.

22. "Meeting with Congressional Leaders," March 9, 1953, Eisenhower Papers, Legislative Series, box 1; Dulles, "Conclusions on Trip," undated [May 1953], Dulles Papers, box 475.

23. "Dulles Says U.S. Aim Is to Gain Friends," *New York Times*, June 2, 1953, p. 1.

24. Special to the New York Times, "Cairo Sees Gains in Dulles' Report," *New York*

Times, June 3, 1953; Special to the New York Times, "Israel Asks Dulles to Clarify Report," *New York Times*, June 10, 1953; and Dana Adams Schmidt, "Sensitive Israelis Concerned Over Shifts in World Opinion," *New York Times*, June 28, 1953.

25. Copeland, *Game of Nations*, pp. 101–2.

26. "Memorandum by the Deputy Assistant Secretary of State," September 28, 1954, *FRUS, 1952–1954*, vol. 9, pt. 2, pp. 2305–6.

27. "Memorandum of Conference with President Eisenhower," April 21, 1954, Dulles Papers.

28. "'Byroadeism' Held Blow at Zionism," *New York Times*, June 24, 1954.

29. "Byroade to Department of State," March 1, 1955, U.S. Department of State, *Foreign Relations of the United States, 1955–1957*, vol. 14, *Arab-Israeli Dispute, 1955* (Washington, DC: GPO, 1989), pp. 78–79 (hereafter cited as *FRUS, 1955–1957*, vol. 14).

30. Love, *Suez*, pp. 200–202.

31. "Mallory to Department of State," March 16 and October 12, 1955, U.S. Department of State, *Foreign Relations of the United States, 1955–1957*, vol. 13, *Near East: Jordan-Yemen* (Washington, DC: GPO, 1988), pp. 4–5, 6–7.

32. Townsend Hoopes, *The Devil and John Foster Dulles* (Boston: Little Brown, 1973), pp. 320–23; and Love, *Suez*, p. 88.

33. Laura M. James, "Whose Voice? Nasser, the Arabs, and 'Sawt al-Arab' Radio," undated, www.tbsjournal.com/jamespf.html (emphasis added).

34. "Caffery to Department of State," December 11, 1952, *FRUS, 1952–1954*, vol. 9, pt. 2, p. 1908.

35. "Points of Agreement in London Discussion of Arab-Israeli Settlement," March 10, 1955, *FRUS, 1955–1957*, vol. 14, pp. 98–107.

36. Memorandum of conversation, "Economic Sanctions Against Israel and Related Matters Affecting US–Israel Relations," October 25, 1953, Dulles Papers.

37. Henry Byroade to State Department, April 14, 1955, *FRUS, 1955–1957*, vol. 14, pp. 151–53.

38. Hoopes, *Devil and John Foster Dulles*, pp. 315–17.

39. Heikal, *Cutting the Lion's Tail*, p. 69.

40. Love, *Suez*, p. 241.

41. Steven Z. Freiberger, *Dawn Over Suez: The Rise of American Power in the Middle East, 1953–1957* (Chicago: Ivan R. Dee, 1992), pp. 122–24.

42. Freiberger, *Dawn at Suez*, p. 124.

43. Memorandum of conversation, September 26, 1955, *FRUS, 1955–1957*, vol. 14, pp. 516–19.

44. Ibid.

45. Ibid.

46. Rubin, "America and the Egyptian Revolution," p. 85; Eden to Eisenhower,

November 27, 1955; and Hoover to Dulles, November 28, 1955, both in *FRUS, 1955–1957*, vol. 14, pp. 808–10.

47. Byroade to Department of State, November 17, 1955, *FRUS, 1955–1957*, vol. 14, pp. 781–83.

48. Hoover to Cairo, January 31, 1956, U.S. Department of State, *Foreign Relations of the United States, 1955–1957*, vol. 15, *Arab-Israeli Dispute, January 1–July 26, 1956* (Washington, DC: GPO, 1989), p. 117 (hereafter cited as *FRUS, 1955–1957*, vol. 15).

49. "Message to Washington," January 24, 1956, ibid., pp. 60–63.

50. Dwight D. Eisenhower, diary entries for March 8 and 13, 1956, in *The Eisenhower Diaries*, ed. Robert H. Ferrell (New York: W.W. Norton, 1981), pp. 318–19.

51. Dulles, "Memorandum for the President," March 28, 1956, Dulles Papers, Subject Series, box 5.

52. On the domestic complications, Dulles was frequently in contact with a former Wall Street associate, Arthur Dean, who pressed in his letters the Israeli case for arms. Dulles tried to explain that American policy was to discourage an arms race, but that he had allowed NATO allies, especially the French, to sell jet fighters to Israel. He also thought Dean should appreciate that the Israelis, when they asked for security guarantees, were unwilling to specify what borders should be guaranteed—thereby making such a commitment intolerably open-ended. According to Dulles, "They insist on working with us at arm's length and, indeed, are carrying on a very highly organized and high-powered campaign directed to force our hand irrespective of our judgment." Dulles to Dean, March 27, 1956, ibid.

53. "Memorandum of Conversation with the President," July 13, 1956, Dulles Papers, White House Memoranda Series, box 4.

54. Allen to Dulles, July 13, 1956, and July 17, 1956, both in *FRUS, 1955–1957*, vol. 15, pp. 828–30, 849–51.

55. Byroade to Department of State, July 13, 1956, ibid., pp. 832–35.

56. Memorandum of conversation, July 19, 1956, ibid., pp. 863–64.

57. Memorandum of conversation, July 19, 1956, 4:10–5:07 P.M., ibid., pp. 867–73.

58. Dana Adams Schmidt, "Aswan Decision Marks a Turn in U.S. Policy," *New York Times*, July 22, 1956; Osgood Caruthers, "Nasser Says U.S. Lied in Explaining Bar to Aswan Aid," *New York Times*, July 24, 1956; and Love, *Suez*, pp. 345–53.

59. For an account of the motives of the participants, see Ovendale, *Origins of the Arab-Israeli Wars*, ch. 9.

60. "Memorandum of Conversation with the President," August 14, 1956, Dulles Papers, White House Memoranda Series, box 5.

61. "Memorandum of Conversation with Selwyn Lloyd," August 24, 1956, ibid., Dulles–Eisenhower Correspondence, box 1.

62. "Memorandum of Conversation," September 6, 1956, ibid., Subject Series, box 1.

63. Douglas Dillon, "Memorandum for the Secretary," September 19, 1956, ibid., Subject Series, box 7.

64. Dulles, "Memorandum of Conversation with Mr. Harold Macmillan," September 25, 1956, ibid., Dulles–Eisenhower Correspondence, box 1; and Dulles, "Memorandum of Conversation with the President," ibid., Meetings with the President, box 4.

65. Memoranda of conferences with the president, October 29, 1956, 7:15 P.M., and 8:15 P.M., ibid., Meetings with the President, box 7; and Neff, *Warriors at Suez*, pp. 335–37.

66. Memoranda of conferences with the president, October 29, 1956, 7:15 P.M., and 8:15 P.M., ibid., Meetings with the President, box 7.

67. Diary notes, October 26–November 6, 1956, Emmett John Hughes Papers, Seeley G. Mudd Manuscript Library, Princeton University, Princeton, NJ, box 1.

68. Neff, *Warriors at Suez*, pp. 375–76.

69. Diane Kunz, *The Economic Diplomacy of the Suez Crisis* (Chapel Hill: University of North Carolina Press, 1991), pp. 135, 146–47.

70. Heikal, *Cairo Documents*, pp. 119–20.

71. Robert Vitalis, *America's Kingdom: Mythmaking on the Saudi Oil Frontier* (Stanford, CA: Stanford University Press, 2007), pp. 184–88.

72. The exchange can be found in Lloyd C. Gardner, *American Foreign Policy, Present to Past: A Narrative with Readings and Documents* (New York: The Free Press, 1974), pp. 192–95.

73. U.S. Senate, *Executive Sessions of the Senate Foreign Relations Committee*, vol. 9, pp. 140–43.

74. Ibid., 161.

75. Ibid., 19.

76. Vitalis, *America's Kingdom*, p. 186.

77. Draft communiqué, February 8, 1957, Dulles Papers, Dulles–Eisenhower Correspondence, Subject Series, box 5.

78. Dulles, memorandum of conversation with the British ambassador, February 7, 1957, ibid., Memos of Conversation, box 1; and Salim Yaqub, *Containing Arab Nationalism: The Eisenhower Doctrine and the Middle East* (Chapel Hill: University of North Carolina Press, 2004), p. 102.

79. Yaqub, *Containing Arab Nationalism*, p. 103.

80. Dulles, memorandum of a conversation at the Mid Ocean Club, March 20, 1957, Dulles Papers, Memoranda of Conversations, box 1.

81. Yaqub, *Containing Arab Nationalism*, p. 162; Vitalis, *America's Kingdom*, pp. 186–93; Ben Fenton, "Macmillan Backed Syria Assassination Plot," *The Guardian*, September 27, 2003.

82. Vitalis, *America's Kingdom*, p. 191; and Dulles, memorandum of conversation, October 6, 1957, Dulles Papers, Memoranda of Conversations, box 1.

83. See Walter Lippmann, *The Cold War* (New York: Harper, 1947).

84. Yaqub, *Containing Arab Nationalism*, pp. 205–15; and Dulles, memorandum of conversation with Prime Minister Daud, June 25, 1958, Dulles Papers, Memoranda of Conversations, box 1.

85. Dulles, memorandum of conversation, January 19, 1959, Dulles Papers, Memoranda of Conversations, box 1.

6. Be Careful What You Wish For

1. H.W. Brands, *Into the Labyrinth: The United States and the Middle East, 1945–1993* (New York: McGraw-Hill, 1994), pp. 76–77.

2. Ibid., p. 77.

3. U.S. Senate, Committee on Foreign Relations, *Hearings: The President's Proposal on the Middle East*, 85th Cong., 1st sess., 1957 (Washington, DC: GPO, 1957), pp. 76–77, 99–100, 175–77.

4. Quotations from Lloyd C. Gardner, *A Covenant with Power: America and World Order from Wilson to Reagan* (New York: Oxford University Press, 1984), p. 99 (emphasis added).

5. U.S. Senate, *Executive Sessions of the Senate Foreign Relations Committee*, vol. 9, p. 9.

6. "The Dissembler," *Time*, April 13, 1959, www.time.com/printout/0,8816,810960.00.html.

7. Sergei N. Khrushchev, *Nikita Khrushchev and the Creation of a Superpower*, trans. Shirley Benson (University Park: Pennsylvania State University Press, 2000), pp. 290–91.

8. Nikita Khrushchev, *Khrushchev Remembers*, trans. Strobe Talbott with an introduction, commentary, and notes by Edward Crankshaw (Boston: Little, Brown, 1970), p. 438.

9. Sandra Mackey, *The Reckoning: Iraq and the Legacy of Saddam Hussein* (New York: W.W. Norton, 2002), p. 181.

10. Joe Stork, *Middle East Oil and the Energy Crisis* (New York: Monthly Review Press, 1975), pp. 102–8.

11. Ibid., p. 108.

12. Unsigned State Department paper, "The Situation in Iraq," April 15, 1959, U.S. Department of State, *Foreign Relations of the United States, 1958–1960*, vol. 12, *Near East Region; Iraq; Iran; Arabian Peninsula* (Washington, DC: GPO, 1993), pp. 414–22 (hereafter cited as *FRUS, 1958–1960*, vol. 12); quotation from p. 418.

13. Stork, *Middle East Oil*, pp. 102–8.

14. Richard P. Hunt, "Iraq Drive Perils French Oil Share," *New York Times*, December 26, 1960.

15. Patrick Cockburn, "Revealed: How the West Set Saddam on the Bloody Road to Power," *The Independent* (London), June 29, 1997; and *Frontline*, "The Survival of Saddam: Interviews: James Critchfield," www.pbs.org/wgbh/pages/frontline/shows/saddam/interviews/critchfield.html.

16. Cockburn, "Revealed."

17. Memorandum of discussion, April 2, 1959, *FRUS, 1958–1960*, vol. 12, pp. 402–6.

18. Memorandum of discussion, April 17, 1959, ibid., pp. 423–37.

19. Ibid.

20. Special Committee on Iraq, Memoranda for Record, April 27 and December 8, 1959, Eisenhower Papers, CP Iraq (Philip Halla Files), National Security Council Staff Papers, 1953–1961, box.

21. *Frontline*, "The Survival of Saddam."

22. Ibid.

23. Said K. Aburish, *A Brutal Friendship: The West and the Arab Elite* (New York: St. Martin's Press, 1998), pp. 138–42.

24. Robert Komer to John Kennedy, February 8, 1963, quoted in U.S. Department of State, *Foreign Relations of the United States, 1961–1963*, vol. 18, *Near East, 1962–1963* (Washington, DC: GPO, 1995), p. 342 (hereafter cited as *FRUS, 1961–1963*, vol. 18); and Aburish, *Brutal Friendship*, pp. 138–42.

25. Memorandum to McGeorge Bundy, February 13, 1963, *FRUS, 1961–1963*, vol. 18, pp. 348–49.

26. Aburish, *Brutal Friendship*, p. 141; and Dean Rusk to Kennedy, February 22, 1963, *FRUS, 1961–1963*, vol. 18, pp. 353–55.

27. Komer, "Memorandum for the Record," November 14, 1963, *FRUS, 1961–1963*, vol. 18, pp. 779–86.

28. Department of State to the Embassy in the United Arab Republic, December 24, 1962, ibid., pp. 275–76.

29. Ibid.

30. Memorandum of conversation, December 27, 1962, ibid., pp. 276–83; quotations from pp. 278–79.

31. Ibid., p. 280.

32. The Hawk missile rationale and sale is explored in Warren Bass, *Support Any Friend: Kennedy's Middle East and the Making of the U.S.-Israel Alliance* (New York: Oxford University Press, 2003), pp. 180–85.

33. Ibid., 178–79.

34. Herman Eilts to Department of State, July 27, 1968, U.S. Department of State, *Foreign Relations of the United States, 1964–1968*, vol. 21, *Near East Region; Arab Peninsula* (Washington, DC: GPO, 2000), pp. 877–78.

35. "Memorandum for the Record," June 1, 1967, U.S. Department of State, *Foreign Relations of the United States, 1964–1968*, vol. 19, *Arab-Israeli Crisis and War, 1967* (Washington, DC: GPO, 2004), pp. 223–25 (hereafter cited as *FRUS, 1964–1968*, vol. 19).

36. Walt Rostow, "Memorandum for the President: Our Policy Toward the UAR," April 14, 1964, encl. William Polk to Rostow, "Our Policy Toward the UAR," April 7, 1964, Papers of Lyndon B. Johnson, National Security File, Country File, Turkey, UAR, box 158, Lyndon B. Johnson Library, Austin, TX.

37. Polk, "Our Policy," ibid. The remainder of this discussion is taken from Polk's memorandum.

38. Heikal, *Cairo Documents*, pp. 228–32.

39. Ibid., 229.

40. Ibid., 237.

41. Ibid.

42. "Memorandum of Conversation," February 23, 1966, U.S. Department of State, *Foreign Relations of the United States, 1964–1968*, vol. 18, *Arab-Israeli Dispute, 1964–1967* (Washington, DC: GPO, 2000), pp. 557–60 (hereafter cited as *FRUS, 1964–1968*, vol. 18).

43. Bass, *Support Any Friend*, p. 238.

44. Rusk to Embassy in United Arab Republic, February 28, 1966, *FRUS, 1964–1968*, vol. 18, pp. 562–63.

45. Briefing notes for Helms, May 23, 1967, *FRUS, 1964–1968*, vol. 19, pp. 74–75.

46. Memorandum of conversation, May 26, 1967, ibid., pp. 140–46.

47. Ibid.

48. Quoted in Donald Neff, *Warriors for Jerusalem: The Six Days That Changed the Middle East in 1967* (Brattleboro, VT: Amana Books, 1988), p. 147.

49. Memorandum to Johnson, June 4, 1967, *FRUS, 1964–1968*, vol. 19, pp. 272–77.

50. This is the argument advanced in Lloyd C. Gardner, *The Long Road to Baghdad: A History of American Foreign Relations Since the 1970s* (New York: The New Press, 2008).

51. Rostow, memorandum for the record, November 17, 1968, *FRUS, 1964–1968*, vol. 19, pp. 287–91; quotation from p. 290.

52. President's daily brief, June 6, 1967, ibid., 322.

53. "Memorandum from the President's Assistant for National Security Affairs (Kissinger) to Secretary of State Rogers and Secretary of Defense Laird," July 25, 1972, U.S. Department of State, *Foreign Relations of the United States, 1969–1979*, vol. E4, *Documents on Iran and Iraq, 1969–1972* (Washington, DC: Office of the Historian, 2006), www.state.gov/r/pa/ho/frus/nixon/e4/69514.htm.

54. Roger Morris, "A Tyrant 40 Years in the Making," *New York Times*, March 14, 2003.

55. David Morgan, "Ex-US Official Says CIA Aided Baathists," Reuters, April 20, 2003, www.commondreams.org/headlines03/0420-05.html.

56. *Frontline*, "The Survival of Saddam."

Epilogue

1. Michael R. Gordon, "Afghan Strategy Poses Stiff Challenge for Obama," *New York Times*, December 3, 2008.

2. Associated Press, "Karzai to Obama: Halt Afghan Civilian Deaths," CBS5.com, November 5, 2008, cbs5.com/national/afghanistan.civilian.deaths.2.856777.html.

3. Undated memorandum, "American Position," *FRUS, 1947*, vol. 5, p. 513.

4. Leo Shane III, "McKiernan Sees 'Tough Year' Ahead in Afghanistan," *Stars and Stripes*, February 20, 2009, Middle East Edition.

INDEX